Urban Planning in the Third World

The Chandigarh Experience

Madhu Sarin

An Alexandrine Press Book

MANSELL PUBLISHING LIMITED

ISBN 0 7201 1637 6

Mansell Publishing Limited, 6 All Saints Street, London N1 9RL

First published 1982

Distributed in the United States and Canada by
The H. W. Wilson Company, 950 University Avenue,
Bronx, New York 10452

This book was commissioned, edited and designed by
Alexandrine Press, Oxford

British Library Cataloguing in Publication Data

Sarin, Madhu
    Urban planning in the Third World; the
    Chandigarh experience.
    1. City planning—India—Chandigarh
    I. Title
    711'.4'0954552   NA9016.1/
ISBN 0–7201–1637–6

Text set in 11/12pt Ehrhardt and printed in Great Britain by Henry Ling
Limited, Dorchester, bound by William Brendon and Son Limited, Tiptree,
Essex.

Contents

Acknowledgements

This book is a stage in a journey which started many years ago and which will undoubtedly continue. Many individuals, groups and institutions made the journey possible. When assistance has been so widespread, it is difficult to single out people or institutions for particular thanks. Even so, I would like to express special gratitude to the following.

In Chandigarh, to the people living, working and suffering in the non-plan areas of the city who allowed a stranger to gain some insight into their predicament, offering warmth and friendship when they had so many reasons to be hostile; to the staff and officers of Chandigarh Administration for their generously given time, assistance and information even when we had strong disagreements on several issues; to Dayal, Sunil, Neena, Kavi, Channi and others for joining in a new learning process; and to my family, who not only bore with me as I brought increasingly discomforting tales and reflections into the midst of their comfort but also, without whose support and tolerance the final stages of writing would not have materialized.

To the Fondation Le Corbusier in Paris, for providing housing accommodation for three months and giving free access to their archives for studying the historical and conceptual basis of the Chandigarh master plan in 1973.

To the staff of the Development Planning Unit in London, particularly to Professor Koenigsberger, Patrick Wakely and Michael Safier for patient encouragement and help in the earlier stages of studying Chandigarh's planning, and to the Ministry of Overseas Development in London who financed the original research for two years and four months from 1973 to 1975 and to the Development Planning Unit for providing one month's salary towards costs of preparing the manuscript during 1976.

However, by far the greatest gratitude is due to Josefina, Das, Sandra, Gita, Andreas and others, friends and colleagues, only long discussions with whom based on their practice, enabled a development of the analysis presented here. Josefina, Neena, Dayal and Dr Mulkh Raj also helped with reading through parts of the manuscript and giving their critical comment.

The views and arguments presented in the book, with all their flaws are mine, and none of those who have assisted in their development necessarily agree with them.

1

Introduction

This book is concerned with some of the critical issues underlying urban planning in the Third World. Although essentially based on a detailed study of the new town of Chandigarh in India, together with a review of a number of other new towns, it is hoped that much of the analysis will help to highlight the fundamental nature of the conflicts and contradictions confronting urban planning in the Third World in general. The advantage of focusing on the new town situation is that it makes possible an analysis of the impact of planning intervention as an *external* factor influencing the settlement process.

As practised in market economies, urban planning has consisted of the imposition of a framework of rules, presented as being neutral, and legitimized on the grounds of being in the 'public' interest. However, within the urban Third World, characterized by extreme social and economic inequalities, it is not difficult to show that the neutrality of planning is a myth. Invariably, its impact on different sections of the population is far from equal. But evidence of this alone does not help in identifying the means by which that situation could be transformed. This study is an attempt to add to the understanding of the role of planning in perpetuating the differential distribution of wealth and power in Third World urban areas; the instruments it provides for legitimizing the *status quo*; and the historical and economic factors which are its mainspring. In analysing the mechanisms by which planning contributes towards worsening the conditions of the working poor, emphasis is placed on identifying the alternative social and economic parameters on which it must be based if this situation is to be changed. Within this framework the problems of housing and employment, particularly the possibilities for their resolution through a more pragmatic approach towards squatter settlements and the so-called 'informal' sector of employment, will be considered in greater detail.

In 'developed' Western countries, whatever expectations people have of urban planning, it is soon evident even to the casual observer that these are not being met. Debates, often heated and sometimes emotional, reflect a state of crisis in the field. Recurrent themes hold planning directly or indirectly responsible for the problems of inner city decay, for inhuman concrete jungles with high rates of crime and vandalism, for the isolated and frustrating life of the housewife in sprawling suburbs, and the destruction of community networks. Planners and planning are frequent targets for public resentment and attack.

Not surprisingly, many Western observers are dismayed to find the reproduction of similar environments in the 'planned' parts of Third World cities and
in Third World new towns in particular.

In countries such as Britain and Holland, where the State has been playing
an increasing role in the provision of such basic necessities as housing, the
characteristics of corporate organizations of both the government and private
sector are blamed for destroying 'individual freedom' and 'local autonomy' [see,
for example, Turner (1976) and C. Ward (1976)]. What is less frequently
discussed is the degree to which local autonomy, particularly in low-income
areas, is really possible within the socio-economic frameworks of these
societies.

In the Third World, the preoccupations with respect to urban problems are
very different. Articulate sections of the population demand more, rather than
less, planning action by State agencies. There are appeals to government to
intervene in the deterioration of the urban environment caused by the lack of
planned infrastructure and services. There are demands to remove the 'eye
sores' or 'ugly blotches' of slums and shanty settlements, which are seen not
only as marring the 'beauty' of cities, but also as breeding grounds for disease,
immorality, crime and other social ills. The problems of dismal environmental
conditions and extremely low standards of living are commonly perceived in
terms of a need to 'educate the poor' about hygiene, nutrition, education and
civic responsibility. Public authorities are pressed to provide cheap but
'modern' housing. When public housing is provided, however, allegations of
corruption, bad management, poor standards and unfair allocation abound.
Hawkers and street traders are seen as requiring control so that they do not
'litter the streets, selling unhealthy foods and creating traffic problems.' There
is relatively little of the criticism, so preoccupying Western urban dwellers, of
the monotony of mass housing or the problems of community severance.

While neither of these typical, but contrasting attitudes towards planning
reveals very much about the structural nature of urban problems in the two
different contexts, they do reveal a good deal about the ruling perceptions in
them – and it is these perceptions which dominate public policy formation.
They are inevitably founded in the ideas and ideals of the dominating sections
of society, and in this context it is important to remember that low literacy rates
and problems of sheer survival exclude many in the urban Third World from
participating in such discussions. In fact, it is not uncommon to be unable to
communicate even the meaning of the term 'planning' to an average citizen.

The planned new towns manifest the contrasts and contradictions of Third
World cities most markedly. It is difficult to find a single example where
planning has succeeded in meeting its stated goals and objectives. Duality of
social and spatial structure – a theme prominent in discussions of Third World
cities – is more pronounced in them than in the older 'unplanned' urban
centres. In Tema, the new town and port planned in 1950 as the heavy industrial sector of the Accra/Tema Metropolitan Region in Ghana, about 50 per

cent of the population lives in the unplanned settlement of Ashaiman, outside the master plan area (Mitchell, 1975:2). By 1964, 57 per cent of the population of Brazilia, planned as the new national capital of Brazil in 1957, was living in satellite towns built in contravention of the pilot plan, and a further 10 per cent was living in squatter settlements (Epstein, 1973:10). The case of Chandigarh, planned or rather 'designed' as the new capital of Punjab in 1951, is no different. By 1971, leaving aside those totally homeless or living in neigh-bouring villages, 11 per cent of the population was living in partially or totally illegal settlements (Census of India, 1971a). Ciudad Guayana, planned in the early 1960s as part of a major regional development programme of Venezuelan Guayana, by 1974 had 39 per cent of its housing stock developed totally outside the planning framework and a further 22 per cent in semi-planned areas (MacDonald and MacDonald, 1977:34).

The case of Ciudad Guayana is particularly remarkable. Here attempts were made to incorporate 'incremental improvement' of dwellings by the low-income households within the planning framework (Corrada, 1969). At the same time, its planning was a product of combining local technical ability with that of a large team of 'experts' from the Joint Centre of Urban Studies of MIT and Harvard University. Receiving the attention of sociologists, architects, planners, demographers, anthropologists and others using computer-aided studies (Rodwin, L. and Associates, 1969), Ciudad Guayana did not suffer from the simplistic planning approach blamed for the distorted outcomes of other Third World new towns. However, its emerging social and spatial structure is equally, or perhaps more distorted than that found in other new towns. This lends strength to the argument proposed here that the resolution of Third World urban problems does not lie in substituting one set of planning techniques by other more 'sophisticated' ones. A start in that direction can only be made by identifying the alternative socio-economic parameters on which planning must be based if it is to contribute towards improvement for all sections of the population.

The living conditions and standards of infrastructure and construction in the 'non-plan' areas of the new towns manifest the very problems that planning was supposed to overcome. What is more, and what appears to be a greater anomaly, the agencies responsible for enforcing the respective plans have not only been unsuccessful in achieving their objectives, but have to varying degrees *themselves* participated in enabling the unplanned areas to continue to exist. Effectively, this has meant their *defacto* acceptance of a dual set of standards for the two components that have emerged – plan and non-plan. Thus, the Tema Development Corporation (TDC) has slowly been directing a small proportion of the public resources for infrastructure and services to Ashaiman. Not only this, TDC has actually 'planned' the layout of future growth there (Mitchell, 1975:15). The satellite towns of Brasilia have similarly been 'planned' and managed by its Development Authority (Epstein, 1973:70). The residents of Chandigarh's 'labour colonies' have no less been living in areas 'authorized' and laid out by the authorities. The relationship between the apparently separate components of these new towns is intrinsically one of integration and unity, but on very inequitable terms. The unplanned parts are second class partners to the planned; the hallmark of their condition being manipulation, insecurity and dependence.

If such developments are taken as an indication of the 'failure' of planning for Third World requirements, what remains inexplicable is why such planning ventures are on the increase and why more and more new towns continue to be planned and built on the basis of the same parameters. Nigeria is in the process of building a new national capital. Tanzania, a country committed to socialist ideals, is building its new capital at Dodoma, planned by Canadian consultants based on critieria no different from those used in Chandigarh or Brasilia*. Egypt, facing severe economic problems, is building a number of new towns in the Canal Zone. The list could be continued. Planned new towns fall mainly into the categories of new capitals, industrial or commercial centres, or those built for strategic or geo-political reasons.

However one of their most significant aspects, and one which seems to have escaped the notice of those who dismiss them as aberrations or unique and bizarre ventures, is that their creation has frequently coincided with an increased State participation in urban and regional planning. Indeed, some of the new towns, particularly the most spectacular and well publicized ones, have represented major landmarks in this direction. State support for new town projects has been accompanied by an evokation of national pride and this nationalist sentiment has in turn been used for legitimizing and increasing the acceptability of planning as a new and major instrument for State control and regulation of urban areas.

While public opinion has been moulded in favour of the desirability of planning *per se*, the impossibility of its achieving its stated goals has gone by relatively unscrutinized. For example, simple economic analyses are sufficient to show that the high standards chosen for planned development cannot be obtained for all sections of the population†. At the same time, by granting privileges to those groups seen by the State as necessary to economic development within the the new framework (post-colonial) of world capitalism, planning and planned new towns have been instrumental in the creation of new social classes. The nature of these social classes, be they private industrialists, public technocrats, or members of the defence establishment, has depended on the historical, political and social factors operating in the particular context. The point of departure for a meaningful analysis of the function of urban planning in the Third World lies in these factors.

Against this background, it is useful to look briefly at the most common

---

*For a discussion of how some of the urban planning proposals by foreign consultants in Tanzania are based on assumptions of a social structure which are irreconcilable with socialist aims, see Bienefeld (1970; 44–8).

†For a good study along these lines, see Prakash (1969).

explanation for the distorted results of planning practice, and the alternative proposals put forward. The obvious inequalities and the contrasts between high-standard 'planned' areas and their inevitably low-standard 'unplanned' appendages have largely been explained in terms of the 'inappropriateness' of Western planning models transferred to fundamentally different contexts. While this assessment can hardly be disputed, its apparently logical extension, namely that the application of planning models and techniques based on prevailing socio-economic conditions and ethnic life styles would resolve the most critical problems of the urban Third World, has very severe limitations. What it is unable to account for is first, why what appears to be such an obvious solution is resisted so vehemently by the authorities concerned and secondly, why wherever at least some effort has been made in this direction, as in the case of Ciudad Guayana, are some of the same problems reproduced?

Among the alternative strategies emerging from this approach are the upgrading of squatter settlements, the provision of housing sites with minimal services, and encouragement of employment within the informal sector. These essentially attempt to amend planning frameworks to enable them to reflect the *status quo*, with all its inequalities, rather than changing it. The 'needs' of different sections of the population become defined in terms of what they can afford to pay for. Thus the housing 'need' of an impoverished labourer is best met by an improvised shack and the employment 'need' of one unable to find any other job can be met by polishing shoes.

If Third World governments resist changing their policies in this direction it is considered desirable to persuade them to do so. Agencies such as the World Bank even attempt to pressurize them by making loans conditional upon such changes. Although these policies seldom suggest the allocation of a higher proportion of total resources to meet the needs of the majority of the population, they do bring that majority within the ambit of State control and management through minimal welfare intervention. The resulting image of State parternalism works as a palliative for the political organization of the base of the population. However, in so far as this approach does not attempt to alter the socio-economic relationships which *produce* large-scale deprivation and poverty, its limitations are clear.

What then is a more useful conceptual framework within which we can not only analyse the forces shaping the outcome of such planning, but also identify the processes by which it can be transformed? And, where does urban planning fit within the wider processes of development (or underdevelopment) taking place in the Third World? Further, what has been the impact of urban planning on the life situations of the working poor? If, as is proposed here, planning serves the interests of the wealthy and powerful, while militating against those of the already deprived, what are the mechanisms by which it does this? Finally, what is the role of planners in this process and what are the preconditions which must be met if their intervention is to be made more positive?

First, it is essential to identify a framework within which the state of underdevelopment can be defined in relation to that of development. One of the major problems in analysing even a very specific situation today is the close integration of different parts of the world through a complex structure of economic and political relationships. It is thus necessary not only to determine the relationship of that situation with its national context, but also with that of the international one. This is important as the interpretation of the nature of these relationships will have a profound influence on the diagnosis of the problems under discussion and, therefore, the potential for their resolution by the alternative strategies now being proposed.

Without going into a detailed review of the different schools of thought on the characteristics of underdevelopment and the nature of problems confronting Third World countries, it is useful to outline the two main, opposing approaches to the subject.

Dualism is a theme of much of the literature on underdeveloped countries, not only in discussions of urbanization, but also of regional characteristics, minority and ethnic relations, and cultural and economic development [see, for example Boeke (1953), Higgins (1961), Ellsworth (1962), Dasgupta (1964)]. The most recent addition to this theme, arising from an increased preoccupation with the problem of high rates of un(der)employment, is the model of two sectors in the economy – the so-called *formal* and *informal sectors* (Hart, 1973). The underlying error of the dualist approach is to look at the social segments which manifest these contrasts as if they were isolated from one another. Thus, solutions sought to problems of squatter settlements and slums relate to them alone, while support for the informal sector is sought through strategies based only on its apparent internal and external characteristics. As Epstein has expressed it,

> The dualist picture of contemporary national societies is often projected into an image of history that is a contemporary version of 19th century evolutionism – what Hoetink (1965) refers to as 'new evolutionism' of the unilinear variety. While making some allowances for differences between individual countries and regions, this unilinear school describes contemporary world history as the progression of each country from underdeveloped or traditional to developed and modern, and postulates a series of two or sometimes more stages through which all countries are alleged sooner or later to pass. Thus, the more 'traditional' of the dual segments is seen as historically more archaic or less advanced, and it can see in the less traditional of the two segments the image of its own future. (Epstein, 1973:1–2)

Rowstow, perhaps the most well known of these *unilinear* theorists, postulates five stages: (1) traditional society; (2) the preconditions for take-off; (3) take-off; (4) the drive for maturity; and (5) high mass consumption (Rostow, 1960:2–12). The logical conclusion of this perspective is to interpret the visible characteristics of economic inferiority as a reflection of 'lag' or of not having 'caught on' to the singular path of modernization. The concept of *marginality*, which is rooted in this view, has led to various development strategies aimed at 'integrating' the so-called marginalized sectors with the modernized core of society*. Writers of this school deny, or more frequently ignore, the possibility that the causes of underdevelopment lie outside the individual society or section of society, and have to do with the international structure of economic and political relationships.

The unilinear view of development has been challenged by a growing body of literature, which bases its alternative analysis on a different interpretation of recent world history leading to different perspectives on development. Frank (1967a,b,), probably the best known exponent of this alternative view, has produced an analysis of the political economy of Latin American countries, based on 'relations of dependency'. This analysis can be applied, in varying degrees, to other parts of the Third World. The world 'metropolis' or dominant centre at the present time is the United States, which has both internal 'satellites' or dependent regions and international 'satellites' located in the underdeveloped countries. Each satellite in turn dominates regional centres in individual countries, and similar chains of dependence and domination link these regional centres with smaller units, down to the most impoverished and apparently isolated peasant. This is a single, integrated system; and the backwardness of each dependent unit relative to its dominating centre is accounted for as a product of the dynamics of the system as a whole (Frank, 1967a). Thus development and underdevelopment are seen not as independent phenomena, but as linked to each other by virtue of their relationship within the system.

Extending the analysis to the urbanization process, Castells (1972, 1975) and others have made important contributions to the development of this alternative perspective. Its theoretical basis lies in Marx's fundamental theses that the material economic base of society determines the superstructure of social, legal and political institutions, rather that vice versa, and that each historical society is characterized by struggles between the opposing social classes arising from the particular processes of production within it.

A society (or social formation) is made up of several 'modes of production', one of which is dominant. In turn, a mode of production consists of a combination of several 'systems', e.g. economic (base), political, legal and ideological (superstructure). Thus in the capitalist mode of production, the economic system consists of three elements: labour, means of production, and 'non-worker' (i.e. capitalist), linked by two relationships, ownership and real appropriation, which are 'homologous', i.e. the capitalist not only owns labour power and means of production, but also controls the technical process by which they are combined together. A social formation is not a functionally-integrated, harmonious whole, but is characterized by contradictions (between its component modes of production, systems, elements, etc.).

Within this framework, the urbanization process is historically rooted in the growth of Western capitalism. The expansion of capitalism in Europe was accompanied by a progressive destruction of other modes of production. The

*For a critical examination of marginality theory, see Perlman (1976).

labour thus released was available for the burgeoning industrial and commercial enterprises in urban areas. The backward state of medical knowledge took care of some of the most pressing problems which characterize the urbanization process in the Third World today. The slow rates of population increase seldom threatened the foundations of capitalism in eighteenth and nineteenth-century Europe. At the same time human labour could not be dispensed with as it can today through automation. This is not to say that the horrors of capitalist exploitation were somehow avoided in the early stages of European industrialization. The scale of human misery, deprivation and exploitation of the working class is vividly documented in the writings of the period [Engels (1892), Jones (1971), Mayhew (1861)]. Nor did the emerging ruling class consolidate its power without experiencing intense insecurity from the potential revolt of the working class. Even the problem of the casually employed, the equivalent of the informal sector today, did not escape nineteenth-century London, and the insecurity experienced by the educated and propertied classes being surrounded by a sea of human misery led to the coining of such terms as 'the dangerous classes' or 'the residuum' (Jones, 1971).

The resulting spatial structure of European economies, involving an increasing number of cities, although not 'planned' by planning agencies, nevertheless followed a particular rationality, namely the demands of capital. Colonialism led to the linking of areas geographically separated by thousands of miles, and marked the beginning of an increasing separation between zones of production and zones in which the products were consumed. The characteristics of individual urban centres were determined not simply by whether they were centres of trade or manufacture, but by who *controlled* that trade or manufacture. Thus the growth of Calcutta was intimately linked with the growths of London and Liverpool, but while the latter could be termed primate cities in British spatial economy, the primacy of Calcutta in India's geography was 'satellitic'.

Colonial urbanization in Third World countries produced spatial distortions in their economies because they were geared to the needs of Imperialist exploitation. Today, when most countries have obtained national independence, their urbanization is a product of the changed and more international structure of economic and political relationships. While the capitalist mode of production, already established under colonialism, has continued after independence, it remains dependent on conforming to the dictates of the transnational capital of metropolitan economies. A key problem in this process is the fact that while progressively destroying other modes of production, capitalist development in Third World countries has no need for the large labour force inevitably thrown onto the market. Imported capital-intensive technology leads to a form of economic development capable of absorbing only a fraction of the available labour force. Thus ever increasing numbers of workers, displaced from their traditional (albeit backward or even bonded) occupations, become *condemned* to independence. Although made individually free, they become dependent on realizing the exchange value of their labour in a surplus labour market. Therefore, their bargaining power remains extremely poor and frequently results in wages barely sufficient for subsistence. The generality of this outline is not to minimize the wide variation *between* Third World countries in terms of social formations, degrees of stability, independence of states, or the specific characteristics of the urbanization process or economic development*.

It is within the cities that the conflicts and contradictions generated by this process are most critically and visibly brought together. Concentration of non-agricultural means of production is inherent in capitalism and, according to Lojkine (1976:127), the capitalist city 'can be seen as a spatial form which, by reducing indirect costs of production, and costs of consumption and circulation, speeds up the rotation of capital'. While the individual owners of the means of production find it unprofitable to invest in such basic necessities as housing and health, the State is increasingly called upon to provide these in order to minimize the social problems arising from political discontent, environmental deterioration and housing shortages.

The origins of modern urban planning are rooted in this process and evolved in industrialized countries out of the need to regulate and minimize some of the worst by-products of capitalist urban development. However, the dominant rationality shaping urban systems continues to follow the requirements of capital or, according to Lamarche (1976:103), planning can only be 'real' if it fits in with the plans of property capital.

A good example, well documented by Jones and illustrating the planning role of commercial and property capital *prior* to the institutionalization of planning agencies, is the transformation of central London during the second half of the nineteenth century. Until that time, central London had a residential population. With the consolidation of the colonial empire and the consequent increase in capital accumulation and commercial activity in the metropolis,

> demolition and commercial transformation in nineteenth century London must have involved a greater displacement of population than the rebuilding of Paris under Haussmann. (Jones, 1971:161)

Historians may judge Haussmann in terms of the greatness of his vision or the brutality with which he razed the homes of large sections of the Parisian working class. However the blame or responsibility for the transformation of London cannot be ascribed to any one individual or body. It was the cumulative effect of the actions of a large number of people and bodies engrossed in maximizing profits and capital accumulation. In its wake, this brought an acute housing crisis in the city and a worsening of the overcrowded and insanitary living conditions of the poor. In terms of the threat that this situation represented to the survival of the social structure as a whole, it also represented the birth pangs of modern town planning as we know it today.

---

*For a detailed discussion of the general theme presented here see Castells (1975).

Understood in this context, the role which urban planning must play within Third World urbanization today is far more demanding. It is in the Third World city that the effects of the consolidation of capitalism in its most developed stage are most critically brought together. As the owners of capital in the private sector (be they national or transnational) are not accountable to those whose sources of livelihood they are directly or indirectly destroying as a result of their investment policies, the State becomes 'responsible' for all those excluded from direct participation in production processes. The hyper-inflated tertiary sectors of Third World urban economies provide an uncomfortable refuge for a multitude of poor or un(der)employed trapped in this situation.

The pattern of social development produced by the international structure of production relationships and the increasing concentration of ownership of capital is one of extreme polarity between a small minority of those who *control* production and its distribution and the rest who must accept a subservient role of conforming to the parameters dictated by that minority. There is a further sub-division within the working population. The traditional 'working class', directly linked to the dominant production process, is able to negotiate certain privileges which the State and owners of capital are willing to provide to contain the risk of discontent and political militancy. The rest, the worst sufferers, are those unable to enter organized production and therefore condemned to struggle for survival by means of casual employment in tertiary occupations in the 'informal' sector.

The informal sector of employment is closely related to the housing problem in Third World cities, primarily in the slums and semi-legal or illegal settlements. The conditions in these settlements reflect the limitations of their residents defined by the wider structure of domination and dependence. The potential for autonomous growth and development in the informal sector or of 'incremental improvement' in the settlements cannot be examined without taking into account the constraints imposed on them by the global structure.

To ensure survival of the present structure of society within this framework, urban planning must perform two functions. First, because of the importance of urban centres to capitalist economies, it must provide a system of urban management whereby national or transnational capital may acquire easy access to locations well supplied with modern infrastructure and services, frequently at public expense. In 'unplanned' cities, growing by accretion, some of the best locations are occupied by low-income housing or small enterprises long before they become attractive to big capital. 'Acquiring' such sites can involve considerable expense, lengthy legal negotiations with numerous interested parties, and political problems. In addition, such 'unplanned' growth does not make it easy to establish a modern and efficient transportation network at a later date. To perform the management function, urban planning must ensure that such obstacles do not develop either now or in the future. Land-use planning, by *reserving* land in particular locations for particular uses in *advance* of settlement serves this function well.

Secondly, planning must devise instruments for diffusing the potential social and political conflicts arising from the worsening situation of an increasing section of the un(der)employed urban population. This is the negotiating role of planning in which it is called upon to *explain, resolve,* and *justify,* to the mass of the population, the emergence of increasingly blatant anomalies. This may be done partly by moulding public opinion towards accepting lower living standards for the majority as a permanent feature, and partly by pre-empting a growth of mass political conciousness by making emerging collective organizations dysfunctional by the introduction of minimal welfare intervention. It is into this pattern that the recently increased preoccupation with minimally 'upgrading' squatter settlements and legitimizing the growth of 'informal' employment clearly fall. As pointed out by Castells (1975:29–30), with reference to Latin America:

> The new structure of dependence generates a series of economic transformations that have to be simultaneously imposed on the traditional oligarchy and on a good portion of the working class. These transformations necessitate an a-social legitimation, capable of establishing its actions on technical imperatives presented as necessary and undebatable, by means of an ideological coherence and guarantee of rationality that a plan expresses . . . Furthermore, this planning apparatus is the only one that can impose the use of a certain language common to all interests, which, in the new situation of dependence, ·necessarily transcends the framework of a single social formation.

We can now return to relating this highly summarized theoretical framework to the role of urban planning in the Third World and the detailed examination of the Chandigarh experience. The reason for placing the study within the wider context is that the emerging problems of squatter settlements and a growing tertiary sector of employment cannot be understood by looking at them in isolation. On the contrary, they are a product of the interaction of predefined frameworks of physical and legal controls with the wider processess of social and strucural change being undergone by the societies of which they are a part. The key points of interest are:

1. The historical and economic factors which led to the selection of the particular criteria used in the formulation of different planning frameworks.
2. The decision-making and perceptual processes which legitimized the planning frameworks.
3. The ways in which most of these frameworks have been inherently incapable of being fully implemented in their respective contexts.
4. Precisely how the frameworks have been modified in the process of their implementation in order to meet emerging conflicts and contradictions.
5. The impact of these modifications on the living and working opportunities of the working poor.
6. The ways in which planning has contributed to the legitimation of these processes and the mechanisms by which those adversely effected have been able to challenge the constraints imposed on them.

7. The identifiable agents and processes of change towards an alternative pattern of production relationships centred around the needs and capabilities of the majority of the *people* rather than on maximizing economic growth or some such objective whose benefits continue to evade them.

These are some of the issues which are explored through a detailed examination of the planning and development of Chandigarh. The experience of some other planned towns is discussed in relation to particular aspects, but lack of space and the non-availability of suitable studies make their detailed examination unviable.

Chandigarh was planned as the new capital of Punjab early in 1951, and its planning was presented as a symbol of the aspirations of Independent India. To place it in a historical perspective, chapter 2 to 4 are devoted to the Indian context at the time of Independence, the Western origins of the planning concepts applied in the city and the process by which the plan was finalized by Le Corbusier in a matter of days.

Chapter 5 shows how the abstract concepts and assumptions underlying the master plan were incapable of being fully implemented. The growth and development of the city is described in chapter 6, which focuses on the form the inherent conflicts in the plan have taken and the social forces determining their temporary resolution. The role of the plan in justifying the unequal allocation of public resources and in de-politicizing and mystifying the nature of social conflicts involved is identified.

Chapters 7, 8, and 9 explore some of the issues underlying the growth of squatter settlements: the relationship between Chandigarh's 'non-plan' settlements and its planned part: the impact of the master plan on the social, economic and political status of settlement residents; who they are and the processes by which they have been housing themselves. In this section the role of the plan in worsening the legal status of non-plan residents and thereby enabling the justification for their relocation so that the land they occupied could be handed over to more 'desirable' uses is highlighted. Equally, the role of relocation in destroying collective organizations in their nascent stages is discussed.

Chapters 10 and 11 consider the growth and functioning of non-plan employment in Chandigarh (the so-called 'informal' sector); the impact of the master plan on the status of non-plan occupations; and the considerations on which official policies towards them have been based. Again, the underlying official preoccupation with preventing the growth of non-plan activities in commercially remunerative locations is highlighted.

The final chapter attempts to synthesize the findings of earlier chapters and to identify the alternative social, economic and production relationships for which the working poor must strive if they are to obtain real improvement in their status and conditions. The role which planners and planning actually play and the role which they can potentially play if they are genuinely committed to social change are also examined in this chapter.

2

The Historical Setting

Chandigarh was a product of the crisis and disorder prevailing in north-western India immediately after Partition and Independence in 1947. The State (then Province) of Punjab had been cut in two; its eastern half ceded to India, was left without a capital. Lahore, the ancient and historic city of the Punjabis, became a part of Pakistan, thus adding to the great sense of loss among the millions of uprooted, homeless refugees who fled east in the wake of appalling Hindu-Muslim riots which accompanied Partition. This, from the common man's point of view, was a tragic end to a long and heroic struggle for independence, during which the Indian National Congress had succeeded in gaining the support of the mass of the population. In the process, expectations of a better life for all had been raised, and independence had come to be seen as synonymous with the end of want, exploitation and poverty.

To retain the confidence of the people, the leaders of independent India had to show that they could fulfil at least some of the promises made during the freedom movement. The Punjab Government itself was homeless and was temporarily based in Simla, the old summer capital of the British, but the city's inaccessibility and extreme winter climate made it unsuitable as a permanent capital. Most other Punjabi cities, besides experiencing problems from faction-ridden local pressure groups, had already doubled their populations, thereby stretching their infrastructures to the limit.

In this context, the building of a new city took on additional significance; not only could it provide a suitable seat for the displaced Government, but it could become a symbol of the new national conciousness and thus a focus of hope and reassurance for the suffering refugees. Further, starting afresh on land free of existing encumbrances could provide an opportunity of initiating a new and model approach to Indian urban planning. The new city could become a training ground for young Indian architects and planners capable of managing future urban development and planning projects in the country. Taking all these factors into account,

" in consultation with the Government of India, it was decided to build a new capital to cater ultimately for a population of 500,000 and to locate it at Chandigarh. (Punjab Government, undated)

Once it had been decided to build the city, the next problem was to find a planner and architect capable of fulfilling the requirements of the Government.

Figure 2.1. Location of Chandigarh.

As a result of this search, the internationally renowned architect and planner, Le Corbusier and three other European architects became associated with Chandigarh; Le Corbusier in the capacity of Architectural Adviser to the Government of Punjab. His controversial ideas and international reputation immediately made Chandigarh the focus of worldwide attention – at least among architects and planners.

India and Independence

To place the planning and development of Chandigarh in perspective, it is necessary to look at the wider context of India at the time of Independence and the changes which have taken place within Indian society since then. The way in which power was transferred from the British determined not only the priorities of the independent State, but also influenced the decision to look abroad for architects and planners capable of providing the populist image of national expression.

To look West for architects and planners might have appeared an unlikely proposition to many at that time. Yet, the decision to ignore the existing conditions and problems of the mass of the population, and actually to invite outside professionals to lay the foundations of architecture and planning in the independent nation was itself an indication of the nature of the new State*. The circumstances which enabled this to take place had a decisive influence on the course the city's development took and continues to take today. The subsequent growth of the city also needs to be seen within the broader framework of poverty, unemployment and urbanization in the country.

The freedom movement, culminating in independence from the British in 1947, was in the main led by the Indian National Congress. It was the first mass mobilization in the sub-continent on a common issue, and provided the first experience of national consciousness to a culturally-diverse and geographically-scattered people. The Congress leadership, nurtured in the tradition of British liberal philosophy, adopted parliamentary democracy for India based primarily on the British model. Throughout the struggle for independence, there had hardly been 'any original theoretical conception of a new type of state and administrative machinery adapted to the needs of India, a backward colonial country (further with its own peculiarities) when it emerged as a sovereign state' (Desai, 1960:56). Eventually when the transfer of power took place it was through negotiation, 'mass pressure' being used only to strengthen the negotiating capacity of the Congress. Thus, the transfer of power which took place was in the nature of a constitutional revolution; it involved no breakdown of government or administration as happens after a violent revolution.

The new State retained the inherited administrative machinery which British imperialism had created for ruling India. The most significant characteristic of the British Civil Service was the concentration of executive power in the hands of a small proportion of senior officers. They were trained to maintain their distance from the mass of the people whose problems were their responsibility, and were conferred with numerous privileges distinguishing them both in social status and lifestyle from the common man. While the key positions in the civil service were reserved for the British, towards the end of colonial rule more and more Indians had been inducted into senior posts. All had received their education in Britain. By granting them privileges, the British ensured their loyalty to the Imperial government and thus alienated them from their own culture and people.

After Independence, the vacancies left by the British were soon filled by a

*In comparison, it is significant that the neighbouring People's Republic of China, which was formed just two years after India obtained dominion status and which was confronted with comparable problems of poverty and underdevelopment, chose to *evolve* a totally different planning framework based on local conditions and needs rather than importing techniques developed by the industrialized countries.

new Indian elite, but the structure of the administrative machinery remained intact and has since been modified only marginally. It was State decision-makers trained in this tradition and their perception of social structure that found expression in the planning of Chandigarh. Thus it is easy to understand how the hierarchical order of status and privilege was translated into physical form in the new capital, which was to be a centre of government bureaucracy. While Independence signified the transfer of power into Indian hands, the form the change took also ensured the retention and continuity of institutional and social structure.

The Constitution for the new State was framed by a Constituent Assembly, which was not elected on the basis of adult franchise. It specified that the Indian Union was to be a secular State having a federal structure with a strong centre. The conception of a good society, as incorporated in the Constitution, is expressed in the preamble, fundamental rights and directive principles for the State. It enunciated the principle of equality for all citizens irrespective of caste, community, race or sex, and provided for wide-ranging civil liberties. However, while it granted the citizen the right to ownership of private property, it did not guarantee the right to gainful employment. In a country where unemployment, both rural and urban, ran into tens of millions, the absence of such a right inherently laid down the future course of development of the new nation. The Congress Government overtly subscribed to the Gandhian doctrine that the rich and property owners had a right to retain their wealth, but should behave as 'trustees' of the poor, and thus become 'humanitarian capitalists' through moral appeals and social pressure.

At the national level, the new government expressed its commitment to 'plan' the country's economic development through a series of Five Year Plans. Since this was to be undertaken within the framework of a mixed market economy, the role of such 'planning' could only be expressed in terms of a series of regulatory devices which attempted to influence private investment in the direction of general public good. This, in essence, was the acceptance of an economy where the main motive for investment in agriculture or industry remained personal profit, but where the State applied regulatory measures to avoid the total neglect of the poverty-stricken masses. There could be no *direct* planning of employment or of the labour market. State planning relied on the assumption that problems of unemployment and poverty would somehow take care of themselves as economic growth took place, and hopes were pinned on industrialization generating new employment opportunities.

Poverty and Unemployment

A National Planning Committee, appointed by the Indian National Congress in 1938 under the chairmanship of Jawaharlal Nehru, had divided itself into twenty-five sub-committees, one of which related to population. The report of this sub-committee, released in 1948, discussed the issue of population and poverty and the need for industrialization as a means of reducing the pressure of population on land. The sub-committee recognized that

> the growth of industrialization would mean, not only a redistribution of population as between town and country which has been proceeding silently but slowly in the last half century . . . (but) also better alternative employment, so as to take off the burden on the soil of a disproportionately large population.
>
> With a large variety of employment for the adult population that planned industrialization and economic development in all fields of national life would provide, it would necessarily bring a dimunition of the pressure on the soil side by side with increasing services, utilities and amenities of life. And these in turn would necessarily mean a higher standard of living. (National Planning Committee, 1947:15–16).

After Independence, the Planning Commission was set up in 1950 under Nehru's chairmanship. The First Five Year Plan (1951–56) reiterated the need for reducing the pressure of population on the land. The state of the Indian economy at the beginning of the First Plan was summed up by the Planning Commission as follows:

> Agriculture is still the mainstay of life for 70 per cent of the population, and productivity in this sector is exceedingly low. The size of agricultural holdings has progressively diminished; the old cottage and small scale industries have been decaying, and the rural population which constitutes about 83 per cent of the total suffers from chronic under-employment and low incomes. Population has increased by more than 50 per cent in the last fifty years, but the growth of alternative occupations either in the rural areas or in the towns has not been on a scale which could absorb this growing population. In the limited spheres which have registered expansion, the level of productivity and the level of incomes have naturally been higher. But for the community as a whole, economic development of the last few decades has brought no significant improvement in standards of living and opportunities for employment, and has perhaps accentuated to some extent inequalities of income and wealth. (Government of India, 1952:12)

In terms of the pattern of urban settlement, the independent nation had to contend with the legacy left by colonialism. Perhaps the best description of urbanization under British rule is given by William Digby, who wrote in 1901,

> There are two Indias; the India of the Presidency and the Chief provincial cities, of the railway systems, of the hill stations . . . There are two countries: Anglostan, the land especially ruled by the English, in which English investments have been made and Hindustan, practically all India fifty miles from each side of the railway lines. (Digby 1901:291–2)

In fact, what Digby said about India as a whole, namely the polarization between Anglostan and Hindustan, was also true of individual cities in India. On the basis of his experience as the chairman of the Allahabad Municipality for two years (1921–23), Nehru wrote in his autobiography:

Most Indian cities can be divided into two parts: the densely crowded city proper, and the widespread area with bungalows and cottages, each with a fairly extensive compound or garden, usually referred to by the English as the Civil Lines. It is in these Civil Lines that the English officials and businessmen, as well as many upper middleclass Indians, professional men, officials, etc. live. The income of the municipality from the city proper is greater than that from the Civil Lines, but the expenditure on the latter far exceeds the city expenditure. For the far wider area covered by the Civil Lines requires more roads, and they have to be repaired, cleaned up, watered and lighted; and the drainage, the water supply, and the sanitation system have to be more widespread. The city part is grossly neglected, and, of course, the poorer parts of the city are almost ignored; it has few good roads, and most of the narrow lanes are ill-lit and have no proper drainage or sanitation system. It puts up with all these disabilities patiently and seldom complains, and when it does complain, nothing much happens. Nearly all the Big Noises and Little Noises live in the Civil Lines. (Nehru, 1962:143–4)

More than thirty years after Independence, there is little evidence to suggest that the general pattern of inequalities is any different from the past. On the contrary, in the country as a whole, and within urban areas in particular, poverty and inequality have actually increased, in spite of attempts to alleviate the situation through 'planned' economic development.

At the beginning of the 1960's about 40 per cent of the rural, and 50 per cent of the urban population in India lived below the stated desirable minimum per capita consumer expenditure of Rs.15 (£1.00) and Rs.22.5 (£1.50) per month respectively. Over half (42 million) of the urban population and more than one-third (135 million) of the rural population had calorie deficient diets (Dandekar and Rath, 1971:8–10).

The incidence of poverty in rural areas is predominantly confined to agricultural labourers and small cultivators, constituting about 25 per cent of rural households. In 1963–64, nearly three-quarters of them worked as casual labourers and the remaining quarter as attached labourers. The two groups would also include village artisans progressively thrown out of their traditional employment (Dandekar and Rath, 1971:13).

Concluding on the performance of the economy between 1961–69, Dandekar and Rath observed:

> During the past decade, the per capita consumer expenditure increased by less than half a per cent per annum. Moreover, the small gains have not been equitably distributed among all sections of the population. The condition of the bottom 20 per cent rural poor has remained more or less stagnant. The condition of the bottom 20 per cent urban poor has definitely deteriorated; and for another 20 per cent of the urban population, it has remained more or less stagnant. Thus, while the character of rural poverty has remained the same as before, the character of urban poverty has deepened further. This is the consequence of the continuous migration of the rural poor into urban areas in search of a livelihood, their failure to find adequate means to support themselves there and the resulting growth of road-side and slum-life in the cities. (*Ibid.,* 32–3)

With 72 per cent of the population remaining dependent on agriculture, the distribution of land among rural households has long since been recognized as a crucial factor in promoting socio-economic development in the country. Since the beginning of the 1960s, ceilings on agricultural landholdings were introduced by most State governments with the intention of redistributing the land thus acquired among the landless. Twenty years on, these avowed objectives are still far from being realized.

However, even assuming a successful redistribution of agricultural land, its contribution towards the alleviation of rural poverty remains questionable. The per capita availability of land in India is less than in most other countries*; besides, land per person has been declining because of the increasing population.

With the introduction of advanced technology in agriculture for increasing productivity, the demand for rural labour is likely to decrease. Thus, on balance, employment is bound to decline and the number of un(der)employed, landless labourers will increase. A clear example of this is the change in the working population of Punjab between 1961 and 1971, when the 'Green Revolution' took place. In 1971 compared to 1961 the percentage of agricultural workers to total workers increased from 9.6 per cent to 20.1 per cent (D'Souza, 1976b:351).

Urbanization in India

From 1901 to 1971 the urban population increased from 11 per cent to 20 per cent of the total, with the most significant increases taking place during the last three decades of this period. During 1961–71, while the proportion of urban to total population increased by only 2 per cent the rate of growth of the urban population was as high as 37.8 per cent. In sheer numbers it increased by 29 million in only ten years.

As the overall rate of population growth during this period was 25 per cent, the net rate of urban growth due to migration alone was 12.8 per cent. Further, the brunt of this increase was in class 1 cities (populations above 100,000). While in 1901 23 per cent of the urban population was living in class 1 cities, this had increased to 52 per cent by 1971. Between 1961 and 1971 the number of class 1 cities increased from 113 to 142. Thus the process of urbanization has essentially consisted of cityward movement.

Analysis of the Census data suggests that the 'net' migration evident through dicennial Censuses does not give a true picture of the extent of population movement. The 1961 Census revealed considerable mobility; about one-third of the total population was enumerated outside its place of birth. According to Bose (1973:104)

We are led to the conclusion that there is a large 'turnover migration' in India. In

*In 1961, land per capita in India was 1.8 acres compared to 181.9 in Australia, 26.5 in the USSR, 12.8 in USA, 4.9 in China and 2.5 in Pakistan.

other words, many people move from one area to another without being able to settle down. The mobility need not necessarily be voluntary. It is possible that persons from rural areas are 'pushed' to the urban areas but what is more significant is that, probably, many of them are pushed back from the urban areas or pushed out to other urban areas.

He also points out that:

The implication of our analysis in terms of economic development is that urbanization in the face of rapid population growth (both urban and rural) has built in obstacles in the form of a surplus labour force in the urban areas which has to be employed before there is any scope for a significant shift of population from the rural to the urban areas. This not only slows down the tempo of urbanization, but also worsens the situation in rural areas. While the pressure on land goes on increasing, the channels of rural–urban migration are closed or narrowed down on account of the 'push-back' from urban areas.

Even during 1951–61, when intensive industrialization programmes were undertaken, the number of employees in large factories only increased by one million. In 1961, while 10.75 per cent of the urban working population was employed in mining and manufacturing, service occupations accounted for 20.12 per cent. Even at the end of the 1960s the Planning Commission concluded that the already high rate of growth in tertiary* employment was likely to accelerate in the coming years (Government of India, 1970:429–34).

The literature on Third World urbanization is replete with discussions on the correlation between industrialization and urbanization and the push and pull factors in rural to urban migration. A thesis propounded by some Western writers on the basis of the negative correlation between industrialization and urbanization in Third World countries, i.e. the 'tertiarization' of their urban economies, is that they are suffering from 'over-urbanization'. This essentially derives from a comparison of present Third World urbanization patterns with those which occurred in industrialized countries during supposedly 'comparable' periods of development. A widespread conception arising from such a thesis is that of a 'human avalanche' (Ward and Dubois, 1972) of migrants streaming into the big cities, creating enormous problems for the urban authorities. This has led to a belief, common among planners, of a need to curb this mobility by discouraging or preventing further migration through action at the urban end.

Both Sovani (1966:1–13) and Bose (1973:77) have challenged the over-urbanization thesis, demanding fresh thinking on the role of urbanization in economic development in the Indian context in particular and in the Third World context in general. The comparatively lower rates of unemployment found among migrants that non-migrants in Indian cities leads to the probable explanation that a large number of migrants unable to secure jobs in the

---

*That is trade and commerce, transport, storage and communications, and services.

city either return to their places of origin or move somewhere else*.

At the same time, it is true that more people come to the cities in search of *some* employment than *better* employment. On the basis of the National Sample Survey data, Bose (1977:116) has estimated that for every 100 persons who migrate to urban areas because they have found better employment, 254 come in search of employment. He argues that the popular view that rural–urban migration is creating serious problems and that such migration should be curbed is an over-simplification. The question to be asked is: a serious problem for whom? Certainly not for the rural migrants in spite of all the hostilities of the urban environment. In fact poverty and unemployment in rural areas drive them to the city. One cannot in the name of 'orderly urban development' look upon cities as the exclusive preserve of those already there.

Industrial Investment and Unemployment

In terms of the structure of the international economy, within which the problems of the Third World were presented in the first chapter, the pattern of Indian economic development, as evident from its employment problems, is clear. Registered unemployment was 2.6 million in 1966 and 8.2 million in 1973 (NIB, 1976:9). By 1974 it had reached 8.4 million and is now estimated as being in excess of 10 million (EPW, 1976b). Estimated unemployment was already 18.7 million in 1971 (according to official sources reported in NIB (1976)) and in 1977, the estimate had risen to 40 million (Palkhivala, 1977:9). (In 1961 the total population of India was 439 million and this had increased to 548 million by 1971, when the number of people of working age (15–54 years) had reached 280 million.) Until the late 1960s it was thought that a sufficiently high rate of economic growth would automatically raise the living standards of even the poorest sections of society. As this proved incorrect, it was felt necessary at the time of the formulation of the Fifth Five Year Plan (1974–79) to take specific action to improve the conditions of the bottom 30 per cent of the population. The Draft Plan defined the two crucial objectives of planned development as the 'attainment of economic self-reliance and the removal of poverty'. Further, it stressed that 'growth and reduction in inequality are both indispensable to a successful attack on mass poverty' (Government of India, 1974: Vol. 1, 1).

By the early 1970s the growth of poverty and unemployment in the country had become such a major social issue that Indira Gandhi's Congress Party swept the polls in 1971 on the populist *Garibi Hatao* (eliminate poverty) slogan.

*In urban India, the unemployment rate was 8.2 per cent among the resident (non-migrant) population while it was 6.4 per cent among the migrant population (Government of India, 1962). In urban Dehli it was found that, while 4.2 per cent of the work force in resident households was unemployed, only 2.7 per cent of the work force among migrant (excluding refugee) households was unemployed (Rao and Desai, 1965:380). In Bombay city 7.1 per cent of the resident males were unemployed, while only 4.5 per cent of the immigrant males (non-refugees) were unemployed (Lakdawala *et al.*, 1963:482).

Yet, six years later, including the intervening experience of 20 months of 'emergency' rule*, the budget speech of the Finance Minister of the new Janata Government admitted that:

A significant consequence of low and unevenly distributed growth has been that the proportion of people living below the poverty line is today higher than it was in 1960–61 . . The magnitude of the problem can be assessed from the fact that in 1975–76, the economy did not have the capacity to absorb the production of even 120 million tons of food grains. This low level of purchasing power is a reflection of the chronic state of underemployment and unemployment which is faced by a large number of landless workers and small and marginal farmers. (*Times of India*, 1977)

This pessimistic picture should not be allowed to detract from what may appear a paradoxical fact that, along with the three major countries of Latin America (Brazil, Argentina and Mexico) and South Africa, India now has the most highly developed industrial sector in the Third World, comparable to that of parts of Southern Europe. According to Frank (1977:463):

Since Independence, investment, much of it by the state, has preferentially gone into industry and particularly into very capital-intensive heavy industry. Despite the public attention and private effort devoted to industry – or perhaps rather because of the over-investment in industry without 'walking on two legs' *à la* China to develop concomitant inputs and market demand from the agricultural sector – Indian industry and with it the Indian economy has suffered from a chronic crisis, marked by stagnating production, widespread under-utilisation of installed productive capacity and low or purely speculative investment since the mid-1960s. The result is the institutilization of economic, political and military repression under 'emergency rule' designed to favour Indian and foreign monopoly capital still further without solving any of the structural problems of the Indian economy.

Although Frank wrote this paper when the 'emergency' was still in force, as the title of the paper—Emergence of permanent Emergency in India—suggests, his main argument is that irrespective of which government is in power, it will have to resort to repressive measures to deal with the crisis in the Indian economy unless the social structure undergoes very major changes.

An example of the nature of contradictions generated by big industry's control of key sectors of the economy is the structure of the cloth industry. India is the third largest exporter of cotton textiles and ranks first in installed capacity. Yet the per capita cloth consumption in the country fell by nearly 15 per cent between 1965 and 1976. This is attributed mainly to the steep rise in

---

*Among the key 'achievements' of the emergency was a 10 per cent rate of growth in industrial production during 1976–77. However, the employment and 'distributive' effects of this increased production are evident from the fact that during the first year of emergency rule, an estimated 700,000 workers were laid off (EPW, 1976a), strikes were banned, workers' annual bonuses were reduced, and already declining wages were either frozen or actually lowered.

cloth prices, particularly from mid-1972. The government initiated several schemes to ensure adequate availability of cloth for the masses. One of these, introduced in 1964, was the Controlled Cloth Scheme and according to Nambiar (1977)

> the textile industry was dead set on frustrating the scheme. The government succumbed to the pressures from industrial houses and the scheme failed. When it was introduced in 1964, the share of controlled cloth to the total cloth output was fixed at 50 per cent. In 1967, it was reduced to 40 per cent and further to 25 per cent the following year. By 1976, the percentage of controlled cloth to the total cloth production was only a little over 10 per cent.

By 1978, the obligation to produce controlled cloth had been removed altogether. While more and more Indian textiles flood the international markets, the Indian masses have even less cloth than before.

The same is true of food production. After the bumper harvest of 1975–76, the government considered the export of 'surplus' food as 'aid' to other countries despite the fact that four out of ten people live below the poverty line, and another four at or just above it.

An end to destitution or poverty in the near future seems nowhere in sight.

3

Origins of the Planning
Concepts Applied in Chandigarh

'Town planning' as a profession was virtually non-existant in India at the time
of Independence. Local government intervention in the physical growth of
towns had originated from the same problems as it had in Britain, namely
public health. As early as 1859, deteriorating environmental conditions in the
growing urban centres had led to the appointment of a Royal Commission by
the British Parliament. A number of preventive measures were introduced as an
extension of municipal functions, the emphasis remaining on the maintenance
of essential services. Worsening conditions led to the creation of Improvement
Trusts in a number of cities at the beginning of the century. The limited
administrative and financial powers given to them, however, restricted their
activities to piecemeal efforts at urban development. Following Patrick
Geddes' visit to India in 1915, some States, particularly Bombay and Madras,
enacted Town Planning Acts on the lines of the British Housing and Town
Planning Act of 1909.

However, progress in town planning and improvement remained minimal.
The impetus given to industrialization by the First World War led to the
construction of a number of industrial new towns, including Jamshedpur which
was planned by Fred Temple, a British sanitary engineer. It was not until after
the Second World War, with the attainment of independence on the horizon,
that urban improvement and planning were given any serious thought. Then,
for the first time, an effort was made to view the problem from a national level.

Urban development by the British had been confined to the construction of
separate residential 'colonies' outside cities – called 'Cantonments' for their
military staff and 'Civil Lines' for officials and businessmen. These were built
on spacious layouts with large 'bungalows' and were destined to become the
haunts of the Indian elite after the departure of the British*. In all cases, these
had been designed and planned by British personnel. The most recent and
largest British venture had been the building of the Imperial Capital at New

---

*The contrast between the Civil Lines and the densely populated city proper inhabited by the
majority of the Indian population has been vividly described by Nehru in his autobiography
(1962:143 – 4). The Indian parts of cities received little planning attention during British rule.

Delhi, both planned and designed by Edwin Lutyens in 1912 in the *beaux arts* tradition.

Thus, at the outset, the picture from the point of view of the availability of technical Indian staff was dismal. Municipal bodies of most cities had posts for Chief Architects but their work was confined to drawing elevations for 'beautification' of building façades. According to Otto Koenigsberger*, 'nobody quite knew what to do with them'. In 1948, when an Indian Board of Town Planners was constituted, it had only eight members, most of whom were architects who had also taken on planning responsibilities.

The first major town planning efforts of the Government of Independent India consisted of the building of a large number of refugee towns by the Ministry of Rehabilitation. Because of the emergency situation, and the inability and unwillingness of refugees to await the preparation of elaborate plans, most of these towns were built around quickly drawn up guidelines. In the absence of rigidly predefined frameworks for physical development, considerable efforts went into genuine rehabilitation; not just physical, but economic and social as well. Already, the unsuitability of European planning methods was being realized. For example, Koenigsberger (1952:95) had observed:

> The people who are to benefit by planning are poor and produce little. Thinking in terms of welfare is of no avail if the aggregate production of the country is not enough to pay for it. The emphasis must be upon increased production and balanced occupational distribution. Improved living conditions, amenities and welfare must go hand in hand with greater productivity, but cannot precede it.

Considering the scarcity of technically trained staff, the refugee towns were planned and built on sound principles and modest lines, with little preoccupation with either 'grandness' of vision or quality of 'style'.

However, during the Freedom Movement, national leaders and intellectuals had been searching for an 'Art and Architecture' which could serve as an expression of independent nationhood. Neither the refugee nor the industrial new towns built immediately after Independence satisfied this need. Many staunch nationalists had favoured a search in the past, and a number of prominent buildings had actually been built in the Mughal style. In the field of town planning, some suggested using the *Mansara Shilpa Shastras*, one of the most ancient Indian treatises on town planning dating back to the third century AD.

With the opportunity to choose any direction at that time, however, the choice was definitely in favour of moving forward; anything to do with 'tradition' being too easily associated with backwardness. Furthermore, there was no Indian tradition of planning upon which the conception of the new

*Otto Koenigsberger came to India in 1939 as Architect and Town Planning Officer to the State of Mysore. After Independence he was appointed Director of Housing in the Ministry of Health. In that key position he was faced with the extraordinary problem of housing millions of refugees and the planning of several refugee rehabilitation townships.

capital could be based. For these reasons, it was decided that the planner for Chandigarh must be sought from outside. It was Le Corbusier and his architectural and planning proposals for the city which provided the new expression being sought by the national leadership. The aspirations of the venture were crystallized in the words of Pandit Nehru, one of the staunchest supporters of the project, who said:

> The site chosen is free from the existing encumberances of old towns and old traditions. Let it be the first large expression of our creative genius flowering on our newly earned freedom. (Punjab Government, undated)

In addition to providing, in terms of symbolism, the new expression in architecture and planning needed politically by the national leadership, Chandigarh also represented a subtle, but important, shift in urban planning and design priorities from those around which refugee towns were being built. Its master plan represented the literal transference and unscrupulous application in the Indian context of building design and physical planning concepts which had been evolved in Europe. These had emerged as a definite response to changes in the socio-economic structures of European societies at a particular stage of technological advancement and growth of monopoly capitalism. As no such transformation of the Indian social structure had taken place, the wholesale transference of these concepts to India represented a more or less complete separation of physical planning and design from economic issues, and the replacement of social and economic considerations as a basis for decision-making by the use of abstract professional norms. Thus, instead of centering planning proposals around enabling the majority of urban households to be engaged in productive occupations, the focus shifted to a preoccupation with visual appearance and aesthetic style, and a virtually total control of land and building use specified on the basis of assumed criteria. In this respect, urban planning in India since Independence has been characterized by a lack of evolution in response to local needs and priorities, and a reliance on imported solutions devised for very different socio-economic conditions. By virtue of this, it has added yet another distorting dimension to the already existing multitude of problems and contradictions confronting the mass of the urban population. To substantiate these arguments, it is necessary to present the social and economic origins of the planning concepts applied in the city – the same concepts which have found wide application in other Third World countries, and also in many of their new towns, such as Brasilia, Islamabad and Tema.

Le Corbusier and CIAM

One of the most formative movements in European Planning was based on the idealism of Le Corbusier and his fellow members of the Congrès Internationaux d'Architecture Moderne (CIAM). In terms of Chandigarh itself, this movement obviously played a key role because of the appointment of Le Corbusier and the other three foreign architect/planners*, all members of CIAM, to plan and design the city. CIAM became a rallying point for the Modern Movement in Architecture and Urbanism between the two wars, and Le Corbusier remained one of its key figures until its disbandonment in 1956.

Born into a Swiss watchmaker's family in La Chaux de Fonds in the Jura region of Switzerland, Le Corbusier was largely a self-taught man. Brought up by God-fearing and nature-loving parents, his own life became a search for the principles of artistic creation and the role of an artist as an individual in society. He made significant contributions not only in the fields of architecture and town planning, but also as a prolific writer, painter and sculptor. One of his main preoccupations remained a synthesis of the major arts.

His interest in town planning dated back to the second decade of this century when Western cities were in dissarray and planning practice was largely confined to a number of preventive controls. There was a lack of direction and the profession was in a formative stage; it had been professionalized in Britain only in 1914. Because recognition of the need for planning had originated in the deterioration of the physical environment, it was predominantly those in the design professions who were attempting to wrest it from the impasse.

It was in this context that Le Corbusier made a bold and dramatic appearence on the scene. In 1923, with the publication of his first book, *Vers une Architecture*, he created a sensation among architectural circles. In 1925, his first book on town planning was published under the title *Urbanisme*. Seeking to define the principles of both modern architecture and town planning, he quickly took the lead of the Modern Movement which was to dominate architectural and town planning thought up to the 1950s.

Le Corbusier's interest in town planning was a natural consequence of his involvement with architecture. That, with the onset of the industrial era, the whole basis of traditional society had undergone revolutionary changes, demanding radically different solutions particularly with regard to the City, became for him a central concern in life. In a manifesto accompanying the presentation of his first major planning project 'A Contemporary City of Three Million Inhabitants' in Paris in 1922, he attempted to focus attention on the changed circumstances in relation to the city:

The great city is a recent event and dates back barely fifty years. The growth of every city has exceeded all provision . . . The new phenomenon of the great city has arisen within the framework of the old city. The disproportion is such that an intense crisis has been brought about.

This crisis is only at its beginning. It's a constant source of disorder . . . In order to transform our cities we must discover the fundamental principles of modern town planning. (Le Corbusier, 1971:86–7)

*Besides Le Corbusier, the team comprised Jane Drew and Maxwell Fry from Britain and Pierre Jeanneret, Le Corbusier's French cousin.

In *Urbanisme* he attempted to lay

the foundations of modern town planning, based on four direct and concise requirements which are capable of meeting effectively the dangers which threaten us:

1. *We must decongest the centres of cities* in order to provide for the demands of traffic.

2. *We must increase the density of the centres of cities* in order to bring about the close
contact demanded by business.

3. *We must increase the means whereby traffic can circulate,* i.e. We must completely
modify the present-day conception of the street, which has shown itself useless with
regard to the new phenomenon of modern means of transport; tubes, motors, trams and
airplanes.

4. *We must increase the areas of green and open spaces*; this is the only way to ensure the
necessary degree of health and peace to enable men to meet the anxieties of work
occasioned by the new speed at which business is carried on.

. . . The technical apparatus and the organization of this age are such as to offer a
satisfactory solution; it is at this stage that the wholē question becomes exciting, and
that we can envisage the advent of a new age of grandeur and majesty. (*Ibid.,* 102)

The 'Contemporary City' provided a new startling image of the city of high
density consisting of tall skyscrapers for both living and working, set in vast
areas of parkland, with segregation of different speeds of traffic. Buildings
covered only 12 per cent of land area, the remaining 88 per cent having been
rescued for parks and circulation.

The first CIAM Congress attempted 'to establish a general programme of
action aiming to wrest architecture from the academic impasse and to place it in
its general economic and social setting'. To the declaration signed by the
participants were attached four extracts, in which were collected the
conclusions of the Congress, the fourth of these dealing with 'Architecture and
its relation to the State'. It reflected, with insight, the realization that an
up-to-date architecture was largely a question of the political power of the
Academy, the educational establishment, which had to be attacked, and less of
its 'false views and equally false products'. Le Corbusier had originally put
down these thoughts on a long strip of paper on the right side of which a
fortress tower was drawn: the State. He expressed the meaning of his drawing
with the slogan 'We must reach the State' (Le Corbusier, 1955:vol.1,175).
This directly political claim gave to the first epoch in the history of CIAM its
special character. Its purpose was described in the statutes as follows: to
establish the demands of the New Building; to champion the demands of the
New Building; to carry the ideas of the New Building into technical,
administrative and social circles; to see that building projects are resolved in the
spirit of the day.

A section of the declaration on 'General Economy' elucidates the architectural problem by starting with the economically-founded demand for standard-
ization in building. This would operate in three respects:

It demands from the architect conceptions which bring with them a simplification of the work processes in the factory and on site; it demands from the building contractor a curtailment of the trades involved in the building work process, and it demands from the consumer a clarification of his requirements in the sense of a far-reaching generalization of his dwelling habits in favour of the most general possible realization of the — at present neglected — requirements of the great mass of the population. (Quoted by Steinmann, 1972)

During the whole of the nineteenth century mass housing remained outside architecture; it belonged to the 'mere buildings' of the working classes and had no right to architecture which remained the prerogative of the cultivated bourgeoisie. After the First World War, with the near economic collapse of most European countries, a change in this situation came when the State had to intervene increasingly in the house-building industry. For the members of CIAM, this also became a kind of weapon by which the academics could be fought politically, for: 'the Academics induce the State to spend considerable sums on the erection of monumental buildings to the detriment of the most pressing problems of housing and urban development', as the fourth extract attached to the declaration of the First Congress remarked.

The Second Congress, held in 1929, was committed to establishing the biological and sociological foundations of the 'minimum' or 'ration dwelling'. As pointed out by Steinmann (1972:52):

The description of the 'Ration Dwelling' in biologically and socially comprehensible terms appears to debunk the human being to serviceable needs, which can be satisfied by constructional measures, without recognising or acknowledging, that these needs are moulded by society. Without wishing to underestimate the tendency of functionalism to regard itself as an end in itself, there were other reasons for the standpoints (of CIAM participants). They consisted of the suitability of the demands to the conditions of the means of production most appropriate to the provision of the 'consumer house', the house as a commodity, in large quantities: industrialised production.

Thus effectively, the Modern Movement in architecture and building was a vehicle for adapting existing traditions, methods of construction, and building form to the changed conditions brought about by increasing mechanization; in fact of moulding institutional practices to the needs of modern industry. The attacks on the Academy, or the old establishment, were rooted in its having become an obstacle in the path of enlarging the market for the products of the building industry. The growth of large industrial firms was also eliminating the small builder, or the artisanal mode of production in the building industry, which enabled construction on a one-off basis with wide diversity in building details. The role of the architect was similarly being transformed into one enabling mediation between the economic demands of standardized production methods in the factory and the diverse requirements of individual clients.

Building regulations, the means at the disposal of the State to realize similar demands of uniformity in the private sector, also constituted an important topic of discussion at the Second Congress.

> The existing regulations are partly contradictory to present needs. . . The amendment of such regulations can only be carried out on the basis of new architectural and urbanistic proposals, which include the acquisition of new techniques. These proposals must be worked out. (Le Corbusier, 1930)

The notion that human progress is brought about through technical advance, has considerable weight in Le Corbusier's writing. It also defines his opinions on the proceedings of the Second Congress, 'that we must draw our efficacy from alliance with industry'.

By 1930, having refined his earlier projects, Le Corbusier produced the concept of 'The Radiant City', which, according to him, contained the elements of a doctrine of urbanism to be used as the basis of our Machine Age civilization (Le Corbusier, 1967:3). It was first publicly exhibited at the Brussels CIAM Congress of 1930. Here, he set the city of concentration (1000 persons per hectare) against the city of dispersal in order to avoid 'waste of time, of energy, of money, of land'. He termed the Garden City a 'pre-Machine Age utopia' and took a bold stand for 'urbanization rather than disurbanization'. In his own words, 'to urbanize the town and to urbanize the country' rather than to disurbanize both was the correct technical approach for the immediate future. While he denounced the American suburb as 'the organized slavery of capitalist society (*Ibid.,* 38), as leading to isolated individualism and to the destruction of the collective spirit and, by virtue of an inherent increase in journey time, as being an actual attack upon human freedom, he also saw Soviet disurbanization as being an uneconomic and inhuman technique of urban colonization.

The socio-political structure, within which the 'Radiant City' was set, had as its ideal absolute respect for the individual subject only to the sanctions of universal, social and cosmic law, and to the dictates of a plan collectively conceived and administered. The three main *decisions* set out as indispensable preconditions to the establishment of a planned economy as they appear in the text are:

1. To undertake a wholesale reorganization of land tenure in the country as a whole and in the cities in particular.

2. To take an inventory of our cities' populations: differentiation, classification, reassignment, transplantation, intervention, etc.

3. To establish a plan for producing permissible goods; to forbid with stoic firmness all useless products. To employ the forces liberated by these means in the rebuilding of the city and the whole country. (*Ibid.,* 148-52)

Le Corbusier was well aware that this represented a simplistic view of the socio-political structure of European industrial society and its decision-making processes, for in his address to the Brussels CIAM Congress he said:

> Let's not go into politics and sociology here. . . We are not competent to discuss these intricate questions. . . I repeat: here we should make known. . . the possibilities afforded by modern techniques and the need for a new kind of architecture and planning. (*Ibid.,* 37)

The 1933 Congress in Athens formulated a treatise on town planning in the form of the *Charter of Athens* which became a work of reference for CIAM members dealing with urban problems. Its most significant contribution was the formal definition of four basic functions of the city as *living, working, recreation* and *communication* and establishing that:

> Planning determines the co-ordination of these four basic functions and determines their place in the master plan. (*Marg*, 1949)

It proclaimed that the materials of urbanism are Sun, Space and Greenery and that 'conditions of nature', forgotten, abandoned and lost, should be reintroduced into urban life. The Charter deplored the chaotic picture presented by most towns, dominated by private interests since the beginning of the Machine Age. In the epilogue, it clarified:

> The individual right has nothing to do with the mean interest which benefits a minority and condemns the remaining social masses to a mediocre life. Therefore private interests require severe restriction. They must remain subordinate to collective interests. Each single person should be in a position to take part in the joys of life.
>
> Comfort of the house = Beauty of the town. *(Ibid.)*

Functional Segregation of Land Use

As in the case of the 'New Building', the rationale underlying the physical separation of the four functions with the help of unifunctional land-use controls was a response to the changed socio-economic structure of European society brought about by the First Machine Age. The growth of monopoly capitalism had led to increasingly large industrial enterprises and a clearer polarization between the organized working classes and other sections of society. The larger industrial units were leading to an increasing socialization of production processes, resulting in a separation between zones of production and zones of reproduction (or consumption). The family as the unit of both production and consumption was no longer the dominant norm. This, of course, is not to say that small family enterprises, particularly in trading and services did not continue on a considerable scale where the 'home' remained the place of both production and consumption. But it was the problems produced by rapid industrial growth under private ownership, where the industrialist remained unaccountable for the social costs of poor working environments and pollution, that led to the necessity for segregating industrial areas from residential ones. This was a part of the wider process leading to an increasing separation between zones of production and consumption, and an alienation of the State decision-makers from the labour process.

As mentioned in chapter 1, the capitalist city 'can be seen as a spatial form which, by reducing indirect costs of production, and costs of consumption and circulation, speeds up the rotation of capital' (Lojkine, 1976:127). Concentrating industrial and commercial uses in clearly demarcated zones reduces the costs to capital. It is interesting that the land-use proposals arising out of the Charter of Athens did not focus so much upon preventing environmental pollution by industry as on isolating pollution-prone industrial zones from other sections of the community. Sun, space and greenery, thus, could only become the preserve of those not directly engaged in industrial production, and would leave industrial workers to suffer from pollution without even the benefit of support for better conditions from other sections of the community.

That land-use planning, based on a clear separation of functions is unsuitable for societies where the dominant production processes have not resulted in a similar change in socio-economic structures is all too obvious. The problems arising out of an unquestioned application of this doctrine in Chandigarh's master plan will be discussed later.

'The Three Human Establishments'

Returning to Le Corbusier, during the war years he produced the concept of 'The Three Human Establishments' with the French group L'ASCORAL*. This was basically an extension of the physical re-ordering of the internal spatial structure of cities (underlying his earlier city planning proposals) to a larger system of global land occupation. It proposed different forms and functions for different types of settlements, specifying the relationships between them. Accordingly, the three human establishments of the 'machinist' civilization were classified as:

1. The unity of agricultural exploitation;
2. The linear industrial city;
3. The radio-concentric city of exchanges (Le Corbusier, 1959b)

In the midst of rural areas of agricultural production, *linear industrial cities* along major routes of communication were to be established. According to Le Corbusier, this implied 'the coordinated redistribution of industrial establishments of proper size' and allowed 'residence in proximity of work, dwelling and work henceforth being installed in "conditions of nature"'. These industrial cities maintained 'contact with the cultural exchange centres that have always been installed at road crossings'.

The *city of exchanges,* according to the system, is of a radio-concentric nature.

Here, are merchants who distribute goods. Here, transactions are made. Here, are the large schools and universities. Here, authority has been established when necessary. Place of concentration and diffusion; place of exchange, place of distribution. (Le Corbusier, 1953b)

Chandigarh thus became classified as a 'radio-concentric city of exchanges'.

*Assemblée de Constructeurs pour une Revolution Architecturale.

Within this (simplistic) schematic framework of spatial organization, the 'cities of exchanges' were visualized as centres of decision-making and consumption, as also of areas devoted to cultural and creative activity. The physical separation between zones of production and zones of consumption was seen as being extendable from that proposed within cities, by the Charter of Athens, to even *between* the three types of settlements classified by Le Corbusier. Because of a lack of any provision for a productive base in the 'cities of exchanges', these were implicitly visualized as consumption centres, where the 'elitist meritocracy' in which Le Corbusier believed, would reside.

Until the early 1950s, Le Corbusier had been demonstrating the application of his doctrine through planning proposals, largely of redevelopment, for several major cities of the world. Not a single proposal, despite some promising opportunities after the Second World War, had reached the stage of materialization. In fact, besides Chandigarh, it was only in Brasilia, the new capital city of another Third World country, that the basic principles of Le Corbusier's doctrine were uncompromisingly applied.

He presented his proposals and the principles underlying them in numerous books which were the basis of a vast and successful propaganda machine which kept the world informed of his latest ideas and their fate in reality.

His prolific creations in the planning field with their almost complete lack of success in finding materialization made him see himself more and more in the role of a persecuted prophet. He projected this image in much of his writing with a unique combination of wit and irony.

It was against this background that, late in 1950, Corbusier was approached by Thapar and Varma, the two Indian officials in charge of recruiting architects/planners for Chandigarh, to work on the new city (see chapter 4).

Le Corbusier and the Modern Movement in Perspective

To summarize, Le Corbusier's search was for a new philosophy in harmony with the Machinist Era, which he viewed with supreme optimism. His call was for a bold expression, through urbanism, of society's confidence in the future. For him, city planning, besides being a science, was the noblest of the Arts; the 'expression of the activity of an epoch'. He had an abhorrence for the crude materialism by which he found himself surrounded. Faced with the conflict between individual freedom and collective interests in capitalist society, he displayed a firm belief in an 'elitist meritocracy' of artists and technicians, which he felt should be put in charge of protecting the community from the 'mean private interests'. By so doing, he could evade the internal contradictions in his own thinking; he could use his advocacy for the responsibility of planning being entrusted to 'experts' with 'their strict scientific analysis' as an instrument for disguising his own intuitive and subjective method of working, and for justifying the transfer of decision-making control into the hands of a small elite group of individuals like himself.

His intuitive confidence in the validity of his planning doctrine enabled him to rebuff criticisms with ease, indeed contempt, and he was constantly surprised and impatient when he failed to convince people. His arrogance resulting from this confidence gave him the reputation of being a difficult person to work with. When first asked his opinion about introducing Le Corbusier to the Chandigarh team, Maxwell Fry had replied to Thapar, 'Honour and glory for you, and an unpredictable portion of misery for me' (Fry, 1977:352).

His concern with visual expression, and his belief that his inspiration was underpinned by the laws of nature, made him confident that control of the physical environment was a major, if not *the* major factor in the creation of an ideal society, leading to a kind of 'environmental determinism'. He referred to the physical environment disregarding the totality of the environmental phenomenon which includes people, and most of all, people. He could separate the physical from the social because he could not be bothered about sociology and politics, particularly when taking them into account implied a fundamental reappraisal of his entire philosophy. It was far more convenient for him to refer to social and political matters opportunistically when this aided him in projecting an authoritative image, as in his 'Radiant City', and to dismiss them when taking them into account would have brought him face to face with the contradictions in his assertions (as he did during the Congress in Brussels).

The Modern Movement as a whole (including the standpoints taken by CIAM) adopted in its ideas the techno-scientific language of the First Machine Age, in order to make architecture 'mathematically demonstrable'*, and make itself part of the overall production process. This afforded the Movement its essential *entré* to the 'technical, administrative and social circles'. The necessity of this arose out of the need for members to obtain commissions not only from wealthy clients but also from the State which started increasing its intervention in the provision of housing.

However, the Architects–State alliance did not arise out of the architects having succeeded in influencing State policies towards socially-defined goals, such as solving the housing problem. The State's interest in public housing was a product of political expediency which the Modern Movement latched onto because of its own self-interest. This was clearly demonstrated when most of the German architects, who went to the United States during Hitler's fascism, soon forgot the 'minimum dwelling' and started designing skyscraper offices. American capital was, at that time, particularly oriented towards exploiting the economic boom generated by the war. The same architects turned away from housing there, as after all, their real alliance was with industry rather than housing for the masses.

The valuation of the techno-factual decision as 'good' in the widest sense

*Walter Gropius, letter to Hans Schmidt in preparation for the Second Congress in Frankfurt in 1929.

(for example, the basis on which the 'Ration' or 'Minimum Dwelling' was worked out) did not remain unopposed within CIAM. It is useful to quote, finally, the conclusion which Hans Schmidt (one of the active participants of CIAM) drew from the situation of the New Building in the capitalist West, as it reveals the overtly apolitical standpoint of CIAM as a pre-requisite for the collaboration of leading modern architects at that time:

> It is not to be contested, that the so-called New Building has drawn its architectonic demands from the scientific, technical and cultural activities of developed capitalism and is therefore to be regarded as a definite element of progress. On the other hand, however, it is obvious that even the most progressive Western architecture cannot in its potential go beyond the boundaries imposed by capitalism. This is particularly apparent in the case of the social goals, which the New Building has set itself. If, in this situation, the Congress were to take up an anti-capitalist stance, it would obviously lose any possibility of practical everyday work for both its participants and the whole organisation. Yet, if it chooses the path of a politically neutral organization, this obviously implies a limitation of the operational possibilities, which it appeared to have in the first years of its existance. They will have to concentrate all their work on the technical and scientific foundations of the new architecture. (Quoted in Steinmann, 1972:55)

4

Preparation and Framework
of the Master Plan

As described in the previous chapter, the priorities on which urban planning in Independent India was to focus were still undefined when Chandigarh was first contemplated. Confronted by the task of rehabilitating millions of uprooted and homeless refugees, senior government decision-makers were being forced to take into account the socio-economic conditions of the mass of the population. However, the arrival of Le Corbusier and his team with a package of formulae, presented as a universal panacea, significantly altered the focus of their key concern. Instead of taking direct account of existing day-to-day problems of the people, the emphasis shifted to an application of abstract concepts and principles considered capable of solving all urban problems. The accountability of government officials for the social and economic problems of the ordinary citizens changed, instead, to government authorities' holding the citizens accountable for not conforming to the dictates of the plan. Instead of the plan being responsive to the needs of the majority, the majority was expected to adjust to the assumptions contained in the plan.

This was indeed a fundamental change with long-term implications. It affected not only the destiny of the city itself, but also the attitudes of professionals and administrators towards the problems of the average citizen. It also had a major influence on defining the role and status of architects and planners in society; in their acquiring an almost unchallenged right to specify not only the detailed use of land and buildings on the basis of imported professional norms, but also the activities and occupations acceptable or unacceptable in the new city.

This subtle but significant change in planning method and priorities, which almost went by unnoticed at that time, did not occur in a social vacuum; the historical context provided all the prerequisites for the legitimization of such an approach. Le Corbusier simply provided the tools the local authorities were searching for. How this change actually took place can be best understood by examining the way in which Chandigarh's master plan was prepared and finalized.

The First Chandigarh Plan

By the time Le Corbusier and his team became associated with Chandigarh, a considerable amount of ground work had already been done by the Punjab Government. A site had been selected, a brief for the planner drawn up, and a budget for the initial stages of construction finalized and approved. In fact, a plan had already been prepared for the city.

Two Indian officials were in charge of the project: P. N. Thapar, a former member of the British Civil Service in India, and P. L. Varma, the Chief Engineer of Punjab. At the time of Independence, Varma was in the United States as head of an Indian mission studying road construction. In view of the anticipated construction of the new capital, in October 1947, he was asked by the Punjab Government to investigate city planning in the United States. He had studied the project planned for United Nations Headquarters on Lake Success which he later recalled as having proved for him a 'valuable book of reference'.

The site for Chandigarh was literally selected by flying over various tracts of land. It was seen as offering almost ideal conditions. Locationally, it was close to a road junction and a railway line. The lack of any existing cities in the immediate vicinity was considered a great advantage with regard to the city's potential for future expansion. Topographically, the site was almost flat, but with a gentle slope ideal for drainage. Two seasonal rivers, Sukhna Cho and Patiali Rao, formed its natural boundaries on the east and west respectively. Situated at the foot of the Shivalik mountain range, the permanent background of the Himalayas gave it great scenic beauty. The land was fertile with an abundant natural supply of underground water. The site was also close to sources of building materials like sand, cement and stone (Punjab Government, undated).

Planning the town had originally been entrusted to Albert Mayer of Mayer, Whittlesey and Glass of New York. Mayer had served as a Lieutenant Colonel in India during the Second World War, was acquainted with Nehru, and had some familiarity with India and its problems.

Late in December 1949, the contract for the first master plan of Chandigarh was completed and the work began. According to the brief, the plan was to be prepared for an initial population of 150,000 with indications of future expansion for a population of 500,000. The detailed plans would include a master layout for the city, areas of residence, business, industry, recreation and so on. Plans were to be made for special areas including a capitol complex containing the provincial assembly, the governor's palace and the high court. Locations for special buildings, such as hospitals, schools and shopping centres, were to be shown. Landscaping and architectural control were to be indicated for typical parks, principal avenues, and major building complexes. A site for the university was to be designated. Areas to be placed under temporary or permanent land-use controls were to be identified. Finally, sites were required for service industries which might spring up with the growth of the town (Evenson, 1966:12)*.

This brief had been prepared on the basis of the subjective judgments and perceptions of the officials in charge of what a modern capital *should* have. The dislocation and upheaval caused by Partition had made the existing statistics or socio-economic data unusable. To estimate the demand for plots in the new city, applications were invited from the public in 1948. The response was overwhelming. This had justified going ahead with the project. The detailed contents of the brief reflected the image of 'modernity' and 'progress' held by senior officers, such as Thapar and Varma, although they had to respect the severe financial constraints of the project budget. Chandigarh was never intended to be a social experiment or a vehicle for altering the adminstrative structure inherited from the British.

The initial work on the plan was to be done in Mayer's New York office. He engaged a number of specialists, including a consultant on city economics and transportation, an expert on utilities, roads and site engineering, an adviser on landscaping, and a climatologist. For working on problems of architectural design, he invited a young Polish architect, Mathew Nowicki, to join the team.

In May 1950, in an address given in Washington DC, Mayer described his aims at Chandigarh. He felt that the basic purpose must be to create a sense of pride in the citizen, in the city, and in India. After the political and economic problems following the partition of India:

> we are seeking symbols to restore pride and confidence . . . We are trying not so much to express ourselves or to obtrude ourselves, but to develop the city as modern self-confident Indians would, if there were such a group. We cannot only do a more viable job, but a more Indian job than they could, because I think we can really enter into their spirit. Practically all forward looking Indians have been educated in and dazzled by the Western world, so that for a considerable time to come, they will be doing Western work. (Mayer, 1950)

The basic unit of Mayer's plan, the 'super-block' (or neighbourhood unit) was described as particularly suitable for India, where 'many city dwellers are still villagers and small community people at heart and fairly recently by origin'.

While planning for traffic separation within and around the 'superblocks', Mayer experienced certain problems peculiar to the Indian situation, for the mixtures of traffic found on Indian roads is unknown in Europe and America. As Mayer (1951) put it, it 'demands a prognostication for which, I believe, no Western example is applicable'. The plan ultimately developed provided accommodation for pedestrians, cyclists and animal drawn vehicles.

The question of whether or not Chandigarh would grow to the projected population seriously worried Mayer. In a letter to Maxwell Fry he wrote, 'A big

*Quoted by Evenson from a letter sent by Albert Mayer to P. L. Varma on December 28, 1949, giving written acceptance of a verbal contract of December 20, and also in the official contract of January 15, 1950.

problem and question mark is whether this city will reach its initial figure of 150,000, let alone 500,000'. He reasoned that Chandigarh had no compelling impetus for growth. It was not a centre of natural resources nor of a large purchasing area, nor was it at a natural and much used transportation crossroads or river confluence. The only sure factor would be the provincial capital function, and that Mayer (1951) felt, was 'demonstrably not enough to make a city of the size contemplated'. In order to stimulate population growth, he believed that industry should be given immediate encouragement.

Essentially, the Mayer plan was based on humane ideals and sprang from an almost anti-urban aesthetic, owing its origins to the Garden City Movement begun by Ebenezer Howard at the end of the nineteenth century.

However, before construction in accordance with Mayer's plan could begin, Mathew Nowicki was killed in a plane crash in August 1950. His death left the Punjab Government with a completed master plan*, on the basis of which a detailed project estimate had been prepared. This included budget allocations for specific buildings and development costs, including thirteen types of houses for government employees in accordance with their salary scales.

The problems experienced with having the planner based in New York when a local technical organization barely existed led to a change in the terms of agreement with the second team. Hardly a month after Nowicki's death, and taking with them the completed master plan, Thapar and Varma set out for Europe. Their mission was to engage two good architects, who were not tied to a particular style and who would be willing to devise an architectural expression in harmony with local Indian conditions. A pre-requisite of signing a contract this time was that the foreign architects would have to reside in India for a minimum of three years to help build up a local organization and train Indian architects to take over responsibility for the project after their departure.

Le Corbusier and Chandigarh

Le Corbusier's association with Chandigarh was the outcome of this trip. When first approached in Paris, he told the Indians 'Your capital can be constructed here. You can rely on us at 35 Rue de Sèvres to produce the solution to the problem' (Le Corbusier, 1955:87). He was completely unprepared to leave his practice in Paris for three years. Prolonged negotiations resulted in Thapar and Varma returning to India with agreements signed with four architects, three of whom, Jane Drew, Maxwell Fry and Pierre Jeanneret, were to work full time on the project for three years. Le Corbusier was appointed as Architectural Adviser to the Punjab Government for the new capital. According to the contract signed on December 19 1950, he was required to render the following services:

*For further details of Mayer's master plan and Nowicki's architectural designs for Chandigarh, see Evenson (1966).

(a) Advise and actively assist in the determination of the general style of architecture to be adopted for the new capital town.

(b) Advise and actively assist in the preparation of the designs of the Principal buildings and, in this connection, even to furnish the sketch studies for some of them.

(c) Advise and actively assist in the laying down of the architectural treatment and control of the prominent features of the new town, such as important roads, streets, squares, public gardens and water features.

(d) Advise and actively assist in the work connected with the landscaping of public places in the new town and its surrounding areas.

(e) Advise and actively assist in the development and detailing of the Master Plan.

(f) Advise and assist in working out of a programme of work for the architectural branch.

Further it was agreed that Le Corbusier 'may continue to reside and work in France but shall visit India and stay at places nominated by Punjab Government for at least sixty days in every twelve months of the period of the contract'*. The signing of the contract included the acceptance of the Mayer plan and the project estimate as the working basis of the agreement.

However the association of Le Corbusier with Chandigarh resulted in the abandonment of Mayer's plan and a dramatic change in the city's destiny. What might have happened if Mayer's plan had been followed can only remain a matter of speculation. What did take place can be better understood by examining Le Corbusier's method of working, the role he saw himself playing within the Chandigarh team, and the manner in which he applied some of his planning and architectural principles to finalize a new master plan within a week of his first visit to India.

When the possibility of working on Chandigarh first arose, the prospects were exciting for Le Corbusier in several respects. While waiting for Thapar and Varma's arrival to discuss the project, he wrote (Le Corbusier, 1950a):

> It is the hour that I have been waiting for: India, that humane and profound civilization. To construct a capital:
>
> > Urbanism is the activity of a society.
> >
> > A capital is the spirit of a nation.
> >
> > A set of tools, it's a conjuncture.
>
> Le Corbusier is an optimist. His name is not mentioned but in 20 years of urbanism, Le Corbusier is in all the projects.

While negotiations about the details of his agreement were under way, he made his views about his capabilities explicit to the Indian Government. In a

*From the contract between Le Corbusier and the Government of Punjab signed on December 19 1950 in Paris. Source: Archives, Fondation Le Corbusier, Paris.

letter addressed to an official in the Indian Embassy in Paris he wrote:

1. I consider myself the only person at the moment, prepared by 40 years of experience and study on this subject, capable of usefully helping your Government. I greatly insist on this information given without modesty.

2. In my participation in this project, I place the pursuit/desire of my career through a work of harmony, of wisdom, of humanity in precise opposition to the chaos generally manifest in urbanism which is only the expression of the chaos reigning in the minds of people on this subject.

The *raison d'etre* of my life is expressed by one word: *harmony* and this resembles beauty 'first above all', order, serenity, effectiveness, economy: in one word wisdom. This wisdom is, alas, a fruit slow in reaching maturity; it is positive if the heart remains young, failing which, it is only a brake. (Le Corbusier, 1950b)

The role of guide or teacher was particularly to Le Corbusier's liking; he wrote (*Ibid.*):

The Indian youth must take a fundamental part in the enterprise, it is they who will be realizing it in the course of the years; but I shall have been able to provide them with a useful springboard to jump from.

The young Hindus whom you will gather together from various universities of the old or the new continent need a doctrinal point of view from the outset; in a way they need a friendly shepherd: they are young, consequently they have to grow, to be nourished, to be given strength, to find their direction. You can arouse enthusiasm in them; everything lies there. If you do not succeed in this, your enterprise is lost. (Le Corbusier, 1950c)

However, Le Corbusier had seen himself not only as a *berger amical* of these young Indians, but also as the spiritual director of the whole enterprize including the other foreign architects in the team. In another document he had outlined his ideas on the organizational structure of the team as follows:

I have qualified this theoretical conception and in practice I have proposed:

1. To assume spiritual and technical direction of the enterprise so as to give it unity.

2. I shall nominate two architects of our spirit, capable and devoted and sufficiently experienced, who would fulfil the functions outlined below.

3. 3 Hindu architects would be permanently attached to our atelier on the Rue de Sèvres to carry out in turn studies as the work proceeds, in order to give them an education of the university type which remains in full contact with the Hindu civilization.

clarifying that:

The role of M. Le Corbusier will be that of co-ordinator and consultant . . . This contract will be bound to that of the two foreign architects who will be under the control of M. Le Corbusier. He will give them orders of a technical and aesthetic nature. (*Ibid.*)

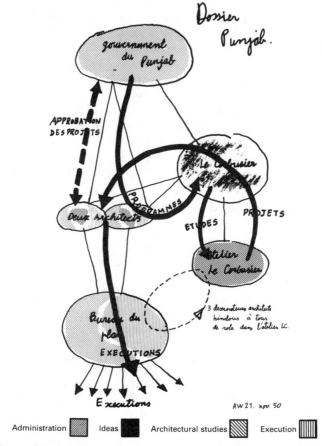

Figure 4.1. Le Corbusier's view of his role in the Chandigarh team.

The role of almost prophet that Le Corbusier saw himself in is best illustrated by the diagram which was attached to the document quoted from above (Figure 4.1). He saw himself as the *sole* supplier of ideas for a city of 500,000 inhabitants.

One of the most significant aspects of working on Chandigarh for the foreign members of the team (all of whom were active participants of CIAM) was that it was going to offer the first real opportunity of applying the thinking on urbanism and architecture developed at the Congresses. Soon after the appointments of all the architects had been finalized, Le Corbusier wrote to Jane Drew and Maxwell Fry in December 1950:

> After 22 years of CIAM action the moment to be heard has arrived, to realize a magnificent work by the productive assembling of talents and efforts.

And after proposing an organizational structure within which to work:

Dear friends Jane Drew and Maxwell Fry, the problem is magnificent. At this moment in the evolution of modern civilization, India represents a quality of spirit particularly attractive. Our task is to discover the urbanism and architecture which is plunged in the vigour of this powerful and profound civilization and give it the modern tools favourable for finding it a place in the present time. It is a task for thinkers and technicians.

The two Indian delegates esteem us; their enquiry in different countries of Europe has demonstrated to them that the grouping described above was incomparable to every other proposition; they are convinced and desirous of signing the contract on these conditions. It is a grand victory for CIAM, it is also an occasion for proving that the CIAM congresses are capable of real action. Without one another, isolated, nothing can be done. Grouped together, everything is possible. (Le Corbusier, 1950d)

With regard to designing for conditions particular to India, Le Corbusier visualized the 'creation of a plans office on the site where the objective is to establish topographic conditions and necessary preparatory statistics for the formulation of the problem and its comprehension' (Le Corbusier, 1950c). According to the programme of work envisaged, he said he could leave for Punjab immediately. He felt he was sufficiently well informed about the Indian civilization, its art, its architecture, and clarifying the nature of services he could give, he said that he

offered a part of his experience in these sort of matters (habitations, offices, urbanization of cities, parks and streets, etc . . .), the benefit of his recent inventions which bring a unity of measure as well as a unity of scale in construction, thus assuring a figure of indestructible beauty.

He brings the 'Modulor', the harmonious measure on human scale universally applicable in architecture and mechanics.

He will also be able to bring the benefit of the 'CIAM GRILLE', which since 1947 has permitted the bringing of considerable means to urban plans. (*Ibid.*)

And as to where the work was to begin:

We will rectify the pilot plan after our trip to India and we will discuss it on the very premises of the plans office on the spot. It will be there that we will give birth to it . . . We must begin from the beginning. (Le Corbusier, 1950e)

On February 18 1951, Le Corbusier left for India and after examining the site of the new city met Fry and Jeanneret in Simla. His method of attacking the problem is best described by Fry (1977:354–6)

The arrival of Corbusier galvanized the situation. We moved down to the Rest House in the lovely village of Chandigarh on the road to Kalka, where the mountain railway starts for Simla. Corbusier, Varma, Jeanneret, myself, and intermittently Thaper were there; Albert Mayer was making his way to us from the South.

Without waiting for Mayer to appear Corbusier started on large sheets of paper to approach a plan by a method of rough and ready analysis familiar to me from the workings of CIAM. First he outlined the main communications with the site on the map of India – air, railway, road. Then he dealt with the site itself – its immediate background of low foothills rising to the sheer mountains of the Himalayas with the peaks beyond; its gentle plain declining at a fall of 1:100; its dry river beds to each side, with a smaller bed intermediate to the left; a diagonal road crossing the plan lowdown and a loop of railway away on the right.

It was a difficult situation. My French was unequal to the occasion. Jeanneret was supernumerary, and Thapar only half aware of what was going forward. Corbusier held the crayon and was in his element.

'Violà la gare' he said *'et voici la rue commerciale'*, and he drew the first road on the new plan of Chandigarh. *'Voici la tête'*, he went on, indicating with a smudge the higher ground to the left of Mayer's location, the ill effects of which I had already pointed out to him. *'Et voila l'estomach, le cité-centre.'* Then he delineated the massive sectors measuring each half by three quarters of a mile and filling out the extent of the plain between the river valleys, with extension to the south.

The plan was well advanced by the time the anxious Albert Mayer joined the group. He must have had an unnerving journey, and he was too upset to make the most of his entry. I found him a high-minded decent man, a little sentimental in his approach, but good-humoured; not in any way was he a match for the enigmatic but determined figure of the prophet.

We sat around after lunch in a deadly silence broken by Jeanneret's saying to Mayer, *'Vous parlez français, monsieur?'* To which Mayer responded, *'Oui, musheer, je parle'*, a polite but ill-fated rejoinder that cut him out of all discussion that followed.

And so we continued, with minor and marginal suggestions from us and a steady flow of exposition from Corbusier, until the plan as we now know it was completed and never again departed from.

Thus, although the contracts with the second team included an acceptance of Mayer's plan, within a week of Corbusier's arrival, it had been abandoned and replaced by the present master plan. On the surface, however, the two plans did not differ significantly, a quick comparison revealing several similarities – in their general layouts, the use of the concept of neighbourhood unit and the functional segregation of land use. The new plan had a slightly reduced area, a marginally increased density, and replaced the winding and curvilenear roads of Mayer's plan by a geometrical grid of fast traffic roads. The 'superblock' was replaced by the 'sector', with a different layout for local shopping centres.

A more fundamental difference lay in the personalities and aims of the two planners. Whereas Mayer had tried to give elements 'of splendour, of greatness, but not overwhelming greatness' for Corbusier, a city was 'the grip of man upon nature' and a 'mighty image which stirs our minds'. To him pursuit of the picturesque represented an abdication of the responsibility to impose discipline for which the architect is trained, and geometry, the foundation and 'the material basis on which we build those symbols which represent to us perfection and the divine' (Le Corbusier, 1971).

Le Corbusier's refusal to accept Mayer's plan created a difficult situation for the Punjab Government who had paid for and approved it already. Besides, Mayer was upset by the turn of events. The problem was eventually resolved by the second team agreeing to develop two 'sectors' in the new plan on the 'superblock' principle as detailed by Nowicki. As the work proceeded, however, the architects found themselves more and more reluctant to use Nowicki's designs. In explaining the situation Fry wrote to Mayer in August 1951,

> Le Corbusier, Jeanneret and I are all architects heavily involved in town planning. Any architect worth the name in charge of building on the scale of this city must have strong ideas on planning as being undisputably an extension of architecture. It is indeed difficult to say where one ends and the other begins. We were therefore forced by our beliefs and ideas to present as completely as possible our conceptions in modifying what you have prepared . . . *What has taken place is inevitably the result of a change over from town planners to architects without a period of joint consultation.* (emphasis added) (Fry, 1951).

Once the dispute with Mayer had been resolved, some conflicts arose between the members of the second team, with Fry and Jeanneret protesting to Corbusier against the way in which he had assumed complete direction and responsibility for the whole enterprise, including the detailed layouts for sectors and designing of all major buildings. They complained that they intended to work in a spirit of *collaboration* advocated by CIAM and were not prepared to simply obey his orders. This was soon resolved and it was agreed that the overall plan of the city, the general control of architectural character of all sectors, including landscaping and the general layout of the city centre would be the joint responsibility of all the architects. Le Corbusier was given complete personal responsibility for the whole complex of administrative buildings to which he then gave his wholehearted attention. The layout of individual sectors and buildings in them, including the thirteen categories of government houses were made the responsibility of the three senior architects, Fry, Jeanneret and later, Jane Drew.

Once the division of responsibility had been clarified, work proceeded briskly, each member trying to give of his best to the enterprise. After his second visit to India, Le Corbusier expressed some of his thoughts to the three senior architects in a letter dated December 12 1951:

> I have meditated a great deal at Simla as well as at Chandigarh and on my way home. I think that none of us, including myself, realizes what will really happen when work really begins . . .
>
> The intellectual conditions are good, for (you will agree with me), *the urbanistic problem of Chandigarh has been solved on doctrinal bases so obvious and unquestionable that the drawings are clear, harmonious and real. Doctrine triumphs and leads all along.* You mustn't forget it. You mustn't lose sight of it for a single moment, as it is precisely Doctrine that is often forgotten on account of 'small sins' (as Maxwell Fry calls them), those small sins that we all love, including myself, but, look out! . . .

I would like to share with you my impression as I went through India on my way home. India has, and always has had a peasant culture that exists since a thousand years! India possesses Hindu temples (generally in carved stone) and Muslim temples in red stone whose architecture is very geometrical. India also possesses Maharaja's palaces and gardens. But India hasn't yet created an architecture for modern civilization (offices, factories, buildings). India is suddenly jumping into the second era of mechanization. Instead of sinking into the gropings and errors of the first era we will be able to fulfil our mission; give India the architecture of modern times (modern techniques, modern mind and adaptation to the surrounding conditions that are extreme over there).

Nowhere in the whole world could a more captivating and positive task be offered to thinkers, aestheticians, and constructors. It is our task and it is worth while!

I will give you my friendly impressions: the first phase of our approach to the problem (March–December 1951) launched us in the study of a thousand little sensitive problems, charming, friendly for the population, delicate and original; but we haven't yet reached the axis of the question, that is to say a fundamental organic architecture, unquestionable, which is neither English, nor French nor American, but Indian of the second half of the twentieth century. So I think we must endeavour to find a fundamental principle.

But I add immediately that I advise and insist that all our efforts and propositions should be accompanied by experimentation . . .

I must tell you that I hope to be able to give you very soon, as well as Messrs Thapar and Varma, some doctrinal principles concerning habitation which will be as clear as the doctrinal principles of urbanization which have allowed us to elaborate so quickly and efficiently the plan of Chandigarh. (Le Corbusier, 1951b, emphasis added)

Thus soon after his association with Chandigarh, Le Corbusier used the force of his personality and the air of supreme confidence in his urban doctrine as instruments for assuming complete control of the decision-making process concerning the basic concept and layout of the master plan. The contradictions running through his earlier writing and between his verbal assertions and his method of working were all too evident in Chandigarh. He could talk about searching for 'unquestionable doctrinal principles' and 'the need for experimentation' in the same breath, just as he could advocate the desirability of 'collective efforts' and expect to be the sole supplier of ideas for a whole city.

The change from the first team to the second was essentially one from town planners to architects who had assumed planning responsibilities as well. Whereas Mayer, as a planner, had been concerned about such aspects as the socio-economic base of the planned city, its potential for growing to the projected population, the need to provide for small-scale industry, the special Indian problems, with Le Corbusier's arrival, it became a matter of the application of 'obvious and unquestionable' basic principles which relegated all other matters to the background. The findings of the different experts engaged by Mayer were completely ignored as far as is evident.

Thus the changeover from planners to architects represented a fundamental shift in priorities; a shift towards a preoccupation with visual form, symbolism, imagery and aesthetics rather than the basic problems of the Indian population. By concentrating on providing Indian architecture with forms suited to the Second Machine Age, the existing Indian situation could be more or less totally ignored.

Le Corbusier had such faith in his abstract principles that he did not acknowledge the glaring anomalies between the bare subsistence levels and deplorable living and working conditions of the labourers building the city and the idealistic assumptions upon which his plan was based. There was clearly no room in the city for the very people engaged in building it. The 'here and now' became completely subordinated to the 'there and then'; to a hypothetical future somewhere in the distance.

From the team of foreigners, Le Corbusier found acceptance and support for the basic concept of his plan and they accepted the role of concentrating on the 'architectural design' problems of the sub-components of the city.

From the Indian side, he received perhaps the best response of his lifetime. His grandness of vision, clarity of purpose and use of vivid imagery and symbolism evoking lofty ideals, harmonized completely with the aspirations and requirements of the new leadership of Independent India. Mayer and his modest goals were soon forgotten. Jawaharlal Nehru, Prime Minister of India, took considerable personal interest in looking after the welfare of the project. As long as Le Corbusier respected the stringent financial constraints of the budget, he was given complete freedon to develop his ideas. The young Indian recruits took to the work with freshness and vigour, and were enthusiastic about the opportunity of learning directly from working with the Master. They soon acquired the attitudes of rebuffing criticism of their work with ease in the confidence of the unquestionability of the Master's teachings.

The Master Plan

The basis of Le Corbusier's master plan is a grid iron of V3 (fast-traffic) roads intersecting at half a mile across and three-quarters of a mile up the plan, enclosing areas known as 'sectors'. The planned area stretches between two river beds defining its natural boundaries on both sides. It is crowned at the top by the monumental complex of administrative buildings with no future construction being envisaged beyond the road separating the capitol complex from the rest of the town, all future extension being projected southwards. The city centre is located 'centrally' in the first phase area with an industrial zone to the right and the university on the left. A smaller river bed forms a continuous stretch of park from top to bottom referred to as the 'leisure valley'. Each sector is divided horizontally by a bazaar street and vertically by a band of open space, these continuing from sector to sector up and across the plan.

The essence of the plan lies in preserving the true functions of seven types of

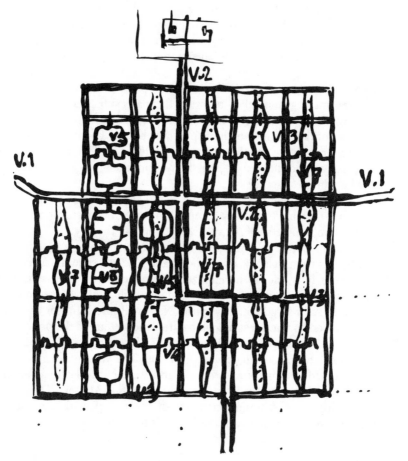

Figure 4.2. Le Corbusier's sketch showing the system of 7Vs (*les sept voies*).

roads, called 'the 7Vs' (*les sept voies*) by Le Corbusier, and their expected operation in relation to the 'sectors'. The assumed functioning of these two interdependent components is best explained in Le Corbusier's own words. Of the sector whose dimensions were the outcome of studies made between 1929 and 1949 of the Spanish *cuadra* of 100 to 110 metres, he said:

> The 'Sector' is *the container of family life* (the 24 solar hours cycle which must be fulfilled in perfect harmony) . . .
>
> A useful reclassification of them [*cuadras*] led me to adopt a ratio of harmonious dimensions and productive combinations: seven to eight *cuadras* on one side, ten to twelve *cuadras* on the other, that is to say 800 m × 1200 m. And this was the 'Sector' issued from an ancestral and valid geometry established in the past on the stride of a man, an ox or a horse, but henceforth

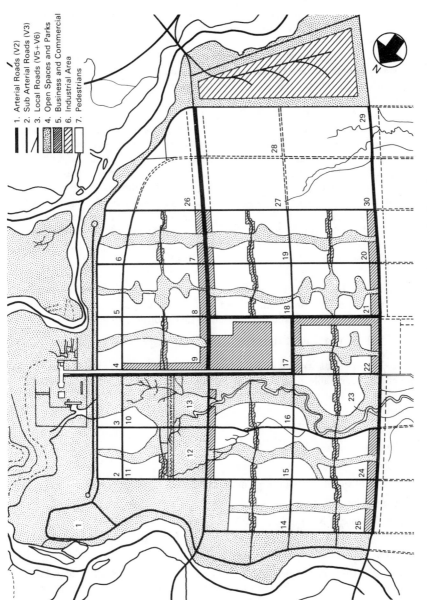

Figure 4.3. Chandigarh master plan: land use in the first phase.

1. Arterial Roads (V2)
2. Sub Arterial Roads (V3)
3. Local Roads (V5+V6)
4. Open Spaces and Parks
5. Business and Commercial
6. Industrial Area
7. Pedestrians

adapted to mechanical speeds . . . The entrance of cars into the sectors of 800 m × 1200 m, *which are exclusively reserved for family life*, can take place on four points only: in the middle of the 1200 m; in the middle of the 800 m. All stoppage of the circulation shall be prohibited at the four circuses, at the angles of the sectors. The bus stops are provided each time at 200 m from the circus so as to serve the four pedestrian entrances into a sector. Thus, *the transit traffic takes place out of the sectors:* the sectors being surrounded by four wall-bound car roads without openings (the V3s). And this (a novelty in town-planning and decisive) was applied at Chandigarh: *no house (or building) door opens on the thoroughfare of rapid traffic.*

The sector is crossed through inside, at its half-way point, by its shopping street (the V4), reassembling on a line the functions which are necessary to daily life (24 hours): food supply, artisans, police, fire-brigade, circulating library, cinema, restaurants, stores, or co-operatives etc . . . These services are set up in a line of 800 metres on one side (facing the north) to avoid dispersion and frequent road crossings as well as the sun's heat. The cars can take this road at a reduced speed and park there. This shop-street continues in the neighbouring sectors on the right and the left: in this way is realized a continuity of the needs and resources of daily life and a connection through the whole town from East to West. (Le Corbusier, 1961)

Each sector has a green space oriented in the direction of the mountains constituting a vertical band connecting a series of sectors. In these bands will be located the diverse schools and playgrounds. (Le Corbusier, 1959a).

He explained the working of the system of 7Vs (*les sept voies*) as follows:

The '7V Rule' was studied in 1950 at UNESCO's request (to try to constitute an eventual acceptable proposition of urbanism for general world application). One discovered that with 7 types of roads the man of the mechanical civilization could:

cross continents: the V1

arrive in town: the V1

go to special public services: the V2

cross at full speed, without interruption, the territory of the town: the V3

dispose of immediate accesses to daily needs: the V4

reach the door of his dwelling: the V5 and V6

send the youth to the green areas of each sector where schools and sport grounds are located: the V7

But the '7V Rule' was to be the object of an assault: the onrush of bicycles in different countries. The 'V8' was subsequently created, the 'V8' independent of the others. Effectively, the 'two-wheels' have customs which are antagonistic to those of the 'four wheels'. At Chandigarh, the 'V8' were created a little later on. The latter was then honestly formulated: *'The rule of the 7Vs . . . which are 8!'* (Le Corbusier, 1961)

Qualifying the technical statement of principle, he said that the V1s are immediately succeeded by the V2s at the beginning of the city. Some V2s can be chosen by the municipality to combine usefulness with grandeur.

In the Chandigarh master plan, two V2s form the two major avenues of the city, one connecting the university to the station and the other connecting the capitol complex to the city centre. The third, V2 south, demarcates the boundary of the first phase. Wide belts of land along all three are reserved for specialized markets and commercial establishments. The V7s, meant exclusively for pedestrians, are located in the vertical green belts. Le Corbusier envisaged the V7s crossing the V2s and V3s with foot bridges, which could be built when the situation permitted but insisted that they be drawn on the plan immediately. The V8s, meant for two wheeled vehicles – bicycles, scooters and motorcycles, go along the green belts. ·

Once the elaborate network of the V7s had been established, Le Corbusier envisaged an efficient public transport system serving the city. Three different types of buses were planned; larger buses connecting it to its hinterland; medium-sized buses for longer runs within the city, and mini-buses for a kind of shuttle service over shorter runs. As he said:

> The greatest clarity of the solution is the reciprocal independence of the pedestrian and the automobile. The private automobile, which encumbers and blocks up cities, shall only enter the city in exceptional cases. Mechanical speeds are assured by a new type of autobus circulating at full speed exclusively in the V3s and partially in the V4s. (Le Corbusier, 1953a)

Le Corbusier's Vision of Chandigarh

In a document entitled *For the Establishment of an Immediate Statute of the Land* addressed to a High Level Committee on Chandigarh, he described his vision of life in the city and the process by which its detailed physical fabric had evolved:

I. DEFINITION OF USE OF CHANDIGARH

(i) Chandigarh is a city offering all amenities to the poorest of the poor of its citizens to lead a dignified life.

(ii) Chandigarh is a Government city with a precise function and, consequently, a precise quality of inhabitants.

On this presumption, the city is not to be a big city (metropolis) – it must not lose its definition. Some people say that life must come in the city from other sources of activity, especially industry – but an industrial city is not the same as an administrative city. One must not mix the two. It seems that the original definition should be complemented by the possibility of introducing elements which can reinforce the functions of the city, rather than create a conflict of rivalry. We must take care that any temptations do not kill the goal which was foreseen at the time the city was founded. Therefore, naturally, old doors must be opened to unknown initiatives. It appears that the future of

Chandigarh will be open to all cultural factors in different manifestations:

Teaching
(schools, university, new science of teaching, audiovisual training etc. – in one word all kinds of knowledge).

Means to express and disperse thought
(editions: books, magazines and eventually, their printing etc.)

Modes of expression and dispersion of the arts
(in time and space – history and geography)

All kinds of reproduction of art-witnesses
(editions: visual means – photographs, diagrams etc. to different scales.)

Diverse kinds of exhibitions, shows, theatres, festivals, creations of the highest modernity etc.

For the culture of the body, an organism can be created having at its disposition possibilities of meeting for competitions and tournaments.

All this will afford the creation of a 'Chandigarh label' which will be the guarantee of quality and will be worth emulation.

II. THE FOUR FUNCTIONS

The CIAM 'Charter of Athens'.

The force of this charter lies in giving the first place to the dwelling: the environment of living – the family under the rule of '24 Solar Hours'.

The second place is given to 'Working' which is the daily act of human obligation.

The third is the culture of body and spirit on the one hand and an intellectual leisure on the other.

When all these goals have received their definite containers, it is possible to give to each of them its respective rightful place and at this moment can occur the problem of realizing the contacts: that is circulation!

III.

With this line of conduct the urbanism of Chandigarh emerged. (Le Corbusier, 1959a)

In explaining the methodology followed in the preparation of the master plan, he explained that each of the four functions *asks for precise locations on the grounds of the city* . . .

Each function is to be contained in one container, i.e. one building.
    The first problem is to give the specific size to this building according to each function. Modern life has to locate all its activities in containers of conforming sizes – *unité de grandeur conform.*
    Each of these tools ('containers of conforming size') have to find their right place on the land. *Their location must be fixed on the paper (plan) with their necessary surroundings. Contact will be provided in direct or indirect ways, which have to be foreseen and fixed from the beginning.*

Some of these containers constitute a concentration, the others dissemination. At Chandigarh, family containers were given a place in the sectors; and the work containers in the Capitol Complex, the University, the City Centre and in a limited Industrial area. (*Ibid;* emphasis added)

Once each function, its location and size of its 'container' had been determined, only the technical and aesthetic problem of physical design remained to be solved. This had to be done within climatic, technical and budgetary constraints. Chandigarh's architecture emerged as an attempt at functional design of buildings within these three constraints.

Thus, the master plan essentially consisted of the provision of a *physical* framework based on the predetermination of the precise locations of assumed functions, and the built forms in which these were to be contained. Implicit in this process was the exclusion of a whole range of activities and occupations not taken into account by the designers. The assumption that all major activities must take place within buildings designed on the basis of aesthetic considerations took into account neither the economic consequences of this on various activities, nor allowed for the use of open land or minimal structures as a means of lowering overheads for low-income enterprises in an economy of scarcity.

In terms of the planned city's relationship to the surrounding region, little was taken into account other than a concern with maintaining a clear rural/ urban dichotomy with its immediate hinterland. In order to prevent haphazard growth on the periphery, control over land within a radius of ten miles of the plan was envisaged. The objectives of doing this were stated as follows in the project report:

Approaching the problem from outside one may imagine the city as lying within a region of traditional agriculture which, as it approaches the city boundaries, will be increasingly affected by the pressures of 500,000 people. It should be the aim of planning to do two things:

(a) to prevent the creation of bad semi-urban conditions on the boundaries of the new city, drawing away the strength of the city by unfair competition immediately beyond the area of local taxation; these conditions are already springing up in Mani Majra*.

(b) to protect the rural community from degeneration by contact with urban life, and to lead it towards a harmonious partnership, in which, without loss of rural status it may improve its living conditions supplying the necessities of the city in the form of milk, eggs, chickens, vegetables, etc . . .

To bring this about it will be necessary first to include an area around the city in a regional town planning scheme that will safeguard land use for rural and agricultural purposes and prevent exploitation.

This would be a negative safeguard. In addition a development scheme should be initiated that will:

*A village in the vicinity of Chandigarh which has now become a service town.

(a) Organize the supply of fresh milk, butter, etc. both at the rural and the city end.

(b) Provide light roads without which nothing will work.

(c) Educate the villagers so that they will make early use of the opportunities offered and close the fatal time gap. (Punjab Government, undated)

Le Corbusier expressed his confidence in these objectives being achieved as a consequence of his planning at a conference in Paris in May 1951:

To build on open ground, of easy topography, filled with natural beauty, Chandigarh, thanks to its urban and architectural layout, will be sheltered from base speculation and its disastrous corrollaries: the suburbs. No suburb is possible at Chandigarh. (Le Corbusier, 1951a)

Finally it is useful to mention the significance Le Corbusier attached to the institutions of authority of the new state. Towering above the grid-iron framework of the city's plan is located the capitol complex, the seat of the Punjab Government. It is designed to house the three major institutions of parliamentary democracy – the Legislative Assembly, the High Court of Justice and the Secretariat. The Governor's Residence was also planned to be located there. In addition, Le Corbusier proposed the inclusion of a fifth element – a monument to 'The Open Hand'. To him this represented an important symbol of the affluence and harmony which he felt the second era of the 'machinist civilization' was going to bring. Explaining its significance to Nehru, he wrote:

Abundance seems to be the sign of the epoch. The open hand to receive, the open hand to give, could be chosen as a symbolic materialization of all these victories!

India could estimate precisely the conjuncture of erecting in the Capitol of Chandigarh, actually under construction, in the midst of palaces sheltering her institutions and her authority, the symbolic and evocative sign of *The Open Hand*.

Open for receiving the created richness . . .

Open for the distribution to her people and to others.

The Open Hand will affirm that the second era of the machinist civilization – has started.

Chandigarh today, offers providentially to bring this to witness. (Le Corbusier, 1954)

Symbolism and Monumentality in Other Capitals of the Third World

The importance given to symbolism and monumentality is a recurrent theme in the planning and designing of the capitals of most newly emerging nations. It is interesting to compare the processes by which the plans of a number of other Third World capitals were prepared with those applied in the plan for Chandigarh.

In the case of Brasilia, Lucio Costa's plan was selected out of a total of twenty-six entries in a national competition. The only information given to the competitors by NOVACAP, the State agency which set the competition, was the topographical setting, an open plain and a large artificial lake (Wilheim, 1960). There was no mention of the size of the city's population, its economic base or sociological or regional questions. Those who entered the competition, which began in September 1956, were required to plan an urban system and a technical structure which could be inaugurated in April 1960. Three and a half years were allowed for the planning and construction of a city which was to serve a nation for centuries (Hardoy, 1967:247).

The terms of the competition left a great deal to the discretion of the contestants. As a result, the proposals ranged from the detailed one of the firm M.M.M. Roberto, of which William Holford (1957:397), a member of the jury, recalls, 'I have never seen anywhere in the world a more comprehensive and thorough-going master plan for [a] new capital city', to Lucio Costa's submission, presented on five medium sized cards without a single mechanical drawing, model, land-use schedule, or population chart (Epstein, 1973:49).

It was nevertheless Costa's proposal which was selected by five members of an international jury of six. Costa's plan called for a city in the form of a cross, variously described by commentators as an airplane, a bird, or a dragonfly. The very desire, to command, to 'take possession' as Costa put it, inspired the plan's symbolism; the solution 'was born of the primary gesture of one who indicates a place and takes possession of it: two axes crossing at a right angle, or the very sign of the cross' (Costa, 1957:41).

Louis I. Kahn, to whom the design of the Second Capital of Pakistan*, seven miles from Dacca, was entrusted, similarly described the process by which his plan emerged:

> I was given an extensive program of buildings: the assembly, the supreme court, hostels, schools, a stadium, the diplomatic enclave, the living sector, market, all to be placed on a thousand acres of flat land, subject to flood. I kept thinking of how these buildings may be grouped and what would cause them to take their place on the land. On the night of the third day, I fell out of bed with the idea which is still the prevailing idea of the plan. This came simply from the realization that assembly is of a transcendent nature . . .(quoted in Nilsson, 1973:195)

In contrast to such mystical preoccupations, Constantinos A. Doxiadis, the architect/planner of Islamabad, the new national capital of Pakistan, declared that

> I have an obligation to follow only that road ahead of me that is not obstructed and cluttered up with monuments, a road whose largest shadows will be cast by simple plain human buildings. (Doxiadis, 1963:194)

The planning of Islamabad was a regular application of Doxiadis' theories

---

*This was in 1962, long before the emergence of Bangladesh as an Independent State.

and he used it as a school example several times. According to him, when constructing on virginal soil, the ideal conditions were all within reach; there was then no need to pay heed to anything except the building programme for the new city and the existing landscape (Doxiadis, 1960:412). And the building programme and the physical linear grid-iron layout of the city emerged out of his vision of what the world was going to look like in the year 2160, in the era of Doxiadis' ecumenopolis.

What is lacking in the preoccupations of all these 'great' planners is any direct consideration of the material reality of the people for whom they were designing these splendid creations.

5

Conflicts and Contradictions
Implicit in the Master Plan

Beneath the grandiose ambitions and idealism of the planners lay the bare, socio-economic reality of the future population of the city. The project report included remarkably little information about the economic base of the new town. An extremely crude breakdown of the anticipated number of people dependent on different types of economic activity and forms of employment during the first phase was provided (table 5.1).

According to this distribution, the majority of people (those employed in categories 1, 2, 3, 4, and 6, representing over 75 per cent of the total population) were to be dependent on fixed salaries, a large proportion with very low ones. Little else was mentioned in the project report about employment and incomes, particularly with respect to the limited purchasing power indicated by the anticipated economic structure and the plan proposals aimed at achieving a high standard of services and civic amenities in the new city.

It is interesting to note that in the case of Brasilia, in many respects a sister new town of Chandigarh though on a much larger scale, Costa's plan did not include as much consideration of the economic base as even this. No provision was made in the plan for an industrial zone. The civil service and construction

Table 5.1. Planned distribution of employment.

Type of employment	Number of persons dependent on it
1. Punjab Government employees	50,000
2. Municipal employees	15,000
3. Domestic servants	20,000
4. Large concerns such as the railways, power house, transport, banks	15,000
5. Professions such as medicine, law, building and teaching	15,000
6. Industry	15,000
7. Trade and commerce	20,000
Total	150,000

industry were supposedly to be the main sources of employment in the short term, and banking, commerce and cultural activities in the longer term (Hardoy, 1967:242).

In contrast, in the planning of Ciudad Guayana, which was part of a major regional economic development programme of Venezuelan Guayana, while major attention was given to the city's economic base of heavy industry, the scale of employment generation resulting from it did not receive much attention. As the distribution of the benefits of economic growth is essentially determined by the number of employment opportunities generated in the process, even the comprehensive planning exercise for Ciudad Guayana did not provide for a balanced income and employment structure for its population*.

The Inherent Conflicts

To show how inherent were the conflicts and contradictions implicit in the implementation of the plan the following aspects are examined:

1. Land policies: development, disposal and control;

2. The short- and long-term sources of finance for development and maintenance;

3. The framework for housing provision
   (a) government housing,
   (b) private housing;

4. The framework for the provision of consumer goods and services
   (a) city-scale provision,
   (b) local provision;

5. Spatial form and population distribution;

6. Development and administrative authority;

7. The 'Statue of the Land'.

1. Land: Development, Disposal and Control

It was decided that *all* land within the plan area should be acquired, developed (provided with basic infrastructure) and sold by the government. Private development was to be restricted to the construction of buildings and infrastructure within the boundaries of individual plots acquired from the Capital Project Organization (CPO). (The CPO was a semi-autonomous development authority created by the Punjab Government to develop and manage the city.)

Chandigarh was one of the first cities in India in which complete land

---

*For a detailed discussion of the planning of Ciudad Guayana, see Rodwin (1969).

development and disposal control by a public authority was attempted. This decision had two major objectives.

The first was apparently, to control and regulate the growth of the city in accordance with the master plan. Within the plan area, in order to control speculative purchase of land, a condition was attached to the sale of all private plots that construction must be completed within three years of the date of purchase. In the case of a violation of this condition, the government was given statutory powers to repossess the plot and resell it. At the same time, complete control over land imposed heavy responsibility on the government to anticipate the nature and scale of the city's growth and to make land available to meet the effective demand of all sections of the population.

The second was concerned with the rise in land values as a result of development. Public intervention in the urban land market is designed to serve two functions: first to modify a situation in which land prices go beyond the reach of large sections of the population, and secondly to control unearned incomes from increased land values going to property owners without any benefit to the community. This aspect had been a central concern of CIAM.

The foreign architects attempted to persuade the government to adopt a policy of selling land on a leasehold basis, but it was decided to sell freehold. As described by Fry (1955a):

> We urged that they [CPO] should recoup on the increased value which would be likely to flow from planning and that land should be sold leasehold, but so great was the need for the necessary cash to carry out the project estimate that the decision was made to sell land freehold and to part with the benefits. This was very sad but there was nothing we could do about it.

In addition to the financial constraints, the psychological implications of offering land on leasehold to potential settlers, many of whom were insecure and uprooted refugees, was used as a justification for selling freehold. This decision was essentially designed to win the support of the top echelons of the bureaucracy, and of the upper middle classes in general; it was implicitly a disbenefit to the impoverished masses.

In spite of the assumption of total public control over land, the potential responsibilities of the CPO in minimizing the distortions in the land market were not clearly spelt out. Neither was the CPO's responsibility towards ensuring an adequate release of land with the growth of the city specified. Public control over land was explained as being desirable *per se.* Indeed, Le Corbusier's supreme confidence in his planning doctrine projected urban planning as a profit-making venture. Even in *The Radiant City,* where on the one hand he had talked of the virtues of a planned economy, he had emphasized his conviction that city planning is not a way of spending money, but of *making money* and bringing in a *profit.* In explaining his views to the Chandigarh authorities, he said:

> When the following operation has been started in a city:

buying of the necessary land
obtaining the money

framing of the first bye-laws permitting the beginning of construction
selling of the first plots
arriving of the first inhabitants, etc., etc.

a phenomenon is born: it is the appreciation in the value of a piece of land. A game, a play, has begun. One can sell cheaply or at a high price; it depends on the kind of tactics and the strategy employed in the operation.
One phrase must be affirmed:

Good urbanism makes money: Bad urbanism loses money! (Le Corbusier, 1959a)

All the same, he cautioned;

The problem is also to be vigilant; one must sell a true merchandise; nothing must be allowed to provoke circumstances which will bring loss to every single inhabitant. (*Ibid.*)

As rising land values were seen as a means of making money, the financing of the city became inextricably linked with the CPO's land sale policy. The considerable section of the population unable to participate in financial land transactions, because of very low incomes and unstable employment, remained 'invisible' to the Punjab Government decision-makers, and to the celebrated architect/planners – just as it had remained invisible to the colonial rulers. In fact, the decision to release land for use only *after* it had been developed, expecting all those gaining access to it to pay the development costs, excluded an even higher proportion of the projected population from legal access to land than would have otherwise been the case.

It is interesting to note that today land acquisition and development rights being in the hands of government authorities seems automatically to accompany the building of planned new towns in most countries. It has certainly been so in the cases of Brasilia, Tema, Islamabad, and Ciudad Guayana. Using the sale of developed land to finance new town development is also fairly common. Brasilia was supposed to pay for itself through the sale of lots whose value was expected to rise as a consequence of development (Epstein, 1973:40). In Islamabad, the plan was that private investment should be concentrated in construction and in the purchasing or leasing of land, dwellings and shops which the government had developed (Hardoy, 1967:246). In the case of Ciudad Guayana, the product of a much more technocratic planning approach, private developers were to be sold land freehold at reduced rates to encourage them to build housing in the new city. Selling land leasehold was not seriously considered as that would have been against 'national practices'. But, while there were no controls to stop large private construction companies indulging in land speculation, under the 'progressive urban improvement scheme' lots were *leased* to lower-income households until they had replaced their shacks with modern houses, in order to prevent them from such speculation (Corrada, 1969:244). Tema was an exception among these new towns as the development authority was expected to build the bulk of the town and to lease its properties to the public (Government of Ghana, 1952:22). In none of these cases did the basic contradiction between relying on the market mechanism of rising land values, with its concomitant effects on legal access to land use for different sections of the population, and the basic objectives of regulating urban development through planning receive particular attention.

2. Finance for Development

During the first stage of Chandigarh's development, estimated expenditure on the capital project was calculated to be Rs. 167.5 million (£10.5 million). Of this, more than half (Rs.86 million) was for development of the town and the provision of civic amenities. The balance of Rs.81.5 million represented the cost of government buildings and the water supply system.

The sources of finance were as follows:

Rehabilitation loans from the Government of India during 1950–53	Rs. 30 million
Assistance from the Government of India during 1953–56	Rs. 30 million
Contribution by the Government of Punjab	Rs. 25 million
Estimated receipts from the sale of plots	Rs. 86 million
Total	Rs. 171 million

In estimating receipts from the sale of plots, the guiding principle was to try to recover as nearly as possible all development costs. Taking into account the estimated recovery of rent from government buildings during the first phase, the net expenditure amounted to Rs.81.2 million (£5 million).

'Development costs' included a whole range of items – land acquisition, survey, roads and bridges, landscaping, the dam across the Sukhna Cho river, railway facilities, publicity for the sale of plots, establishment charges, maintenance costs for the first five years, and the major item of civic works. This last item included thirty-five educational and eight medical institutions, six community centres, six swimming pools, a stadium, a *serai* (cheap lodging house), a museum and art school, a public library, municipal offices, and a number of administrative offices. Water and electricity supply schemes were not included in development costs as these were to be run on a self-financing basis.

The picture presented by the authorities, and which has continued to be projected with considerable force, is that of Chandigarh being, in the main, a self-financing city. However, there were considerable inequities and anomalies in the financing procedure and method of cost-calculation adopted. The self-financing aspect was to be confined to the private sector. Government expenditure was accounted for on a different basis, incorporating considerable amounts of subsidy, particularly for government housing. This was not to be confined just to the initial stages, but was to be on a recurrent basis. The anomalies inherent in the financing procedures are worthy of closer examination.

Essentially the sequence of preparing the project estimate was as follows. The senior government officials selected a range of services and amenities which they felt were desirable in a new city. As the project report stated, 'every effort has been made to provide all the civic amenities which a modern capital *should* have' (emphasis added). Estimates for each item were prepared and included in the development costs. These were then used as the basis for calculating the price of developed land to be charged to private buyers. Thus all developed land used for government construction was to be subsidized by the private sector. This subsidization of government construction and civic amenities took no account of the limited purchasing power of a large part of the private sector. The only means by which these people might have obtained legal access to land and housing would have been through government subsidy. But this would have raised the issue of where such large subsidies were to come from. The accounting procedure used in the project estimate simply evaded this problem by ignoring it.

In estimating costs of government housing, it was felt necessary to incorporate an element of subsidy for almost all salary groups to provide them with accommodation 'consistent with their status'. This subsidy was partly provided out of government funds and partly out of receipts from the sale of plots to the private sector. While passing the problem to the private sector could be continued over time, little consideration was given to how even the government housing programme was to be sustained once the grants and loans from the central and state governments had been used up.

In working out the fixed price per square yard for private residential plots, a sliding scale was adopted for different sizes on the grounds that smaller plots 'involve a higher incidence of development costs per acre than larger ones'. This logic overlooked the fact that even if development costs per acre were greater in areas with smaller plots, a greater proportion of the developed land is put to productive use, leading to higher returns over time. Even if the development costs per acre in areas with larger plots were lower to start with, the high costs of maintenance and services per plot would make them much more expensive in the long run. (This was essentially the anomaly noted by Nehru in the differential taxation structure enforced by the British between the Civil Lines and the city proper during his tenure as Municipal Commissioner of Allahabad (Nehru, 1962:143–4).) In any case, assuming that smaller plots were going to be bought by those with lower incomes, charging a higher price per square yard from them implied that they would have to make the same, if not a greater, contribution towards subsidizing government housing than those with higher incomes. In other words, private sector households with lower incomes would be forced to subsidize government housing dis-proportionately to their earnings.

Recovery of the development costs of infrastructure and civic amenities at the same rate from all sections of the private sector implicitly assumed that they would be used equally by all. But since the lower income groups then, as indeed now, were not in a position to benefit from sophisticated amenities such as museums, art schools and higher educational institutions, the costing procedure really meant a subsidization by the poor of amenities predominantly used by the rich.

Lastly, there was no long-term financial policy which took account of how the high standards of infrastructure, services and amenities were to be sustained. The project estimate made an allocation for maintenance for the first five years; it was simply assumed that a municipal authority would take over the burden later.

3. The Framework for Housing Provision

Chandigarh aspired to set an example in environmental improvement over conditions prevailing in other Indian cities. Although there was no questioning of the disparities of the existing social order, minimum housing standards were specified even for the poorer sections of the population. A dwelling unit, consisting of two rooms, a verandah/kitchen and a courtyard, equipped with piped water, water-borne sewerage, and electricity, was adopted as the minimum accommodation per household. By making this minimum standard mandatory, it was assumed that the conditions of overcrowding prevailing in most urban areas would be eliminated.

In this context it is worth noting that of the four other Third World new towns referred to earlier, only in the planning of Tema and of Ciudad Guayana was the relationship between higher physical standards and the economic circumstances of different sections of the population openly acknowledged. In the case of Tema, it was attempted to overcome the problem by providing fully-built housing to desirable standards on subsidized rents (Government of Ghana, 1952). In Ciudad Guayana, the response was to accept the lower housing standards, which are the by-product of lower incomes and unstable employment, as inevitable and to incorporate opportunities for incremental improvement of dwellings within the planning framework. This, however, was to be permitted only in certain zones of the city (Corrada, 1969), implying spatial social segregation on the basis of housing standards.

In Chandigarh, responsibility for housing construction was to be broadly divided between the public and private sectors. Public housing, intended exclusively for government employees, was to be built by the government and made available on a rental basis. Private housing construction was to be regulated through indirect controls. Access to housing for government and private workers was to be operated through markedly different mechanisms. While government housing was to be made available on the basis of non-market criteria, private housing was expected to conform to the economic dictates of the market.

Provision of Government Housing

At the outset, the project estimate allocated Rs.26.8 million (£1.6 million) for government housing. This included an officers' hostel, 100 flats for members of the legislative assembly, and a detailed programme of thirteen types of houses for different salary groups of government employees. The estimate specified minute details for each house type; area of site, minimum covered area, number of rooms, maximum cost per square foot, and specifications of building materials. The architects were presented with this programme for producing suitable house designs, and the experience of designing within these constraints is best described by Fry (1955b: 143):

> By far the most onerous task before the architects was the design of 13 categories of government houses, graded from the lowest costing only £244 to the highest costing £4875 and excluding the house for the Chief Minister. The accommodation asked for seldom matched the estimate, and most noticeably in the lowest grade, where a long suffering class of office messengers, drivers and the like pleaded for two rooms rather than one, and in which the critical item proved to revolve about the problem of whether or not an individual W.C. could be provided. . .

In the initial stage, 3208 government houses were to be built, at that time representing 90 per cent of the permanent government employees. It was expected that such employees as could not be allotted government houses would be able to make private arrangements (Punjab Government, undated).

According to government rules, these houses were to be let to the employees at a fixed rent of 10 per cent of their salaries. On the other hand, for a building to be classified as productive, it was necessary for it to fetch at least 6 per cent of its capital cost. Since the cost of construction had risen considerably without any corresponding increase in the salaries of government employees, it was considered impossible to restrict the cost of houses to the capitalized value of 10 per cent of the pay of the occupant and at the same time provide him with 'reasonable accommodation consistent with his status' (Punjab Government, undated). A certain degree of loss of rent on government housing was thus considered inevitable.

The economic rent (calculated at 6 per cent of the capital cost) of all government housing in the initial programme worked out to be Rs.1,609,000. Of this the recoverable amount was only Rs.633,000, leaving a balance of Rs.976,000 as a yearly loss to the government. These figures, however, did not represent either the true costs of government housing or the actual yearly losses. First, the estimated cost per house excluded the cost of developed land. Secondly, the maintenance and establishment costs were not included. Thirdly, although the government calculated economic rent at 6 per cent of capital costs, this was based on a rule formulated in 1927 (Prakash, 1969:86). Since then there had been a much greater increase in land and construction costs than the general rise in price level. Thus 6 per cent was unrepresentative of the true economic rent at prices and interest rates prevailing in the early 1950s. Because of these anomalies, in absolute amounts, higher-income employees received the largest subsidy.

All the same, it was perhaps the first time in Indian history that those with low status occupations such as sweepers and peons had received any consideration in the government's housing programme. Much political capital was made out of this, it being claimed that the housing of the sweepers had received as much attention as that of the senior officials and ministers. It all helped to foster the progressive and benevolent image of the new government. But, as pointed out above, it was an artificial situation with no possibility of wider application. Such housing was to be available only to employees of the State, and practically none of the government employees could have obtained similar housing left to their own resources. The public authority had been able to manipulate the project funds in favour of housing its own employees, but this cross-subsidization was not done on economic grounds of channelling funds from the rich to the poor, but on the political basis of getting the private sector to subsidize the public employees. As some of the key beneficiaries of this arrangement also happened to be the main decision-makers for the project, not surprisingly, these anomalies went by unquestioned. That they remained unchallenged by even the poorest sections of the community expected to contribute towards such differential State patronage was a reflection of the level of social and political consciousness of the mass of the population.

Cross-subsidization on these grounds is quite typical as a means of financing housing and civic amenities for State employees in Third World countries. Given the inability to provide comprehensive welfare state services to all sections of the population, the State's own employees are given preferential treatment as a bribe for their loyalty. Subsidized housing for all income groups of government employees has been extensively provided in most new capitals of the Third World, and in Islamabad the framework for the provision of private and public housing seems to have been quite similar to that of Chandigarh.

The Framework for Private Housing

The unit of land made available for housing in the private sector was the 'plot', demarcated by the CPO, and fragmentation of plots was forbidden. Private houses were permitted a height of up to two and a half storeys, with a maximum of two dwelling units per plot. In the case of those desiring to build two units, one could be provided on the ground floor and the other on the first. To prevent use of the second floor as a living unit, provision of services on this floor was forbidden. These measures were designed to prevent 'misuse' of residential plots leading to fragmentation and overcrowding.

Regulation of private construction was sought through an extensive system of controls. The priorities on which these were based were described by Fry (1955b; 147) as follows:

... because we were unwilling and unable to control the design of individual buildings erected by the public, we devised a system of sector planning sheets on which were shown graphically the building lines, permissible heights, building areas of plots, public open spaces, scheduled trees, and controlled building walls, with standard designs for gates. Some frontages on important streets were controlled as to height, profile, materials and setbacks in order to project to some extent the effect such streets would have when finally built. But further we did not wish to go, nor could go, without the aid of a large staff of inspectors in each of whom should burn an equal zeal for architecture. . .

Construction could not be started until house plans had been approved by the CPO and occupation of the premises was to be delayed until a 'completion certificate' had been obtained. This was to be granted only after the premises had passed the desired standard of construction and services, specified in the byelaws.

A total of 20,251 private plots varying in size from 125 to over 5000 square yards were to be offered for sale to the public. They were to be sold at a fixed price by means of a lottery, preference being given to displaced* persons and to those applying in groups. Displaced persons issued with government bonds† could exchange them for plots, others having to pay cash.

Land was to be sold at the cost price of development (see page 62). The price per square yard was calculated to be Rs.12 (then about £1) for the first 125 square yards, Rs.8 for the next 125 square yards, Rs.6 for the next 250 square yards, and Rs.4 after the first 500 square yards. Thus, the price of the smallest plot amounted to Rs.1500 requiring a down payment of Rs.375. Construction costs, of course, were to be over and above this.

To promote private construction, government loans on easy terms were made available to plot-holders. However, to obtain a loan, it was necessary to own a plot already, and to have income sufficiently high and regular to ensure repayment. Many people, such as building labourers and sweepers, clearly could not qualify for them.

The only feasible alternative for acquiring 'planned' residential accommodation for a low-income non-government worker was on a rental basis, providing such accommodation was available within his paying capacity. Because of the high standards of building and amenities adopted for the city, it was inevitable that rents in the private sector would be higher than those of equivalent government housing and closer to true economic rents, if not even higher due to market forces. Thus it was impossible for those in private or self-employment with low incomes to gain access to 'planned' residential accommodation without assistance in some form.

To a certain extent this was realized by the foreign architects while they were

*The term 'displaced person' has been used here and elsewhere in the text to refer to people uprooted by Partition.
†Only those refugees who could prove loss of property through displacement were issued with government bonds as compensation. The rest had to fend for themselves.

working on government housing. On her own initiative, Jane Drew designed an additional house type costing only £154 and persuaded Thapar to make additional allocation for it in the budget. As a result, 800 'cheap houses' were built in the first few years, but their construction was later discontinued. These houses represented the only attempt to cater for the housing needs of low-income households in the private sector, at least until the early 1970s.

4. The Framework for the Provision of Consumer Goods and Services

Provision for consumer goods and services in the master plan may be broadly divided into two groups: (1) services at the city scale, and (2) those catering for daily needs at local levels.

City-Scale Provision

City-scale provision was visualized as being located in the city centre and along the three V2s forming the major avenues of the city.

City centre: The city centre occupies an area of one typical sector (242 acres). As proposed by Le Corbusier, trading and commercial facilities within it were to be divided into two categories:

> *Commercial centre proper:* This has buildings 4-storeyed high grouped around a central *chowk* – essentially a traditional Indian feature. The chief among these will be the Town Hall, Post and Telegraph Office, the Chamber of Commerce, and a few banks. Of these, the Post and Telegraph Office building will be 140' high and all of the rest 4-storeyed rising to a height of 56'. The shop–office buildings will have exclusive shops or restaurants etc. on the ground and in some cases on the first floor with offices only on the upper three floors . . .
>
> *Smaller shops along V4:* Normally, the V4 (shopping street) is the hub of every day activity within a sector. But, in the case of the City Centre,. . . the focal point is the *chowk* with the V4 taking a subsidiary place,. . .
> . . . Development along this. . . will be 3-storeyed structures. . . These will cater for the needs of petty shopkeepers* who are keen to be in close proximity to the commercial centre proper. . . (Prabhawalkar, 1954)

The scheme proposed entire segregation of pedestrian and vehicular traffic in the commercial centre.

Two possible means of development were considered. The first was that the CPO should construct all the buildings and sell them to various buyers and the second, that individual plots or blocks of land should be sold to private developers who would have to build strictly according to specifications.

The land was divided into blocks comprising varying numbers of a standard

---

*It is interesting to note the perception of a 'petty shopkeeper' contained in here. As will be discussed later, few petty traders in the Indian context can ever dream of being able to afford the overheads of three-storeyed commercial buildings.

unit of 200 square yards. On all floors, there had to be a 12-foot wide verandah both on the front and the rear of the building. Heights of floors were regulated at a standard of 12 feet, each developer having to conform to the standard elevations proposed by Le Corbusier. All buildings had to be build in exposed reinforced concrete to ensure uniformity. In 1954, the cost of construction of one typical unit was between Rs.85,000 and 90,000 (£5300 to £5600).

Le Corbusier suggested that if no private developers were forthcoming immediately, the government should construct the Town Hall and the cinema, accelerate the construction of the Post and Telegraph building, and create the *chowk*. It was hoped that once the *chowk* was established, it would act as a spur for other developers to purchase land and start construction. Although this way development could take a little longer than expected, his advice was to *sit and wait*.

Commercial Development along the Principle V2s

In the commercial belts of land reserved along the V2s, specialized markets were visualized. It was planned to develop four or five markets for wholesale business along the V2 Station–University. These were to be for building materials, agricultural goods, machinery, motor cars, printing, etc. Since it was felt that initially there might not be sufficient demand for sites in each of the markets, it was agreed to locate all trades in one nucleus to start with and to relocate them into their respective markets later. Designs for the first market to be developed in Sector 7 specified a standard height of 45 feet for all buildings and an 'architectural control' to which private developers had to conform. Land was again to be sold with a standard 'bay' as a unit. To give a sense of 'grandeur' along these roads, the smallest unit was on a similar scale to that in the City Centre and the height of all buildings along the V2s was to be greater than that of residential buildings in the city*.

Although the exact nature of these markets could not be anticipated, their building form, size and architectural design was specified by Le Corbusier's office in the early years. Along the V2 Capitol, big buildings such as offices, banks, hotels, and other 'important' institutions were to be provided for. The designs for building these were also prepared in the early years.

Local-Level Provision

Local provision for consumer goods and services in the residential sectors was in a linear form. This was to be restricted along one side of the bazaar streets to avoid the necessity for users to cross the road frequently. The architects'

*Interestingly, this physical and visual relationship   between residential and commercial buildings was reversed in the design of Brasilia, with 'grandeur' and monumentality being provided by multi-storey residential blocks, and shops, etc. being housed in single-storey structures.

considerations while designing these shopping streets were described by Jane Drew (1961:22):

> A Sector is a small world but it presents many of the same problems as a big town. Scale has to be established and to this end the 'hub' of the sector, the market, had to dominate a little over the housing areas. The architects, who had a better sense of the importance of physical environment than administrators, laid down that the main part of this centre should be three-storeyed and also be strictly architecturally controlled. Thus shop-owners could build their own shops, but to the architect's design. A variety of shops were provided, so that both small shop-owners and larger ones could be accommodated.

The approved shop designs varied from three-storey shop-cum-flats to small single-storey 'booths'. A little later, a third category of 'semi-industrial' shops was created. The areas for commercial sites ranged from 100 to 1000 square feet. To ensure the availability of all commodities and services considered essential for daily life, it was made mandatory for the purchasers of most sites not only to conform to all physical design and construction regulations, but also to use them only for the particular trade or service specified.

The criteria used for determining the number of sites of each size and the trades or services permitted on them had to be arbitrary as the extent of demand for different sizes could not be assessed in advance. However, in the process, decisions made on the basis of intuitive judgements became final.

The predetermination of the locations and mandatory built forms of *all* commercial and service facilities in the city, combined with the policy of selling land to the highest bidder in open auction, implicitly assumed:

1. that *all* city-scale services could function within the planned framework of pre-designed buildings located either in the city centre or along the V2s;

2. that prospective traders would either have access to capital to pay for land and construction costs, or be able to pay the market rent for premises;

3. that *all* sections of the population would be willing and *able* to pay for essential consumer goods and services involving these high overhead costs;

4. that the CPO's right to withhold land in key locations until it deemed it fit to release it would be used judiciously for the benefit of the majority of the population.

In this last case, the grounds on which the withholding of central city land was to be justified was never openly discussed. Instead, the physical provisions of the master plan became the sole points of reference upon which to base such decisions. The emphasis given by the architects to visual form and scale led to the reservation of the most desirable commercial locations for big business. Le Corbusier's suggestion to 'sit and wait' for land values to rise reinforced the tendency inherent in the planning methodology to exclude small enterprises from such locations. Thus, the CPO would become the instrument for legitimizing exclusive access to remunerative commercial locations to big business, literally handing the sites over when it became sufficently attractive for big business to invest in the city. While private land owners would be prevented from holding on to land without putting it to use within three years of purchase, the CPO would retain exclusive rights to speculate with land developed with public resources.

5. Spatial Form and Population Distribution

The spatial form of the city contradicted some of Le Corbusier's own key assertions about the aims of planning. Contrary to his stated philosophy of 'residence in proximity of work', the major work zones were located in peripheral areas; the industrial area and the university on either side of the grid iron and the capitol complex, the major employment centre, actually *outside* the main fabric of the plan. The criteria used in determining the location of the capitol complex had little to do with the convenience of the majority of citizens. It was more a question of creating imposing and powerful images of the institutions of authority of the new State. In this respect, Chandigarh differed little from the logic behind Lutyens' plan for the Imperial capital of New Dehli. Only the rhetorical statements explaining the plan used a different language – of freedom and democracy, of emancipation and progress for all citizens of free India. The pattern of population distribution within the plan fabric was initially determined by the location of different types of government housing in different sectors. As government housing was not influenced by market forces, its spatial distribution was based on the structure of existing social and economic disparities. Thus, the highest paid government officials, with the largest houses, were provided for in low-density sectors in the north near the capitol complex. The majority of government employees, belonging to the lowest income groups, were provided housing in the sectors at the southern end of the first phase area. The distribution of different sized private plots followed a similar pattern. The planned population per sector varied from 5000 to 20,000, resulting in a hierarchic disposition from the rich to the poor downwards from the capitol. The average population density for the whole city was 16.8 persons per acre, varying from 7 persons per acre for low-density sectors to almost 100 in the high-density ones.

Again it is interesting to compare the spatial form of Chandigarh, arrived at by Le Corbusier's method of 'rough and ready' analysis, with that of Ciudad Guayana planned by a multi-disciplinary team of 'experts'. For the linear spatial form of Ciudad Guayana, finally selected as 'optimal' after a number of alternatives had been tested by computers, it turned out that even when the city's population reached 250,000, the population would be spending 12 to 16 per cent of its disposable income on transport. The distance between the major industrial employment nucleus of the city and its main low-income residential area was to be as much as 15 miles! (Rodwin, 1969). And this in an economy much more committed to free enterprise where the availability of public transport was to be negligible in the city. Clearly, the determination of an optimal spatial form for the city by the 'experts' and the computers was not optimal from the point of view of the majority of the city's existing or projected population.

6. Development and Administrative Authority

Under the Chandigarh Development and Regulation Act 1952, the Chief Administrator of the CPO was vested with powers to frame bye-laws and issue instructions regarding building, land use, sale of developed plots, preservation of trees, regulation of outdoor advertisements, peripheral control and other related matters.

The structure of the organization was along similar lines to that of the development corporations for new towns in Britain. Although eventually the city was to be administered by an elected municipal authority, in the initial stages the functions of both local adminstration and development were to be performed by the CPO. As the CPO was a non-elected organization, its accountability to the general population was limited.

The setting up of similar semi-autonomous State agencies has accompanied the development of the other Third World new towns already mentioned. Their structures, designed to ensure implementation and frequently based on the pattern of the development corporations of British new towns, leave few channels for their being accountable to their populations. What is more, the powers of making decisions relating to matters of even local concern have frequently been left in the hands of remote central authorities, as in the case of Ciudad Guayana and Tema.

7. 'The Statute of the Land'

As one of the major points discussed by CIAM had been the need for planning control, a lot of effort was put into devising legal instruments for such control in Chandigarh. Among others, these included the Development and Regulation Act 1952, the Periphery Control Act 1952, building and sale of sites rules, and several architectural and aesthetic controls. The overall use of all these legislative measures was to be governed by what Le Corbusier called 'The Statute of the Land', which summarized the conceptual basis from which the planning of the city had emerged. Besides describing the process by which the selection of functions and land uses in the city had been, and had to be *continued* to be, determined; the ways in which the locations and forms of the 'containers' of the functions had been, and had to be *continued to be anticipated*, the document *defined how the city had to be used and the kind of life which had to be lived in it for all time to come.* So complete was the confidence that Le Corbusier displayed in his urban doctrine that he assured the authorities that so long as it was meticulously *implemented and enforced* by them, Chandigarh would indeed be a 'city offering all amenities to the poorest of the poor of its citizens to lead a dignified life.' While making a plea for the translation of his Statute of the Land into law, he outlined the role of the authorities in the matter:

> The duty of an authority is to be honest: it is to control things which belong to a regime of rules (existing and understandable) which have to be created by the will of a collectivity . . .
>
> . . .The Statute of the Land is the description of what has been proposed and has to be proposed in the future and a commitment of the authority that such realities will never be destroyed by inattentive resolutions or decisions. (Le Corbusier, 1959a)

Although the Statute of the Land was never made into law, the wide-ranging statutory powers granted to the CPO were justified on the grounds that it would always use them in the 'public interest'. What was going to constitute 'public interest', on what criteria its interpretation was to be based, and how the CPO was going to be accountable to the people for its decisions, was never spelt out.

6

Development of Chandigarh
1951–1981

In the first phase, thirty sectors were planned to be developed for a population of 150,000. The 8919 acres of land required for the purpose were acquired by the CPO to start construction. Land for seventeen additional sectors was to be acquired and developed during the second phase to cater for a total population of 500,000.

Le Corbusier had emphasized that there should be *three* and not two phases of development. He felt that before the development of additional sectors was undertaken, the *real* second phase should consist of increasing the population density of the first phase area by filling in its un(der)used pockets. This was to prevent inefficient and uneconomical use of infrastructure already provided. The physical development of second phase sectors was thus really to constitute a third phase.

Contrary to Mayer's misgivings, Chandigarh has developed into a rapidly growing city. Between 1961 and 1971, its population increased from 89,000 to 219,000, placing it among 142 class 1 cities (population exceeding 100,000) in India. During this decade, the rate of growth of its population was 144.9 per cent, one of the highest for urban areas in the country. According to the provisional population totals of the 1981 Census, the population grew by another 70.06 per cent to a population of 371,992 during the 1971–81 decade, continuing to maintain the highest rate of growth among cities in the country (Census of India, 1981).

Over the past thirty years, the plan framework has undergone significant modifications during its implementation. Many battles have been fought over interpretation of its 'unquestionable' concepts. In the process, the plan has generally been appropriated by the ruling elite to serve its own interests even more than it did originally.

This chapter looks at the nature of the transformations which have taken place and the processes by which they have been brought about. It is confined to developments which were generally able to conform to the physical pre-requisites of the plan. Subsequent chapters will deal with the two major developments *outside* the plan framework.

Political and Administrative Changes and the Regional Context

Chandigarh's high rate of growth has largely been a consequence of a number of political and administrative changes which have taken place since its creation.

The first of these was the merging of the state of PEPSU with Punjab in 1956. This led to a sudden shift of additional government offices and staff from Patiala, the old capital of PEPSU, to Chandigarh.

The second major event was the reorganization of the erstwhile state of Punjab into the present states of Punjab and Haryana in November 1966. The dispute over which of the new states was to get Chandigarh was temporarily resolved by the creation of the Union Territory of Chandigarh. This is administered directly by the central government, with Chandigarh City serving as the administrative centre for *three* governments. This led to a gross accentuation of the administrative functions of the city with many offices of the Punjab, Haryana and central governments being moved to it from other places.

The third major political event, whose impact is yet to be assessed, was the decision of the central government in 1970 to award the city to Punjab in 1975. Haryana was allowed to continue using Chandigarh as its capital during this period to give it time to make arrangements for a separate one. At the beginning of 1975, the implementation of this decision was delayed indefinitely.

The temporary conversion of Chandigarh into a Union Territory has been significant in a number of respects. First, the responsibility for the development, financing, and administration of the city was transferred from the state government of Punjab to the central government, and the CPO was replaced by Chandigarh Administration, part of the central administrative service.

Secondly, the Union Territory under the jurisdiction of Chandigarh Administration, which includes the master plan area and a rural belt, is considerably smaller than that within a ten-mile radius previously covered by the Periphery Control Act of 1952. The governments of both Punjab and Haryana, competing with each other to exploit the economic potential generated by the high investment in Chandigarh, and the proximity to administrative offices, have started the development of two separate townships just outside the Union Territory. Development of the industrial town of SAS Nagar by Punjab, and Panchkula, a market town planned by Haryana, is well underway (see figure 6.1). The concept of maintaining a clear rural/urban dichotomy with Chandigarh as a 'radio-concentric city of exchanges' has thus already become obsolete. Punjab government likes to describe SAS Nagar as the third phase of Chandigarh, and its master plan envisages linking its sectors with those of Chandigarh when the latter is handed back to Punjab. As SAS Nagar is being developed as an industrial centre, even the clear functional definition of Chandigarh as a purely administrative and cultural centre has been destroyed.

Thirdly, a number of additional developments have taken place in the vicinity. These include the establishment of a Military Cantonment and a Hindustan Machine Tools factory within the periphery. A little further out, the

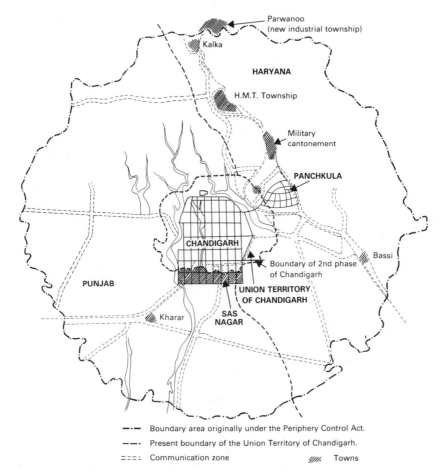

Parwanoo
(new industrial township)

Kalka

HARYANA

H.M.T. Township

Military
cantonement

PANCHKULA

CHANDIGARH

Bassi

Boundary of 2nd phase
of Chandigarh

PUNJAB

UNION TERRITORY
OF CHANDIGARH

Kharar   SAS
              NAGAR

—·— Boundary area originally under the Periphery Control Act.
—–· Present boundary of the Union Territory of Chandigarh.
==== Communication zone   ///// Towns

Figure 6.1. The planned industrial township of SAS Nagar in Punjab and the market town of Panchkula in Haryana, located well within the original Periphery Control Zone.

development of Parwanoo, a new industrial township in Himachal Pradesh, has also reached an advanced stage. The resident staff of all rely heavily on Chandigarh for various amenities and services.

Economic Activities and Employment

The percentage of workers to total population in the city in 1971 was 33.5 per cent, which is above the all India average of 29.5 per cent for urban areas. The distribution of workers among different economic activities during 1961 and 1971 is shown in table 6.1*. Because of Chandigarh's increased administrative

*Details of the 1981 Census were not available at the time of going to press.

Table 6.1. Distribution of workers in different categories of economic activity in 1961 and 1971.

Category	1961		1971	
	Number (1000s)	Percentage of total	Number (1000s)	Percentage of total
Government service	17.0	50.0	45.0	61.6
Manufacturing, processing, servicing and repairs	3.0	9.0	9.0	12.3
Construction	10.0	29.5	4.0	5.5
Trade and commerce	3.0	9.0	11.0	15.0
Transport, storage and communications	1.0	3.0	3.0	4.1
Agriculture and allied groups	—	—	1.0	1.4
Total	34.0	100.0	73.0	100.0
Workers as percentage of total population		37.5		33.5

Source: Superintendent of Census Operations, Chandigarh.

Table 6.2. Income distribution of households.

Household income (Rs/month)*	Percentage for urban areas in India†	Assumed existing percentage for Chandigarh‡
Below 250	40	25
251 to 350	33	30
351 to 500	15	25
501 to 1000	7.5	15
Above 1000	2.5	5

*£1.00 = Rs.16.00 approx.
†These figures are based on various sample surveys of consumption levels.
‡This distribution has been assumed by Chandigarh Administration on the basis of higher per capita incomes in Punjab and Haryana and because Chandigarh is 'attracting prosperous new settlers' from abroad.
Source: Draft proposals for the Fifth Five Year Plan (1974–79) Department of Finance, Chandigarh Administration.

functions, the proportion of government employees to total workers during the decade increased from 50 to 61.6 per cent. In other sections of activity such as trade and commerce, transportation and industry, although the increase in absolute terms was three to four times, the percentage of workers in each of these categories remained much below the average for a typical urban centre in India. Thus, as originally visualized, a majority of Chandigarh's working population has salaried employment with fixed incomes, the economic structure of the city being dependent on its limited purchasing power.

The income distribution of households for the whole of urban India and the adjustments made for Chandigarh by Chandigarh Administration for the Fifth Five Year Plan (1974–79) are shown in table 6.2. In 1974, the Administration assumed that only 55 per cent of the city's households had monthly incomes of Rs.350 (about £21.90) or below compared with the overall average of 73 per cent for urban areas. This assumption was based on Punjab and Haryana having higher per capita incomes than other states and because Chandigarh was 'attracting prosperous new settlers' from abroad (Chandigarh Administration, 1974). This is a reference to a number of families of Indian origin settling in the city following their return from East Africa. Any significant impact of these families on the city's economy is suspect given that according to a 1977 estimate (*The Tribune*, 1977b) they numbered only about 150–200*. The occupational distribution of the working population, accompanied by the steady rise in the numbers of unemployed persons in skilled, unskilled and white collar categories registering with the city's employment exchange, also make the official optimism about the prosperity of the city's population highly suspect†.

The use made of the city's educational and cultural amenities is taken by the Administration as an indicator of its socio-economic standing. But this is a false indicator. While it is the master plan area which is used in assessing this performance, the *actual* area from which those using the amenities are drawn includes all the new developments on the city's periphery mentioned above. The affluent of these developments make extensive use of Chandigarh's civic amenities, while large sections of its own population are unable to do so.

'Use' and 'Exchange' Values of Land

Implicit in Le Corbusier's and CIAM's doctrine was a reliance on the use of rising land values as a means of financing urban development. Initially residential land was sold at fixed prices based on development costs. However, as the problems inherent in the original short-term financing policy (see page 61) became manifest, the auctioning of both residential and commercial land

---

*Probably a much more significant impact on the city's purchasing power has been made more recently by the remittances of Indian skilled and unskilled workers from the Middle East. Unfortunately no statistical assessment of this is available.

†Whereas in December 1970, the total number of persons registering as unemployed was 14,218, in 1972 the number was 22,328 having risen to a total of 44,957 by June 1977, and 57,908 by August 1980. The numbers of graduates, professional and managerial job seekers for the first three respective periods were 3698, 4990 and 5396. (Source: Regional Employment Office, Chandigarh. Those registering with this office have to be resident in the Union Territory and seeking employment within it.)

began to be used as a major means of raising finance for the city's development. The fundamental contradiction between relying on, accepting, and actually promoting a rise in land values, and the very objectives of urban planning were never acknowledged by Le Corbusier and his colleagues. They certainly have not been acknowledged by Chandigarh Administration. This has led to dire consequences for the majority of the city's population in terms of acute over-crowding, a high cost of living, and restrictions on the right to engage in certain financially gainful occupations – in other words, a negation of some of the objectives of the plan. The contradiction lies in the fact that while the plan specified land and building uses on the basis of use values to the community, the very process by which land is made available to private purchasers grants them not only the right, but actually exhorts them to realize its exchange value as determined by the market.

'Use value' is concerned with the satisfaction of personal or social needs. An owner-occupier of a house is interested in its use value in relation to his personal needs. His ability to acquire a certain amount of use value, however, is determined by his ability to pay its exchange value. The exchange value of land, or a house is a function of the allocative mechanism of the market. If there is inadequate land or housing available in relation to the effective demand for it, its distribution will be determined by the distribution of exchange values or the acquisition power among those competing for it. Thus a small family with a large income will be able ot satisfy much more than its basic needs, while a large family with a low income will only be able to acquire limited housing use values. In Third World contexts, where large sections of the population have no exchange values at their command, their access to housing use values has to be through channels which violate the local property laws. Purely technically speaking, the very existence of anywhere between 15 and 70 per cent of Third World urban populations in different countries is 'illegal'.

The relationship between use value and exchange value with respect to land and the improvements on it, within a capitalist economy, acquires additional complications because of the special characteristics of land as a commodity. Three of these characteristics (Harvey, 1975:157–8) are particularly important for understanding the irreconcilable contradictions underlying land-use planning on the basis of use values and the actual determinants of land use in reality.

First, land has a fixed location. Absolute location confers monopoly privileges upon the individual who has the rights to determine use at that location. It is a basic attribute of physical space that no two people or things can occupy exactly the same location, and this principle, when institutionalized as private property, has very important ramifications for urban land-use theory and for the meaning of value in use and value in exchange.

Secondly, land is something permanent and the life expectancy of improvements is often considerable. Land and buildings, and the rights of use attached to them, provide an opportunity to store wealth. Land and structures have historically been the single most important repository of stored assets. In a capitalist economy, an individual has a dual interest in property both as current and future use value and as potential or actual exchange value both now and in the future.

Thirdly, land and improvements on it are commodities which no individual can do without. No one can exist without occupying space or work without occupying a location and making use of the material objects located there.

Rising land and property values, particularly in certain locations, are a function of the scarcity of the attributes of those particular locations relative to the effective demand for them. However, the demand for these locations does not necessarily mean that they will be put to use. By acquiring ownership of a key location, an individual can decide to actually keep it out of use to realize its increased 'exchange value' in the future. This is essentially the phenomenon referred to as speculative land purchase. There is a strong tendency towards an increase in such speculation in a context where alternative opportunities for investment in direct production are limited, and the returns from it do not compare favourably with those from rising land values. Such activities by a minority section of the population with surplus capital entail heavy social costs because they result in the withholding of developed urban land from use and a diversion of potential investment in production into land/property speculation.

Selling land leasehold by the public authority, and retaining the right to specify the use to which it may be put, was the panacea suggested by CIAM to counter the activities of land and property speculators. The apparent objectives were to ensure that land would not be kept out of use by private owners for extended periods of time and that at least a part of the unearned income accruing from rising land values could be acquired by the public authority for investing in items of 'public benefit'.

However, effectively, this merely means that the public authority acquires monopoly rights over land speculation and relies on it as a major source of income, which clearly does not solve the problems concerning the lack of access to land use for those sections of the population unable to pay its 'exchange value'. This is particularly so when the public authority resorts to auctioning land to the highest bidders as the basis for its distribution. In other words, the public authority acquires the role of a capitalist enterpreneur whose source of income is not increased production but speculation. In such a role it can only imitate the functioning of the market and, in turn, must also defend the rights of real estate co-owners to appropriate large amounts of consumer surplus from the rest of the population.

Although public speculation in land is justified on the grounds of its being in the 'public interest', how a public authority uses its resulting increased income is determined by the balance of power prevailing in its particular social context. Where there is a socially conscious and organized working class, a public authority could find itself having to be accountable for the majority of its allocative decisions. On the other hand, in a typical Third World urban context, where frequently the levels of organization and consciousness of the mass of the working population are low, public authority decision-making often blatently reflects the interests of the ruling elite.

Land and Finance Policies in Chandigarh

As described earlier, the sources of finance for the first phase of the city were direct grants and loans from the central and Punjab governments, 'development' costs being recoverable through the sale of plots. Of the original project estimate of a gross expenditure of Rs.174.4 million, the outlay during the first Five Year Plan (1951–56) was Rs.128 million. During the Second Five Year Plan (1956–61), the Planning Commission approved additional funds for the project. Taking into account the approved expenditure on two new government housing schemes and the additional allocation, the project estimate was revised to Rs.241 million.

Further allocation was made during the Third Five Year Plan (1961–66). As this time no specific expenditure was approved for housing, construction of government housing virtually halted. In the meantime, in 1959, 'in order to encourage the construction of private houses', the Chief Minister of Punjab had given the assurance of a twenty-five year tax holiday to the city's property owners.

The CPO then began to experience the first financial strains of continuing with the planned pattern of development. It was decided to try raising additional resources by changing the land sale policy. The practice of selling residential plots at fixed prices was given up in favour of auctioning them to the highest bidder. Commercial plots had been auctioned more or less from the beginning. In 1972, the sale of both commercial and residential plots was changed from freehold to ninety-nine year leasehold, and an annual ground rent of $2\frac{1}{2}$ per cent of the premium for the first thirty-three years, $3\frac{3}{4}$ per cent for the next thirty-three years and 5 per cent for the last thirty-three years was introduced. In addition, 50 per cent of the 'profit' of the leaseholder (increase in the value of the plot above the auction premium) through resale was to be paid to the Administration.

During the three Annual Plans from 1966–69, the Planning Commission approved still further allocation of central resources for the Capital Project. However, pressure started building up against Chandigarh being a continuous burden on the public exchequer.

The budget for the Capital Project approved during the Fourth Five Year Plan (1969–74) amounted to a gross expenditure of Rs.110 million. Of this, the anticipated receipts from the sale of plots were estimated to be Rs.70 million, and the deficit of Rs.40 million was to be fully financed by the central government. Instead, towards the end of the Fourth Plan period, the anticipated gross expenditure on the city amounted to Rs. 126.8 million, out of which as much as Rs.85.5 million had been recovered through the sale of plots.

In Chandigarh Administration's budget proposals for the Fifth Five Year Plan (1974–79), of a gross outlay of Rs.200 million, Rs.95 million were to be recovered through land sales. In the process of pruning the liabilities of the Capital Project on central resources, the Planning Commission reduced the proposed expenditure to Rs.156.5 million, but increased the target of receipts from land to Rs.120 million. This was done on the grounds that the amount raised through selling land during the previous plan period had exceeded the target, and therefore the Administration's estimate of recovery from the same source during the Fifth Plan was on the low side (Government of India, 1973).

With the growth of the city, the expenditure on the maintenance of infrastructure and amenities has also been increasing. In 1971, it was Rs.3.0 million; it rose to Rs.5.0 million during 1971–72 and to Rs.6.0 million during 1972–73. Until recently, even this expenditure was met by central funds, but because of the increasing reluctance of the central government to continue subsidizing the city, no allocation for maintenance was approved for the Fifth Plan period. As a result, Chandigarh Administration introduced local property taxation for the first time in 1976. Its right to levy such a tax, however, was quashed by the Punjab and Haryana High Court in February 1979 (*Indian Express*, 1979). Its appeal against the judgement is pending in the Supreme Court.

The basic approach of the Administration has continued to be that of estimating the costs of chosen standards of physical development first and *then* attempting to extract them from the public rather than assessing the ability of different sections of the population to pay and providing them accordingly. Neither has there been any systematic attempt to promote more productive activities among the mass of the population by allowing an intensive and remunerative use of land and building. The direct relationship between the economic circumstances of the people and the standard of services and amenities within their reach, has continued to elude reflection in the city's policies. Sanctified by law, the physical framework of the plan, with all its contradictions, has been used as a major instrument to prevent such policy changes.

According to projections in the late 1970s, the Capital Project was expected to be 'completed' by 1987. On its 'completion', it was expected to have cost Rs.950 million out of which receipts from the sale of plots were estimated at approximately Rs.550 million (57.9 per cent), the balance being financed largely by central government. However, in October 1979, the Chief Commissioner came out with the startling statement that after a summary survey, it had been realized that 'there are just no more residential plots for sale to the general public' (*The Tribune*, 1979). Since then, only two auctions of 135 and 68 residential plots have been held in August 1980 and October 1981 respectively, at which prices reached an all time high.

Land Auctioning

The original policy of selling residential plots at fixed prices was given up in

1960. Until the beginning of the 1960s, land values in Chandigarh had remained low. In fact, the resale price of plots sold even by allotment was below the price fixed by the government.

All the same, when the Estate Office advertised the first auction of residential plots in 1960, it was very heavily attended and plots fetched high prices. This was due to a number of reasons. The most important was that there were still a large number of refugees who had been issued government bonds in lieu of compensation for property lost in Pakistan. Many of them, knowing that encashment by the government was unlikely for several years, used the device of purchasing auctioned plots as a means of cashing their bonds. They subsequently resold these at prices far below the auctioned ones but were satisfied as far as their objective of getting cash in hand was concerned. A number of purchasers were Indian expatriates returning from East Africa who wanted to invest in property and had ready money in hand.

Table 6.3. Number of residential plots sold per year by Chandigarh Administration from 1961 to the end of the first quarter of 1975.

| Year | Number of plots sold | | |
	by auction	by allotment	total
1961			
1962	218		218
1963	43		43
1964	64		64
1965	36		36
1966	27		27
1967	19	2461*	2480
1968	35	665*	700
1969	19		19
1970	79		79
1971	139		139
1972		1821	1821
1973	92	109	301
1974	275		275
1975 (first quarter)	66		66
Total	1112	5056	6168

*Most of these were sold at concessional rates to members of the armed forces not resident in Chandigarh and to a selected few of the city's elite such as government architects, engineers, doctors and professors.

Note: During the period of fifteen years, the city's population increased by approximately 170,000. In addition to the sale of only 6168 private residential plots, only 3579 government houses were built.

Source: Estate Office, Chandigarh Administration.

Encouraged by the high prices fetched through auctioning, the CPO gave up the system of allotment altogether. Not only that, but the highest average price fetched by each plot category in one auction was used as a basis for fixing the minimum reserve price for a like plot in the subsequent one. In addition, care was taken to release only a limited number of plots for sale in any one year. Between 1961 and 1971 while the population of the city increased by 130,000, only 3805 residential plots were released for sale (table 6.3). Of these, 3126 were sold at concessional rates predominantly to defence personnel not resident in Chandigarh and to a small number of 'selected' high government officials and professionals 'because the high land prices had gone beyond their reach'. Thus, over a period of ten years, in a rapidly growing city, only 679 residential plots were made available to the general public. As these were sold to the highest bidders, it was inevitable that only the wealthier could have bought them. As mentioned above, this coincided with the period when the construction of government housing had virtually halted. Six years after the allotment of plots to the defence personnel, only 10 per cent had been built on. Another six years later, by 1979, this percentage had increased to only 16.6. In April 1979, the Administration permitted resale of these plots by the defence personnel. Since then the rate of construction on them has gone up considerably despite a phenomenal rise in building costs and scarcity of building materials. The Adminstration itself earned over Rs.10 million as its 50 per cent share of the unearned income (through rises in land value) of the defence plot sellers between 1979 and 1981 (*The Tribune*, 1981).

The effect of this policy on land values was staggering. By 1973/74 prices of some of the smaller residential plots had increased by 1000 to 1400 per cent and by 1980, by 4500 to 6700 per cent (table 6.4(*b*)). Ironically, in 1959, just one year before the change in land policy in Chandigarh, a Committee had been set up in Dehli to study the problems of, and to suggest measures for, the control of land values. In its report this Committee had observed that

> The only practicable measure to control land values in a growing city is to relieve the pressure of demand as much as possible. (quoted in Bose, 1969: 33)

Soaring land prices in Chandigarh, however, did not perturb Chandigarh Administration until the early 1970s. On the contrary, there was a general feeling of satisfaction and an explanation of the phenomenon in terms of the 'success' of Chandigarh's 'planning'. One can see Le Corbusier's optimistic views about 'good' urbanism being a 'way of making money' being used to justify the situation.

From the early 1970s, owing to widespread public discontent and unrest, both locally and nationally, Chandigarh Administration began to feel pressurized to reassess its land policy. Following the central government's overt commitment to the removal of poverty and the reduction of inequality, just before the 1971 general elections, the Administration formulated a 'Model Scheme' for two of the second phase sectors. Under this, 1821 residential plots

Table 6.4. Increase in residential land prices after the introduction of sale through open auction. (*a*) Fixed allotment prices up to 1960. (*b*) Prices fetched in auction in 1973–74, and in 1980.

(*a*)

Size of plot in square yards	Fixed allotment price per square yard (Rs.)
First 125	12
Next 125	8
Next 250	6
Above 500	4

(*b*)

Size of plot in square yards	Average auctioned price per square yard in 1973–74 (Rs.)	Percentage increase over allotment prices in 1960	Auctioned price per square yard during last auction, 3 August 1980 (Rs.)	Percentage increase over allotment prices in 1960
125	181	1408	536	4366
187	154	1343	657	6570
250	125	1150	544	6700
375	108	1147	—	—
500	95	1087	466	5475

Source: Estate Office, Chandigarh Administration.

were sold in 1972 to low-income group persons* at fixed prices approximately equal to the cost of development. Since this symbolic gesture, no more residential plots have been released on such terms despite an association of the unsuccessful 1972 plot applicants continuing until the present day to agitate to be allotted plots at 1972 prices.

The only criterion being used by the Administration to decide how many plots to put up for sale, and the frequency of the sales, was the need to raise funds for the budget for any one year. As and when it was running out of money, it put land up for sale. Since permitting resale of plots allotted to defence personnel in 1979, the Administration earned over Rs.10 million as its share of the sellers' profit, it reduced the number of auctions of plots from four in 1978 to two in 1979, one in 1980, and one in 1981 (*The Tribune*, 1981). Now that there is hardly any residential land left for open sales, it is unclear what the policy is going to be.

One positive policy change which was made a few years ago was the decision to limit maximum plot size to 500 square yards. Eighty per cent of all new plots are to be of 250 square yards or less. This should lead to an increase in density and also to a greater proportion of the total land being put to productive use.

The Housing Situation

During the first decade of Chandigarh's development, despite a rapid rate of population growth from almost nil to 89,000, the objective of the average household living in the minimum dwelling of two rooms with services was, to a large extent, achieved. (This, of course, does not include all those who were excluded from access to housing within the planned framework by virtue of their income and employment conditions. Their plight is discussed in later chapters). A majority of government employees were able to obtain government accomodation, and rents of private housing remained low.

Two policy decisions made this possible. The first, related to the private sector, was to induce house construction through incentives and sanctions. However, the majority of private house construction which took place was for owner-occupation. The second was the construction of a large number of houses by the government for its employees. During the first few years, over 8000 dwelling units were built, sufficient to accommodate most employees at that time.

However, in 1956, when there was a sudden influx of additional government personnel caused by the merger with PEPSU, a solution to the resulting housing shortage was sought by allocating two families to a housing unit in the lowest income categories. Thus the aim of providing a self-contained dwelling unit per household was put aside by the government itself within six years of the city's inception.

---

*Defined as those earning Rs.7200 per annum or less (see also table 6.2).

From the early 1960s, when the government housing programme was virtually halted, more and more government employees had to rent private accommodation. They began to experience the problem of housing acutely around 1964. At that time, the 8310 available government houses had been allotted to 11,938 employees, while a further 3041 were on the waiting list. This was at a time when only about 4000 private houses had been built. The result was a substantial rise in private rents. 'To mollify the rumblings of dissatisfaction on the part of its employees living in private houses, the government started paying a house rent allowance of $7\frac{1}{2}$ per cent of the salary' (D'Souza, 1973). This measure only led to a further increase in rents without bringing any real relief to the tenants. A market thriving on conditions of scarcity emerged. It is important to note that this situation had developed before the Administration's change in policy, leading to a restricted release of plots, had created an artificial land scarcity.

The multiplication of Chandigarh's administrative functions further aggravated the housing shortage. Although the total number of government houses had increased by about 3800 over a period of eight years, most of the new units were alloted to those who had previously been sharing houses. Therefore, the total number of employees living in government houses increased only from 11,938 to 13,821. The enormity of the problem is apparent from the government housing waiting list. While there were 3000 on it in 1964, by 1972 the figure had reached 18,000 – a six-fold increase. Some of the lowest income employees have been on the waiting list since 1957. Against this background, Chandigarh Administration proposed the construction of only 604 houses during the Fifth Five Year Plan.

The halt in the government's housing programme, combined with a phenomenal rate of population growth proved a more effective incentive for promoting private construction than all those offered earlier*. While up to 1964, only 4000 private houses had been built, by 1974 another 7000 had been added. Although permission was granted for building two dwelling units per plot, higher income owner-occupiers with larger plots mostly built houses to accommodate one household only and, according to official estimates, only 50 per cent of private plots have been built with two dwelling units. Private accommodation built up to 1974 was thus estimated to be sufficient for 16,500 households, but over 30,600 households had to find accommodation within these houses. Although more dwellings have certainly been added to the housing stock since then, the majority have been built on a limited number of

---

*The same problem of inducing private capital to invest in housing has been experienced in other Third World planned new towns. In Ciudad Guayana, because of an open commitment to make 'free enterprise' work, the regional development authority made a determined attempt to remain uninvolved with the direct production of housing for all income groups. Yet, in spite of land being given to private construction companies at reduced rates and the offering of several other guarantees by the public authority, the response was minimal. Reluctantly, the corporation was forced to organize the direct production of housing for most income groups (Corrada, 1969).

Figure 6.2. Standard upper/middle-income private housing in one of the first phase sectors.

plots released for sale to the private sector or to employers for housing specific groups of employees. The natural consequence of this has been multiple occupation, and that mainly confined to the smallest houses. While comprehensive data on multiple occupation are not available, a number of random surveys indicate its being acute on plots of 250 square yards and below, with each accommodating from two to as many as eight or nine households. As plots of these sizes are in sectors for low-income and high-density development, populations here have already gone well beyond their planned targets.

The increased private house construction after 1964 largely took place on plots sold at fixed prices up to 1960. By virtue of this, those who had purchased plots before 1960, and those allotted plots at concessional rates later, have been able to make their fortunes either through renting their properties at very high rates, or by selling them at phenomenally increased prices.

It is quite common for senior government officials to be paying Rs.200 to 250 per month for spacious government houses while having built equally large dwellings financed by government loans at subsidized interest rates, from which they can expropriate rents of anywhere from Rs.800 to Rs.2500 per month*. By these means, in addition to being able to repay the loans by the time of retirement, they can look forward to having acquired substantial assets which will have further multiplied in exchange value in the intervening period.

---

*According to recent estimates, between 10 and 15 per cent of the government housing stock is occupied by employees owning their own houses.

For the wealthy in the private sector, while the benefit of simultaneously having access to subsidized housing does not exist, ownership of land and housing nevertheless serves as a major means of not only storing their wealth and protecting it against inflation, but also of multiplying it. No such options are open to the majority of tenants, who constituted about 80 per cent of the total households in the city in 1971 (Census of India, 1971a:74).

As a result of the 1972 change in policy of selling auctioned land on leasehold, many of the middle-income group wishing to purchase and build for owner-occupation are often forced to sublet parts of their dwellings at the highest possible rents just to enable them to repay loans or even to recover the high ground rents.

In the case of Tema, where the bulk of the housing stock has been built by the Development Corporation, the same mechanism functions in a different way. TDC has been forced to rent its houses at between 25 and 55 per cent below the economic rent, and even initially heavily-subsidized rents have not been revised since 1954. Among the main beneficiaries of this arrangement are big industrial companies, including those which are totally foreign-owned and remit all their profits abroad. Not only that, but, in the words of TDC's Chief Estate Officer, 'collection of [even these highly subsidized] rents from the tenants of the corporation has . . . been a nightmare'. The end result is that the benefits of TDC's investment in public services are more or less monopolized by this section of the population, leaving TDC unable to recover even the direct investment in housing. The private companies, for their part, have totally failed to respond to TDC's pleas to invest in housing themselves, at least for their own employees, in spite of being given several incentives such as land at concessional ground rents (Bauchie-Kessie, 1976).

In 1976, a semi-autonomous Housing Board started operating in Chandigarh. Its aim is to supply pre-built houses or flats of one or two standard designs for four different income groups, on a hire purchase basis. The Administration has been providing land to the Board at the concessional rate of Rs.40 per square yard when development costs are Rs.55 per square yard. The land is on a ninety-nine year lease, the same as in the case of auctioned plots. Ground rent is calculated as a percentage of the concessional land price. Allotment is by the draw of lots. The applicants have to submit affidavits giving their total household income, which is used as a basis for deciding the type of housing to which they are entitled. The periods for paying for the dwellings, through monthly instalments, vary from eighteen years for the 'economically weaker section' to ten years for the 'middle income group'. In addition, there are front-end costs at the time of application and allotment. (Housing boards in the country do not permit subletting even by owner-occupiers.) By July 1979, the Board had allotted 1260 units and about 1400 were in various stages of construction. It hopes to complete a total of 9000 units by 1983. However, an acute shortage of cement is likely to prove a major impediment in meeting this target. In addition, the cost of all building materials has been escalating making it difficult for the Board to restrict its unit costs to the limits specified by HUDCO.

While this may reduce the housing shortage in the city to some extent, the Board essentially caters for those desiring owner-occupation, who have stable incomes and employment, generating sufficient household savings to ensure repayment. Past experience all over India, as also in other Third World countries, has demonstrated that the housing provided by agencies organized on these lines never goes to the income groups for which it is intended. A recent survey carried out by HUDCO, a central government corporation and the main financing agency for state housing boards, revealed that a majority of the 'economically weaker section' housing financed by it so far, had gone to higher income households. The demand for housing among even the middle class makes it virtually impossible to enforce an effective compartmentalization between different income groups.

The creation of the Housing Board marked an important change from the original framework. It implied a withdrawal by government from the responsibility of providing minimum housing, at least to its own employees, irrespective of their income. Instead, the emphasis has shifted to direct provision of dwellings to both government and non-government applicants in accordance with their ability to pay. While this form of direct intervention is partly in response to the government's inability to provide subsidized housing on a large scale, it is also an attempt to ensure the production of more housing space which the private sector failed to provide satisfactorily even when adequate land had been released*. The present pattern of house production, if anything, will reflect existing inequalities rather than attempt to modify them, resulting in perhaps greater social segregation than before. The element of subsidy in the case of Housing Board dwellings will be a reduced cost of land and some cross-subsidization of the supposedly 'economically weaker section' by charging differential interest rates to different income group applicants.

Several writers have attacked direct house production by public agencies on the grounds of their insensitivity to complex and variable 'dweller' needs, and instead advocated a 'supportive' role for them to enable maximum housing development by private agents, owner-occupiers, landlords, private builders or local groups†. However, an historical examination of the factors leading to direct public intervention in house building in a majority of contexts reveals that it has been a response to the failure of the very policies supporting construction by private agents that these writers advocate. As is clear from the Chandigarh experience, for the majority of households the option of house ownership never existed. Those owning private plots refused to build housing for rent until conditions of immense scarcity ensuring very high rates of return had emerged. The vast majority simply had to accept the terms dictated by

*A similar change towards building for owner occupation, as also of selling previously built housing let at subsidized rents to the tenants, has been noted in both Tema and Brasilia.
†For example see Turner (1976), C. Ward (1976).

these private owners, frequently receiving less or the same accommodation for ever increasing rents.

The inadequate response of the private sector in Ciudad Guayana has been referred to earlier. Even in Brasilia, the pattern turned out to be fairly similar to that of Chandigarh. While the initial provision of housing by the public authority on the basis of 'use values' enabled at least a small proportion of low-income households to have access to good housing, the decision to sell all public housing to the occupants at a later stage pushed all such households into far worse situations (Epstein, 1973:91). In the case of Tema, the TDC is also attempting to move in this direction but with extremely limited success (Bauchie-Kessie, 1976).

The Provision of Consumer Goods and Services

In the initial stages the resident population of the city was too small to warrant the development of city-scale facilities. The first commercial development was in Sector 22, and for ten to twelve years this shopping centre functioned as the commercial centre for the whole city. As other sectors developed, the development of their shopping streets also gathered momentum. The general pattern was that of commercial development following residential development. To induce investment in commercial building, a large number of sites were sold in the early years and loans were made available. In the city centre, the CPO built a number of shops on the V4 and rented them at fixed rents. Development of the commercial centre with the *chowk* was similarly initiated by the government.

In Tema, where the TDC could not resort to similar public investment in the town centre because of the system of development finance to which it had to conform, the private sector has failed to respond at all. In spite of 80 per cent of the town centre land having been allocated to commercial developers, anything substantial is yet to appear on the ground (Hornsby-Odoi, 1976).

In Chandigarh, as in the case of the residential plots, the sale of commercial sites per year was reduced after 1960. With the high rate of growth of the city, demand for commercial premises has also been growing. Consequently, both land values and rents have risen sharply. While in 1954, the cost of construction of a typical bay was about Rs.90,000 now the auctioned premium for just the land can be up to Rs.1 million.

At the city scale, development of the commercial centre and the V4 in Sector 17 is in an advanced stage. Specialized markets planned along the V2s are also being developed. The commercial zone along the V2 Station/University has so far been developed in Sectors 7, 8 and 26. Showrooms to the south, and east of Sector 22 are also in an advanced stage of development. For most other areas, Chandigarh Administration is 'sitting and waiting' for both demand and land values to rise before releasing land for development.

The number of planned shops operating in each residential sector and catering for local needs, and the distribution of planned shops per 1000 people

Figure 6.3. Architecturally controlled development in the city centre. Most of the blocks have shops or showrooms on the ground floor with offices above, while some have only offices. A fly-over for segrating vehicular traffic from pedestrians is in the right background .

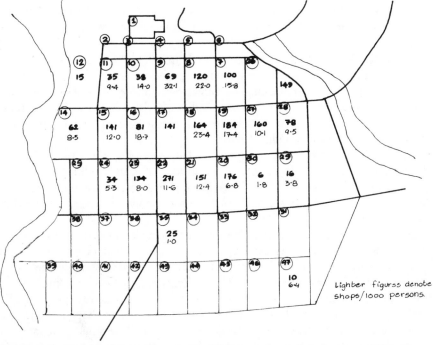

Figure 6.4. Distribution of planned shops (bold numbers) and shops per 1000 persons (light numbers) in different sectors in 1971. (From G. Krishan and S. K. Agarwal (1973) 'Commercial pattern of a planned city: Chandigarh'. *National Geographical Journal of India,* 19, part 2, June.)

Figure 6.5. Local level planned shops in Sector 18 (left), and middle-income private housing (right) with rush hour traffic on the sector's V4 (bazaar street).

in different sectors in 1971 are shown in figure 6.4. As is evident from the figure, the distribution in different sectors is uneven, with a greater number relative to population in the high-income, low-density areas. However, this uneven distribution is nothing compared with the concentration of most commercial and community facilities in only one of the residential neighbourhoods of Tema (Hornsby-Odoi, 1976).

Certain problems have been experienced in enforcing plans for the sector shopping centres. First, the simplistic assumption of locating all facilities along one side of a central street has been inadequate. In the second phase, the Administration is planning a number of 'corner shops' dispersed in the four quarters of each sector.

Secondly, it was realized that the planned shop designs could not accommodate the variety of actual uses. Consequently, a number of semi-industrial shops, suitably designed by the architects were permitted in some sectors. This has not solved the problem either. The architects and planners are finding that if they plan such shops in a particular sector, these are frequently put to regular uses, while semi-industrial uses emerge in other locations in shops designed for regular use. The process of specifying exact uses and designs in advance of occupation continues, instead of permitting the users to build the premises in accordance with their requirements.

Thirdly, as mentioned earlier, sector shopping centres were planned on the assumption of an even spatial distribution of shops catering for daily needs in residential sectors. For certain businesses to function, however, demands a concentration of specialist uses, and there was no provision in the master plan for small-scale units of this kind. Thus they have found an outlet in the form of specialist markets dealing with mechanical repairs, building materials and so on in some of the sector shopping centres.

Fourthly, the restriction of commercial uses to only one side of the sector shopping streets has been the most difficult to enforce, particularly in the high-density sectors where the planned number of shops is in any case inadequate for the population. All the inadequacies of the assumptions of the plan are being rectified by market forces. Locationally, the private housing facing the shopping streets is ideal for small-scale business, commerce and services. Its owners have not been slow to realize the potential exchange values of their property because of its locational characteristics. They also cater for the demand for comparatively lower rental commercial accommodation.

According to a survey conducted by the Administration, among those 'misusing' residential accommodation were 287 government offices, sixty-two semi-government offices, 212 private offices, thirty private guest houses, four-teen hostels and messes, 182 scheduled users such as doctors and lawyers, and 330 miscellaneous establishments such as shops (*The Tribune*, 1977a). Over 90 per cent of these 'unauthorized' uses were located in residential premises facing sector shopping streets.

Figure 6.6. Sector 21 shops which have become a specialized centre for auto repairs instead of catering for the daily needs of local residents because of the lack of facilities allowing concentration of small specialized enterprises.

Figure 6.7. A further example of non-conforming uses of planned buildings –
private housing facing a sector shopping street being put to diverse non-residential
uses.

For years, the Administration has been trying to stop such 'misuse' of
residential buildings, but with little success. Legal proceedings entail heavy
costs and can continue for years.

However, there has been little evaluation by the authorities of the relationship between these developments and their own policies. Because of the
restricted release of commercial land through public auction, not only is there a
shortage of non-residential accommodation, but rents are extremely high.
Should the Administration succeed in forcing all the enterprises violating
planned uses to conform to plan requirements, it will probably lead to a further
escalation in the rents of commercial premises. This will also imply leaving all
the small enterprises at the mercy of the commercial property owners.

Considerable sections of the city's middle class, overburdened as they are
with enormous rents for housing, support the Administration's move to prevent
non-residential uses of residential accommodation. This is because they per-
ceive the high rents as a consequence of 'misuse' of housing by business and
commercial enterprises. But as discussed earlier, the rents for private housing
are largely a result of the Administration's own land and finance policies. While
the removal of unauthorized uses from residential premises might make a
marginal impact on housing rents in the city, it is unlikely to be of a spectacular
nature given the wider situation.

In addition to all these problematic developments, a substantial proportion of the trading and service units functioning in the city have developed totally outside the planned framework. According to a survey carried out by the author at the end of 1974 these accounted for 52.4 per cent of the total trading and service enterprises in the city. This category of activities, which falls within the so-called 'informal sector' of Third World urban economies, will be examined in detail in chapter 10.

Spatial Form and Population Distribution

Chandigarh's spatial form, based on uni-functional separation of land uses has proved difficult to enforce. Besides the land-use violation along sector shopping streets, mixed land uses have emerged throughout the city. Several attempts have been made to relocate all the violating uses into their prescribed zones.

A peculiar example of this was the relocation from residential sectors of a number of activities labelled as 'industrial' to the industrial area. In the mid-1960's, 147 small enterprises engaged in radio assembly, ice production, printing presses, bakeries, soap manufacture, dairies, etc., were moved to the second phase of the industrial area (S.I.S.I., 1970:5). A study by the Small Industries Service Institute had criticized their relocation to a peripheral area as they catered for localized markets within the city and because heavy investment in industrial infrastructure was unnecessary for such small units.

In 1975, the Administration amended its zoning regulations to permit 'cottage' (household) industries in residential areas in line with the recommendations of the S.I.S.I. The argument supporting 'cottage' industries is that they will enable housewives and household members to supplement limited incomes by generating additional employment. The list of the fourteen permitted items which may be produced on residential premises includes candles, dolls, paper, watch straps, thread balls, incense sticks, ink, baskets, non-mechanical toys, pens and spectacles in addition to tailoring and embroidery. However, in return for the 'concession' of being allowed to function from residential premises, such enterprises are not permitted, among other things, to display any sign boards, engage any paid or non-family worker, use industrial power, or set up a sales counter (Industries Department, Chandigarh).

The totally unequal terms on which such enterprises must compete with the large production units allowed to advertise and sell their products openly, is evident. First, the majority of the permitted goods cater for the middle-class consumer market. Secondly, the conditions attached to their being allowed to function leave them totally at the mercy of middle men to reach the market. The imposed atomization of production leaves few opportunities for such cottage industries to establish production relationships between themselves or to have any collective control over what they produce, whose needs they cater for, or over the marketing of their products.

This particular approach towards increasing 'labour intensive' employment,

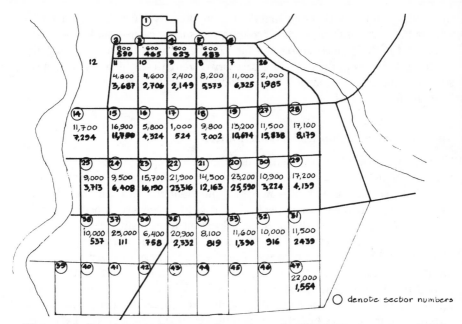

Figure 6.8. Distribution of target and actual populations (1971 Census) in different sectors. (Bold numbers denote actual populations).

which is currently being promoted by national and international agencies as a solution for the employment problems of Third World countries, is incapable of significantly improving the living conditions of those thus employed. Although a quantitative increase in employment opportunities may be possible through such strategies, the framework of production and marketing relationships leaves the small production units open to severe exploitation by those controlling distribution. How 'planning' facilitates such exploitation is clearly demonstrated by the use of land-use controls to justify the imposition of crippling restrictions in Chandigarh.

The distribution of planned populations for different sectors and their population recorded during the 1971 census are shown in figure 6.8. The emerging pattern shows populations below planned targets in northern low-density sectors and already exceeding them in some of the southern high-density ones, further accentuating the social and economic hierarchy originally planned. Some of the major factors which have led to this pattern have been dealt with already.

However the spatial maldistribution of population in Chandigarh is nothing compared to that in Ciudad Guayana. By 1975, barely fifteen years after the sophisticated planning exercise of the city was started, some 78 per cent of the population was living in the eastern, lower income section of the city, and only 22 per cent in the 'smart' western part. The distribution was planned to be 50 per cent on either side (MacDonald and MacDonald, 1977:33).

As far as the objective of preventing suburbanization through the Periphery Control Act was concerned, the degree to which this has failed is evident from the changed characteristics of the villages surrounding Chandigarh. According to the 1971 Census, 20 per cent of the households living in the villages of the Union Territory were one-person households, predominantly males. Further, 67 per cent of their working population had non-agricultural occupations. Both figures indicate that the surrounding villages are increasingly becoming low-income residential suburbs of the city, and reception centres for recent migrants arriving without their families. The provisional data available from the 1981 Census indicate an accentuation of this pattern. While there are 782 females per 1000 males in the city, in the rural areas of the Union Territory, the ratio is only 689 per 1000. This is in contrast to the pattern in the country as a whole. More and more men (either single or married but without their families with them) in the city are being forced to seek housing in neighbouring villages virtually converting them into the city's dormitories or suburbs.

Industry and the Industrial Area

In the initial years, promoting development of even the comparatively small industrial area proved very difficult. Chandigarh's location offered few advantages to industrialists from the point of view of the availability of raw materials, a potentially attractive market, or links with other major industrial complexes. Further, restrictions imposed on the types of buildings permitted and the fuels which might be used were an added disincentive. Persistent efforts directed towards individual industrialists and backed by such inducements as easy credit facilities, allotment of cheap land, scarce raw materials, and import licenses did result in the establishment of a number of industries. But, as a result, industrial development has not evolved along any rational pattern.

According to the 1971 Census, six large industrial units employed 33.4 per cent of the total industrial workers in the city, the remaining consisting of small units. Owing to the high level of automation of the larger firms, some of whom are subsidiaries of multi-national corporations, they have had a limited impact on expanding employment opportunities or producing a multiplier effect on the local economy.

All the same, contrary to original plans, an additional industrial area is being developed during the second phase. The guidelines along which Chandigarh Administration is developing this remain that

> As a planned city, the industrial pattern has to fit in the overall planning and architectural control and cannot impair the aesthetics of the city. (Chandigarh Administration, 1974:53)

The present emphasis of the Industries Department is on promoting small, high-technology units partly to absorb some of the technically trained unemployed and partly to avoid 'labour problems' or the additional responsibility for providing housing for industrial workers.

Among the concessions offered to industrialists is a very low price of land. In the first phase, plots were allotted freehold at Rs.4, Rs.8 and Rs.10 per square yard. After 1971, the rate was changed to Rs.15 per square yard as premium, with ground rent on the same basis of a percentage of premium, as for other leasehold sales. More recently, the price was raised to Rs.35 per square yard.

Compare these rates with the prevailing prices of residential land in the open market (table 6.4). Such are the concessions owners of capital may obtain. Under a central government scheme, public subsidy is provided for housing industrial workers as a majority of the industrialists refuse to house their workers themselves. In Chandigarh, only 880 such houses have been built when the industrial labour force is over 12,000. As three-quarters of this small number of houses has been allotted to the workers of the two or three foreign corporations, they are receiving a further public subsidy in addition to other tax concessions. The same phenomenon, but in a much more extreme form, is evident in both Tema and Ciudad Guayana. In Tema, Valco, a consortium of two American aluminium companies, in addition to paying no ground rent for its 500 acres of developed industrial land, insists on using subsidized public housing for its employees. In addition, Valco's smelter consumes as much power as the rest of Ghana and at a price one-sixth that paid by the residents. All profits are, of course, returned to the parent company (Glover-Akpey, 1976; Mitchell, 1972:21).

The 7Vs and Transportation

Against the background of an acute shortage of living and working accommodation, the network of the 7Vs is in an advanced stage of development. The main emphasis has been given to developing the V2s to V6s designed largely for vehicular traffic. In recent years, a number of V7s (for pedestrians only) in some of the first phase sectors have also been provided. Two overbridges for segregating pedestrian and vehicular traffic have already been built, one in the city centre and one between two sectors. An indication of the priorities on which resource allocation in the city is based is provided by the fact that while there is a phenomenal housing shortage in the city, the road network of today is adequate for ten years hence.

Even after thirty years, development of the road network is dominated by the abstract statements of principle made by Le Corbusier. No attempt has been made at inter-relating the *intensity of actual use* of the roads by existing forms of traffic *to the amount invested in them.* Because of the scarce resources available to Chandigarh Transport Undertaking and the low paying capacity of the majority of the population, it has not been possible to organize cheap and reliable public transport. The low density of population and the resultant long distances of travel increase the costs of running such a system. As a result, the most common form of transport is the bicycle. Hired private transport consists of cycle *rickshaws* and three-wheeled scooters. A large proportion of goods transport within the city is handled either by horse drawn carts or cycle *rickshaws*. Under the circumstances, attempts at enforcing use of the road network aimed at segregating fast vehicular trafffc from pedestrians assumes the existance of a hypothetical situation bearing little resemblance to reality. A whole range of forms of transport and types of vehicles actually in existance are not taken into account in the city's traffic planning. Vast amounts of public resources have been used for the convenience of a small minority of car owners, making the non-motorized vehicles used by the majority, travel longer distances and therefore further increasing travelling and time costs for them.

Chandigarh Administration and Local Government

Although the CPO was to be a temporary body for promoting co-ordinated development of the new city during its initial years, and was to be replaced by an elected municipal government, the creation of a municipality has been progressively delayed. Both development and local government functions continue to be performed by what is now called Chandigarh Administration.

Chandigarh Administration has a highly centralized decision-making structure. Most policy issues are settled by senior adminstrative and technical officers under the overall charge of the Chief Commissioner. As a non-elected body, none of the administrative officers is directly answerable to the public and they do not have to depend on the popularity of their policies to remain in office.

A minimal semblance of local 'participation' in the decision-making process is acheived through monthly consultative meetings with the 'Local Advisory Committee'. This consists of a number of selected individuals nominated by the Chief Commissioner and considered representative of different sections of the population. The Chief Commissioner is not bound to the recommendations of the Committee, and his own decisions are final.

The social and executive status of administrative officers within a highly stratified society inevitably means that they have no direct experience of the life and problems of the underprivileged sections of the population. Their decisions, however well meaning, in the end amount to *their* perception, which is a particular class perception, of the problems and priorities of other sections of the society.

For reasons of history and the association of Le Corbusier with the creation of the city, the Architecture and Town Planning departments have retained a dominant position in influencing major policy decisions. In addition to determining the pattern and priorities of physical development, their views are strongly reflected in the enforcement policies of the Estate Office responsible for looking after the maintenance and use of land and buildings in the city. The Estate Officer has a small staff at his disposal for carrying out enforcement operations. This has become a symbol of fear and persecution for large numbers of people who have become labelled as 'offenders' or law breakers by virtue of the demands made on them by the 'planned' city.

All this, of course, is not to say that the Administration is totally insensitive to public opinion. Within the framework of parliamentary democracy, maintaining a 'democratic' façade, at least amongst the articulate sections of the population, is an important instrument of political control. It is used to manipulate public opinion in favour of executive policies through maintaining a low level of awareness, and by encouraging activities which generate an individual rather than a collective outlook among the base of the population.

It is acutely sensitive about its public image, a phenomenon most markedly evident in recent years. With the changing socio-political environment of local and national contexts, it has generally produced responses in line with the demands of the articulate sections of public opinion.

It is also useful to point out that the Administration by no means has total autonomy in making its decisions. Most of its budgetry allocations have to be in line with central government policy guidelines and have to be approved by the Planning Commission. Sometimes even positive changes proposed by the Administration are rejected by the Planning Commission as was the case when, in the proposals for the Fifth Five Year Plan, the Administration stressed the need to change the land auctioning policy to allotment at fixed prices. The Planning Commission, however, demanded that it raise even more money than before through auction.

The local autonomy of the development corporations of the other new towns is even more limited. The Tema Development Corporation, for example, while being expected to be self-financing, has been forced by central government to let its housing at highly subsidized rents. Even in its attempts to rectify the growing imbalances in the distribution of community facilities, its hands have been severely tied.

The issue here is not the Administration's sensitivity or the lack of it about the needs of different sections of the population, but the nature of economic and political relationships it is required to enforce. One of the fundamental objectives of promoting urban planning in Third World Countries today is concerned with the control and distribution of land use in urban areas. Contrary to frequent assertions about the failure of 'conventional planning' in these countries, the fact is that urban planning in Third World contexts is a very recent introduction. Its history in India was briefly discussed in chapter 3. In Venezuela, the planning of Ciudad Guayana coincided with the introduction of regional and urban planning in the country on a large scale. The situation is no different in the case of most other Third World countries.

What is proposed here is that with the accelerated rate of urbanization, the objective historical function of urban planning in Third World countries is to centralize the control of land use and its distribution in the hands of public authorities. Although it is typically justified on the grounds of the need to ensure orderly development, prevent the growth of slums and traffic congestion etc., the nature of economic and political relationships existing in these contexts, ensures that such planning excludes large sections of the poorer populations from legal rights to land use in the most desirable locations. This is done by justifying the withholding of developed central city land from use till big business and commerce find it sufficiently attractive to take over. Even standards of 'planned' physical development exclude large sections from the ability to acquire legal access to urban land use. While obviously, poorer people cannot be prevented from coming to the cities, or the problems of shanty settlements and slums resolved by these means, the position of such sections of the community is further worsened. The status of the living and working opportunities available to them becomes illegal, making them much more vulnerable to manipulation by the privileged groups and the public authorities.

In the case of those who are able to remain 'legal', there is an increasing polarization between owners of real estate and their tenants. As demonstrated in the case of Chandigarh, one of the roles played by the Administration has been that of ensuring the restriction of real estate ownership to the already affluent or to certain other 'selected' groups such as state employees or defence personnel.

Any challenging of this right through direct land occupation by those unable to acquire legal access is suppressed by preventing 'encroachments' on public land. Increased public ownership of land in such a context also implies that it is the public authority which performs the function of preventing 'encroachments' on land on behalf of the potential wealthier owners or leaseholders of it. Any protests against the terms and conditions of land sales can easily be branded as threats to 'law and order' while the actual channelling of land to the affluent minority can be explained in terms of the public authority's 'lawful performance of its duties'.

Further, since investment in urban infrastructure, services and amenities must take place in a 'planned' way, even this becomes reserved for the benefit of the privileged sections of the community. As demonstrated in the case of Chandigarh, despite the change to selling land through public auctions, the high standards of public amenities and services in the city, including vast areas of public open space, the elaborate network of roads, planting of trees, refuse collection and other services, have been possible only with a continuous allocation of central government resources. In conventional terms, the mechanism of planning has enabled the use of public resources towards subsidizing the higher standards of living of the powerful elite. As they have to be 'persuaded' to invest their capital in various activities desired by the government, they can demand all sorts of guarantees and concessions before being prepared to respond.

The effective power of both the owners of capital and the educated elite, and their influence in the modification of planning frameworks to conform to their demands, is most clearly evident in the planned new towns of the Third World.

As in Chandigarh, so too the senior government officials in Brasilia and Islamabad had to be provided with luxurious subsidized housing to persuade them to move to the new capitals. In the cases of Ciudad Guayana and Tema, this section comprised senior technical and managerial employees, both public and private. In both of these cases, large proportions of such persons belonged to foreign enterprises.

The end product is evident in all the planned new towns referred to so far. The typical argument of several housing experts, economists or even international agencies like the World Bank that housing policies of Third World governments must be based on the principle of cost recovery from low-income households, has to be seen in this perspective. According to their argument, these governments simply do not have the resources to subsidize low-income households. An examination of the development of planned new towns demonstrates why this is so. Their public authorities are busy subsidizing the wealthy and the elite by the mechanisms described. The arguments of those against providing subsidies to low-income households totally evade the relationship between the way the rich in these contexts house themselves and the deprivation of resources to the already deprived. The unequal distribution of incomes and employment is a consequence of such mechanisms.

7

Growth of Non-Plan Settlements

In addition to the housing crisis described in the last chapter, about 15 per cent of the city's population has been living in totally or partially unauthorized settlements which developed outside the master plan framework. These will be referred to here as 'non-plan' settlements, purely and simply to indicate their situation as defined by the city's plan. The terms 'unplanned', 'uncontrolled' or 'squatter' settlements all have connotations not fully applicable to the phenomenon and process represented by Chandigarh's non-plan settlements. In the specific context of what was supposed to be a totally planned city, their predicament is most clearly highlighted by their relationship to the plan framework. Between 1961 and 1971, while the population of the whole city increased by 144.9 per cent, that of its non-plan settlements grew by 230 per cent (D'Souza, 1976a:1526). Between 1971 and 1974, the number of households living in them increased from 6000 to 8000, and there were few signs of a slowing down in this rate of growth. By June 1981, after the Administration had 'resettled' 12,000 non-plan households, over 6000 continued to reside in non-plan settlements (*Sunday Tribune,* 1981).

The comparative figures for Tema are even more staggering. Between 1960 and 1970, while the population of the planned parts of the city increased two and a half times, that of Ashaiman, its non-plan component, increased ten-fold (Glover-Akpey, 1976). The rate of growth of Brasilia's non-plan population is evident from the fact that by 1964, the population living in the pilot plan area comprised only 33.3 per cent of the total population of the Federal District (Epstein, 1973:69). An indication of the rate of growth of Ciudad Guayana's non-plan settlements is seen from the fact that these contained 38 per cent of the city's housing stock by 1974 (MacDonald and MacDonald, 1975).

Whatever name these settlements are given, they represent one of the most typical developments in the Third World urban context today. The last twenty-five years have witnessed spectacular rates of growth in the proportions of urban populations living in such settlements. Depending on the levels of urbanization in different countries, the percentage of urban populations living in 'unplanned' settlements varies from as high as 75 per cent in some Latin American countries to 10 to 15 per cent in the less urbanized countries of Asia and Africa.

Over this period there has been a gradual change in official perceptions of what the phenomenon of their growth represents. From initial hostile reactions – their being seen as a threat to law and order and as unhygienic slums requiring clearance – the continuing lack of success in eliminating them has led to various attempts to interpret them differently. During the last decade they have increasingly come to be seen not as a 'problem' but as a 'solution'. The writings of such people as Abrams (1964), Turner (1963, 1967) and Mangin (1967) have been landmarks in the process of change.

More recently, international agencies like the World Bank, the United Nations through its development programme, and the national aid agencies of developed Western countries, have adopted this changed interpretation as a major component of their aid policies for low-income urban housing and settlements in Third World countries. The World Bank took the lead in encouraging and exhorting many unwilling Third World governments to accept a lowering of official physical and social amenity standards, through providing surveyed sites with minimal or no services to low-income settlers as a viable solution to their housing problems. A more recent addition to the 'site and services' package has been the physical 'upgrading' of existing squatter settlements. This is typically proposed through the provision of minimal services, tailored to match the paying abilities of the residents, rather than in accordance with abstract 'desirable' standards which cannot be enforced without high levels of public subsidy.

Yet in the plethora of writing on the subject, which have been primarily based on micro-studies of individual households or settlements, there is little explicit definition of what is perceived as the problem. Turner was among the first to focus attention away from the low standards of individual dwellings within such settlements towards the *process* by which these were built. His main arguments centred around the 'mismatch' between the demands made on low-income households by official standards of building, infrastructure and services and their ability to pay for these. He demonstrated how individual households consolidated their foothold in the urban economy through an 'incremental improvement' of their dwellings as their socio-economic status improved.

By implication, the problem lay not in the low standards of living frequently evident in unplanned settlements, but in the inappropriate demands made on individual households by the authorities. In other words, if the authorities could be made to understand these processes and therefore to lower standards, what was perceived as a problem could effectively be taken as the solution for the settlement and housing needs of low-income households.

However, by focusing on the housing process at the local level, Turner evaded the question of the relationship between conditions prevailing at the household level and the wider national and international processes which determine those conditions. His model based on 'incremental improvement' could only work if it could be taken for granted that the structural processes within the wider society would ensure that improvement *would* take place for *all* households eventually. In this respect, Turner's model complied with the unilinear view of development (see page 7). In his more recent writing,

Turner (1976), and others thinking along similar lines, have acknowledged that the scarcity of resources accessible to Third World low-income households also demands that central authorities ensure an equitable distribution of resources to all sections of the population. Once this has been achieved, and it is assumed that this can be done simply by persuading the authorities concerned, he focuses on the merits of autonomous organizations determining the local use of resources instead of the highly insensitive, centrally administered ones. He still visualizes this change taking place within the existing framework of the global economy. The basic assumption remains that public authorities are *misinformed* about the inadequacies of their existing policies and that change could be brought through informing them better.

Present policies of agencies such as the World Bank, incorporating 'site and services' and 'squatter upgrading' projects, are essentially derived from the writing of authors like Turner. What they are attempting to do is to pressurize national governments to adapt their regulations to conform to existing conditions.

All these policies ignore the relationship between the growth of unplanned settlements and the structure of the national and international societies which have produced them. However, we cannot even begin to understand the short and long-term implications of their growth or the impact of the policies currently proposed for them without understanding the processes by which they are generated.

The Issues underlying the Non-Plan Settlement Process

There is no denying that the varying degrees of illegality manifested by non-plan settlements constitutes a 'problem' from the point of view of the insecurity of tenure it represents for the residents concerned. At the same time, it also constitutes a major 'problem' for the authorities, in so far as their commitment towards maintaining the existing juridical structures, for which they are responsible, is concerned. Confining the statement of the problem in such terms, however, focuses only on the necessity of amending existing legal frameworks to incorporate the non-plan settlement process. The issues underlying this approach, therefore, are concerned first, with the extent to which it is possible to amend existing legal structures in this direction and secondly, with the likely impact of this very change on non-plan settlements as a whole. In other words, on what terms are public authorities likely to accept such an adaptation and what changes in the non-plan settlement process is this going to imply for the settlers concerned? If they are granted security of tenure within existing societal structures, what will be the social, economic and political costs for them, and to what extent is local autonomy – considered to be one of their characteristics – really possible for them, both now and in the future?

The argument presented here is that within the existing structures of Third World societies, absolute *dejure* security of tenure, or legal rights of land use obtained through the non-plan settlement process is *impossible*. Even where the authorities are conducive to amending their regulations, it can only be done on an *ad hoc* basis for individual settlements *already in existence*. Granting such rights to the residents of non-plan settlements which are *yet to emerge* would imply the authorities themselves participating in a gross violation of local laws relating to property rights. No public authority can do this. In most situations, while unable to prevent the growth of non-plan settlements, they refuse to acknowledge their existence. Even where the granting of *defacto* tenure is evident through the authorities' lack of preventive action, the benefits of this for the settlers can frequently be totally illusory. In this respect, the residents of non-plan settlements enjoying *defacto* security of tenure have no autonomy in determining the future of their settlements. While under certain socio-political conditions their right to settlement may be preserved over extended periods of time, with a change in these conditions, they can suddenly be deprived of it on highly unequal terms. This has been witnessed time and again, in a wide range of different Third World contexts*.

The second aspect of non-plan settlements, the importance of which has recently been increasingly played down, is related to the social and material deprivation and poverty of those living in them. To simply say that this does not constitute a part of the problem is an act not only of academic dishonesty, but a statement of political and ideological values. If the removal of conditions of insanitation, disease, epidemics, malnutrition and dangers of fire and house collapse are not to be a major objective of housing and settlement policies, then there is hardly any need to be concerned with problems of development. If *laissez faire* is all we are aiming at, then everyone can be left to manage as best he may. The degrees of human adaptability witnessed all through history, and most evident in the worst of today's urban slums, like the *bustees* of Calcutta or the hutments of Bombay, are remarkable indeed. But they also take a heavy toll in terms of frequent loss of life, intense human suffering, and a degradation of basic human values. No housing or settlement stategies can be assessed without taking into account their potentials for changing these conditions both in the short and long term.

It is in this respect that the long-term problems of low-income housing and settlement cannot be defined simply by looking at how low-income households solve their housing problems at present. It is here that the cost of short-term gains offered by the World Bank type proposals have to be understood in terms of their long-term implications.

This aspect of the problem will be dealt with in chapter 8 through an examination of the income, occupational, employment and cultural character-

*For examples of a sudden deprivation of long-standing *defacto* security of tenure from non-plan settlement residents under changing political conditions, see the cases of Rio de Janeiro (Perlman, 1976) and Delhi (Dayal and Bose, 1977). For an example fo the eviction of low-income settlers possessing even *dejure* security of tenure for almost twenty-five years in Bombay, see Deshpande (1976:519-22).

istics of the residents of Chandigarh's non-plan settlements. Their relationship with the planned part of the city will be investigated to highlight their economic and political dependence on the dominating sections of the city's population. In addition, the interaction between the conditions prevailing in the national economy, discussed in chapter 2, and Chandigarh's urban economy, will be explored by investigating the reason why non-plan settlement residents migrate to the city.

Chapter 9 looks at the characteristics of the housing process in Chandigarh's non-plan settlements from the point of view of the possibility of 'incremental improvement' through 'dweller control' as witnessed over a period of eighteen years. The material, economic and technical limitations within which non-plan settlement dwellings have been built will be examined particularly in relation to the self-help or self-build process commonly assumed to be their major positive aspect.

The Conflicts between the Master Plan and Non-Plan Settlements

The negation of some of the basic objectives of Chandigarh's master plan (as indeed of the plans of most other Third World new towns*) began at the very start of construction. The majority of the first people to arrive at the site were construction workers. Within the first two years, the site was the scene of intense activity; with 30,000 workers – both men and women – working seven days a week.

In 1953, at a conference in Paris, Le Corbusier (1953a) described the experience of Chandigarh under construction:

> Things were done à l'Indiènne, that is to say with an innumerable labour force and very few machines . . . The picturesqueness of the Indian enterprise is extraordinary; women in 'saris' carry bricks on their heads; the men lay the bricks; the children play in the heaps of sand. In India one does not 'Taylorize' the design to economize on labour since the population is innumerable. Everyone sleeps on the spot under a rush mat carried on four stakes. The gangs of workmen arrive from afar with their families.

The general poverty of the mass of the population and the underdevelopment of the Indian economy made this cheap and abundant labour force available. Financial and technological constraints meant that most of the city had to be built manually, with machinery limited to a few bulldozers and concrete mixers.

Although some of these construction workers had come on their own initiative, the majority were brought by labour contractors holding large contracts for government building and development projects. Such labour

*For an excellent description of the growth of Brasilia's non-plan settlements from the very start of construction, see Epstein (1973).

contractors take a proportion of a labourer's daily wage as their commission for having found him work. They themselves are bound by few obligations towards the labourers. Indeed the minimal labour welfare legislation is normally violated by the contractors.

Thus, some of the earliest settlements to emerge on the site were large clusters of thatch huts adjoining major construction works, built by the labour force to provide rudimentary shelter for themselves. One of the largest of such settlements grew up adjacent to Bajwada village to the south of sector 22 (figure 7.3). The shops and other services increasingly available there catered for its basic requirements.

In the early 1950s, daily wages for unskilled work were extremely low (as they continue to be today after accounting for inflation) – between Rs.1.50 to Rs.2.00 (9.5p to 12p) per day and barely sufficient for a minimum level of subsistence. Reflecting on the cheapest of the smallest planned house, Fry later wrote:

> The low cost of this, indeed of all housing, owes much to the cheapness of bricks at 30 shillings per thousand made without any machinery on the periphery of the site; *and to a labour force of men, women and children, underpaid, unhoused and uncared for* turning the heart by their beauty and cheerfulness under conditions as bad as could be imagined. (Fry, 1955b:143–4, emphasis is added)

That even the cheapest planned house for non-government employees was not going to be accessible to large numbers was also noted by Fry, for he wrote,

> When we began to move about, we realised that there were vast masses of people who were not included in the project estimate, and we tried to make provision for them, but in a certain sense we failed. There was no economy on which we could do it, even with the smallest houses. (Fry, 1955a:94)

Thus the standards of development specified in the plan necessitated its violation from the very start of construction; planned development required non-plan settlements for its very implementation.

During the first seven or eight years, this pattern of planned and parallel non-plan settlement continued without causing much concern to the authorities. However, as construction stretched over larger areas, the labour settlements began to be seen as 'getting in the way of' planned development, and as an undesirable precedent for 'encroachments' on public land in the new city. According to P.L. Varma, Chief Engineer of the project, these, and un-authorized developments on the periphery of the city, were serious problems requiring stringent action from the outset. Accordingly, in 1958, the CPO decided to remove all non-plan settlements. Notices were issued to their inhabitants to remove their huts from Chandigarh at their own cost.

Much earlier, in 1953, the first union registered by the Labour Commissioner of Chandigarh had been the Capital Workers Union. The majority of its members were daily wage construction workers. Formed under the initiative of the Communist Party of India, the Union had successfully

Figures 7.1 and 7.2. The working and living conditions of construction labour (summer 1977). Right: The workplace – desilting the lake in the city. Below: The living place – improvised shelter of an unskilled labour household, 15 minutes walk from the work site.

taken up such issues as the non-payment of wages, a claim for an increase in daily wages, and implementation of the Wages and Factories Act by contractors (Goyal, 1962).

The eviction notices issued by the Estate Office to the residents of the labour settlements manifested a fundamental contradiction typical of today's Third World urban context. Technically speaking, the residents were violating the property laws of the country by occupying land which they had neither purchased nor rented from its owner. The contradiction lay in the fact that the majority of them *could not* acquire legal rights to land occupation by virtue of their economic circumstances. Their extremely low daily wages left no household savings available for the purpose. In addition, the standards of development laid down by the master plan further increased the costs of acquiring legal rights to land use. Conceivably, in a situation of 'unplanned' urban growth through gradual addition to an existing settlement, at least a certain proportion of the non-plan settlement residents could have acquired undeveloped agricultural land on the perphery at a much reduced cost. The planned framework of Chandigarh's development left no such option open. Effectively, the Estate Officer's eviction notices demanded that the construction labour either left the city, which was clearly not intended as without them construction could not be continued, or *that they stop occupying space*, something humanly impossible. It was essentially a political confrontation.

Faced with the situation, the Capital Workers Union demanded alternative settlement sites or built accommodation from the CPO on terms accessible to the labourers but to no avail, and in November 1959, the Union organized a strike in support of its demands. During this period, because of the threat posed by the eviction notices, the membership of the Union increased dramatically. There was a clear recognition among the workers that their only strength lay in organized and collective action.

Unperturbed by all this and backed by the repressive apparatus of the State, the authorities ordered the forceful demolition of all the huts in the city. Left with no other recourse, the settlement residents prevented this by lying in front of the bulldozers, refusing to allow demolition until their demand for alternative accommodation had been met. Only the 'political' costs of bulldozing some residents along with the huts prevented the authorities from going ahead. Such an incident in a new capital on which the attention of the world was focused, in a recently independent nation ostensibly committed to the high ideals of democracy and equality of all citizens, would have cast a major slur on the image of the authorities.

The First 'Temporary' Resettlement

Instead, it was decided to yield partially to the demands of the residents. Three peripheral sites, located respectively in Sector 26, the Industrial Area and just beyond the University in Sector 14, were demarcated as 'temporary' locations

111

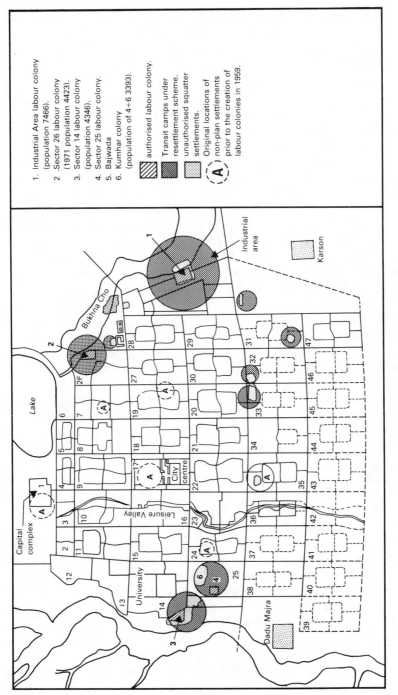

1. Industrial Area labour colony (population 7466).
2. Sector 26 labour colony (1971 population 4423).
3. Sector 14 labour colony (population 4346).
4. Sector 25 labour colony.
5. Bajwada
6. Kumhar colony (population of 4+6 3393).

authorised labour colony.

Transit camps under resettlement scheme.

unauthorised squatter settlements.

(A) Original locations of non-plan settlements prior to the creation of labour colonies in 1959.

Figure 7.3. Location of labour colonies.

for what were called 'labour colonies' (see figure 7.3.). In 1964, after the destruction of another settlement by fire, its inhabitants were moved to a fourth 'labour colony' in the adjoining totally undeveloped Sector 25.

Relocation in the 'labour colonies' was fairly systematic. In each, plots measuring 14 ft 7½ in by 19 ft 6 in were demarcated along parallel streets, some of these facing rectangular open spaces. Each household was allotted a plot at a rent of Rs.1.50 per month. No agreements on terms or conditions of tenure were signed, the implication being that the allottees could be evicted at short notice. However, a verbal assurance was given by the authorities that within a period of five years all the allottees would be permanently rehoused in the planned part of the city. In the meantime, each household was permitted to build any type of improvised structure it could afford. The creation of the labour colonies marked the first participation of the CPO itself in violating the plan, although it was explained as a 'temporary' measure. By means of the colonies' supposed 'temporariness', the CPO retained the right to determine the eventual future of the settlements as well as of their residents. The question of any local autonomy simply did not arise.

The peripheral locations of the labour colonies, although justified on the grounds of their not interfering with planned development, had important implications for the future of their residents. First, it was a clear demonstration of the impact of urban planning on their situation. They were being removed from areas planned to be developed in the near future, so that those who could pay for the higher costs of development could be given legal rights to ownership or use.

Secondly, as they were being removed far from areas scheduled for development in the near future, they would remain 'invisible' to other sections of the community for a long time to come. The exposure of the other sections of the population to their dismal living conditions would remain minimal. 'Out of sight, out of mind' is an appropriate summary of one of the objectives of such relocation.

Thirdly, because of the lack of public transport and road facilities, particularly on the periphery, the labourers would have to walk long distances every day both to seek and go to work.

Fourthly, as the colonies were supposedly 'temporary', not providing even basic services could be justified. One of the major positive objectives of the plan lay in its commitment to ensure access to publicly provided infrastructure and services to all sections of the population. By being granted only a 'temporary' status, the labour colonies were excluded from this commitment, and to start with the authorities provided only a few communal water taps to each colony.

The 1445 plots initially provided exceeded the total number of households at that time, and other people, building huts elsewhere in the city, when evicted could apply for plots in one of the labour colonies. Thus, slowly, the colonies became reception centres for new low-income migrants who were unable to afford planned accommodation. By 1965, following the creation of the fourth labour colony, the total number of authorized plots had reached 2182, but after this no further plots were allotted.

In 1963, the settlement which had emerged adjoining Bajwada village was also removed. The residents were given verbal permission to move to one of the existing labour colonies. The majority of them moved either to the one outside the University or to the one in the Industrial Area. In their case no clearly demarcated plots were allotted and they were not given the status of 'authorized' lessees of the government. All the same, Bajwada evictees built their houses in fairly formal layouts, with straight parallel streets similar to the 'authorized' sections of these colonies. As this group was not 'officially' authorized to settle in the labour colonies, even minimal facilities such as communal water taps were not provided for them.

Attempted Prevention of Growth by Force

The policy decision to stop further allotment of authorized plots in the labour colonies was justified on the grounds that having authorized lessees imposed a certain responsiblity on the government to resettle them in regularly planned houses. A verbal commitment to this effect had already been made at the time of their creation. Up to 1965, although no action had been taken in this direction, their growth and the increasing number of people seeking authorized plots in them was viewed with increasing alarm. Because of the commitment of all available financial resources to developing the city to high standards, it was argued that their continued growth would make it impossible for the Administration to rehouse the increasing numbers of people. Therefore it was decided to try to stop the growth of the colonies. To achieve this, in addition to stopping the allotment of new plots, the enforcement staff was instructed to demolish any new 'unauthorized' structures even in these settlements.

The implication of this was that the new city would legitimatley admit only settlers above a certain economic level. The planned city was attempting to deal with the problems of poverty by keeping the poor out. The status of poorer newcomers was reverted to that of the first construction workers in the city. It is important to note that this policy was adopted *after* the land sale policy had been changed to one of auctioning plots. The ostensible objective of using the income obtained from increased land values for projects beneficial to the 'public' was thus totally distorted to suit the priorities of the privileged classes. While labourers building and servicing the city were increasingly subjected to humiliation and suffering, among the major priorities of the Administration at the time was the planting of extensive flowering trees along the roads and developing a major 'rose garden' containing thousands of varieties of roses, one of the largest in Asia.

In spite of fairly frequent demolition raids, it proved impossible to curb the growth of non-plan settlements. On the contrary, in addition to the 'unauthor-

Figure 7.4. Life goes on in the ruins of a forcibly demolished unauthorized settlement as there is nowhere else to go.

Figure 7.5. A street in the authorized part of a labour colony.

ized' growth of existing labour colonies, a number of settlements emerged on totally unauthorized locations (see figure 7.3). A result of this situation was that an artificial division was created, by virtue of their respective 'authorized' and 'unauthorized' statuses, between people who were essentially in the same situation.

In the meantime, the continued lack of any action by the Administration either to provide alternative accommodation or improve the services in the

Figure 7.6. The deteriorating environment in another labour colony as a result of the pressure of an increasing population on highly inadequate services.

original labour colonies, led to increased agitation by their residents. Slowly, through the years, and only after persistant demonstration and demands, marginal improvements were made in the colonies. First, a few communal dry latrines were provided in each. By 1964, the Industrial Area labour colony had succeeded in getting a primary school. By 1974, all the labour colonies had at least one primary school, the buildings in all cases having been provided by the residents themselves and the teaching staff by the government. Approximately twenty sites were created in each settlement for small shops. All also had minimal street lighting with the added facility to authorized lessees of private electrical connections on the payment of normal charges. The residents had also built temples and in one of the settlements, a charity organization was running a dispensary and in another, a child care centre.

Towards a Policy Change

Towards the end of the 1960s, the continued presence of the labour colonies, and the increasing deterioration of their sanitary conditions as a result of the growing populations became a source of embarrassment to the Administration. Their initial 'invisibility' was beginning to become uncomfortably visible. A number of local and foreign journalists started writing about the deplorable conditions in which a sizeable proportion of the 'City Beautiful's'* population was living.

*This is what the Administration proudly calls Chandigarh.

The 'problem' was discussed in a meeting of the Local Advisory Committee in May 1969. Some members alleged that Chandigarh Adminstration had allowed a large number of unauthorized people to settle in the labour colonies, and a sub-committee was appointed to screen the residents. It recommended that authorized lesssees should be allowed to stay, while all unauthorized occupants, except for those engaged in fourteen selected occupations, should be evicted*.

Unconcerned about the arbitrary nature of this screening exercise, the main preoccupation of the Administration was to move the labour colonies as soon as possible. The Administration's right to continue labelling them as 'temporary' was increasingly under the threat of repudiation. As time passed these settlements were becoming strong communities. Several years of urban experience had heightened the consciousness of the residents to their legitimate status as citizens equal to the rest, and they were beginning to *demand* equal treatment rather than being *given* what the Administration deemed fit for them. They began to make it clear that they would refuse to move except on their own terms.

Among the Administration's proposals for their relocation was a scheme to create 'labour villages' or 'suburban sectors' and 'milk colonies' beyond the two river beds on either side of the plan area. Thus cheap manual labour for the needs of the middle and propertied classes was to be ensured by moving it *outside* the master plan area. There was little concern about the violation of the city's sacred concepts against suburbanization which this represented. On the other hand, the 'temporariness' of the labour colonies was being justified because they violated the plan. In the case of Brasilia, where exactly the same problem was experienced, the development authorities lost little time in violating the plan, and shortly after the start of construction legitimized the creation of 'satellite' towns developed to much lower standards, outside the pilot plan area (Epstein, 1973:66).

On the basis of these proposals, layouts of 'suburban' sectors were prepared and proceedings for acquiring land were initiated. It was proposed to provide plots of 15 square yards to each of the screened residents on a leasehold basis. Basic services such as water supply, electricity and sewerage were to be provided by the Administration but the allottees were to build their dwellings all over again. After 12 or 13 years of rotting in insanitary and insecure conditions in peripheral locations, the residents were to be asked to move still further from the city on equally unfavourable terms. This scheme was, however, eventually abandoned midway, probably because it was realized that it would be extremely difficult to sell it, particularly to the older residents of the labour colonies.

*The selected occupations were: cobbler, doctor/*hakim* (those practising traditional medicine), waterman, tailor, sewerage labourer, milkman, blacksmith, plumber, electrician, barber, washerman, painter, *mali* (gardener), rickshaw puller (Source: Official records, Chandigarh Administration).

Table 7.1. Distribution of authorized and unauthorized structures in the labour colonies, and the division of unauthorized residents according to the Administration's approved job categories.

Colony	Authorized structures	Unauthorized structures	Unauthorized residents approved category	other than approved category
Industrial area	585	1277	234	1043
Sector 26	738	241	233	8
Sector 14	541	676	622	54
Sector 25	196	227	220	7
Total	2060	2421	1309	1112

In September 1971, the Estate Office carried out a survey in accordance with the screening criteria proposed by the sub-committee. The findings of the survey are summarized in table 7.1.

In addition to the total of 4481 dwellings found in the original labour colonies there were 1586 dwellings in six totally unauthorized settlements located in different, as yet mainly undeveloped, sectors. According to the Estate Office, the totally unauthorized settlements were 'primarily constructed by construction labour either employed by the engineering department or big private contrators'. The survey carried out by the author in 1973–74, which covered four of these settlements, however, revealed a different picture. Only 14 per cent of the heads of households were construction workers, while ironically, as many as 50 per cent of them were low-income government employees, working mainly as sweepers.

Thus, despite the attempt to *stop* the growth of non-plan settlements, they continued to grow. The only difference was that by 1971, out of the total of 6067 structures, only 34 per cent were authorized, the remaining 66 per cent being 'unauthorized'. As a result of the screening process recommended by the special sub-committee, 32.6 per cent of the unauthorized dwellings were further classified into a new category of 'approved unauthorized'. The occupants of the remaining 2698 dwellings were to be evicted.

Towards Resettlement of the 'Temporary' Resettlement

During 1972–73, the Administration decided to try and get rid of the problem quickly by building 6000 pucca one-room tenements and moving the labour colony residents into them on a monthly license basis. The costing exercise carried out for the purpose revealed that Rs.50 million would be required. It was proposed to let the tenements at a monthly fee of Rs.30, although to recover the interest alone would have required a fee of between Rs.60 and Rs.70. Accordingly the Planning Commission was asked to sanction the full amount on the following grounds:

1. That the existing labour colonies contrast sharply against the general living standards in the rest of Chandigarh.

2. That their presence militated against the planned character of Chandigarh.

3. That resettlement schemes by way of alternative accommodation had to be found to ensure certain minimal standards to the slum dwellers.

4. That their presence had an adverse effect on resource mobilization as receipts to be realized by the sale of land on which the colonies are located could not materialize till they are shifted. (Chandigarh Administration, 1974:200)

The Planning Commission, however, approved a sum of Rs.15 million only. It recommended that while the 'domestic class' among the labour colony residents could be housed in pucca tenements within the residential sectors, the 'construction labour class' (including skilled labour), which is 'essentially of a migratory nature' could be located on the periphery, and provided with improvised hutments on developed plots (Government of India, 1973).

Accordingly the Administration formulated a scheme under which all the residents of the existing non-plan settlements would be housed in either pucca one-and-a-half room tenements built to master plan standards within residential sectors, or on 'transit' sites located on the periphery of the plan area where lessees would again be allowed to build their own 'temporary' structures to standards lower than the official ones. The scheme was notified in April 1975 under the title 'Licensing of Tenements and Transit Sites in Chandigarh Scheme' but will be referred to here as the resettlement scheme.

At the beginning of 1974, the Estate Office carried out another survey of non-plan settlements and found that the number of dwellings had increased by 25 per cent to about 8000. Under the terms of the resettlement scheme, only those households listed in one or other of the surveys, or who could prove residence in the city since before 1971 or up to the beginning of 1974 were eligible for alternative accommodation. Thus, instead of dividing people on the basis of occupation, their length of residence in the city would be the main criterion in determining their eligibility. Older residents would be eligible for pucca tenements, and more recent ones or those unable to prove their length of stay for transit sites only.

From the residents' point of view, in the case of those offered pucca tenements, the main advantage would be the acquisition of access to such accommodation at about a quarter of the market rent. In addition, the majority would be living in pucca, fully serviced dwellings for the first time in their lives. The main advantage for those allotted transit sites would be the acknowledgement of their existence by the authorities, through the acquisition of *dejure* status, again perhaps for the first time in their lives.

Figure 7.7. Pucca tenements under construction for rehousing older residents of the labour colonies.

The coercive power of these advantages, given the state of insecurity in which the residents had been living, is phenomenal. However,'it would not be without heavy economic, legal and political costs for those involved.

The Terms of Resettlement

The terms of resettlement are entirely biased towards the Administration's convenience, which neither made an assessment of the impact of resettlement on the families, incomes or employment of the residents, nor is prepared to accept settlement leaders putting foreward residents' demands. The leaders are simply labelled exploitative elements 'misleading' the people, and the only 'participation' acceptable to the authorities is total 'voluntary' compliance with official dictates. No physical force is used. The residents *have* to move 'voluntarily' and the Administration is prepared to wait until they fall in line.

For those allotted pucca tenements there are substantial disadvantages. They receive no compensation for the dwellings they built in the labour colonies, which in some cases were good structures. They are allowed to dismantle the buildings and sell the materials, but the value of these is negligible compared with the market value the structures had obtained. Thus the residents lose the right to realize the exchange value of their houses, a mechanism which, as discussed in the last chapter, serves to protect household savings against inflation.

In terms of space, all receive the same standard accommodation, comprising one room of about 100 square feet, a kitchen, bathroom, WC and an open terrace, which as some of the larger households had between two to five rooms is very disadvantageous. In addition, the monthly costs for each household increase from Rs.1.50 to Rs.30.00 (in fact to Rs.45 in more recent allotments) plus water and electricity charges. This license fee can be revised by the Estate Office five years after its commencement.

The terms on which the tenements are allotted represent a unilateral contract involving no long-term security of tenure, and the license can be cancelled in the event of non-payment (or inabililty to pay) if the household income exceeds Rs.500, or if the licensee or one of his dependents acquires land or building in the Union Territory.

The tenements are to be used exclusively for residence, thus many households who were using their dwellings for working (as carpenters, cycle repairers and potters, etc.) will find their livelihood jeopardized, at least from the legal point of view. Further, households, who were keeping pigs, buffaloes, cows and chicken to supplement their incomes or diets, will lose this facility.

Every licensee has to maintain a passbook, with photographs of himself and all members of his household. He has to give details of the age, occupation and relationship of each member and to notify any change in the household to the Estate Officer within fifteen days.

The majority of the above disadvantages also apply to those allotted 'transit' sites, although in somewhat different forms. They are provided with sites of either 15 by 20 feet or 10 by 30 feet, on the 'site and services' principle. The services include minimal street lighting, communal water taps, latrines and baths, brick paved streets, open drains, and the option of electricity connections on payment of the normal charges. Provision is made for a school and a number of shop sites within the camps. In 1979, the standard for future development was raised to a plot size of 37.5 by 10.75 feet on which the foundation for one room up to plinth level and individual water and sewerage connections for a bath and a WC are provided.

The licensees are required to demolish their structures in the old settlements and rebuild on the transit sites. Although they may re-use the materials, in many cases this is not possible as they are required to build to minimum standard, although much lower than those for the rest of the city, and materials such as mud and thatch are not permitted.

The monthly costs for each household are a license fee of Rs.15 (previously Rs.10) and a loan repayment (in the case of those acquiring loans) of another Rs.32 to Rs.70 over a period of four years depending on the amount of loan taken. Initially the period of the lease was to be only one year, renewable on a yearly basis at the discretion of the Administration. However, following a central government minister's support for granting loans of Rs.1500 to enable licensees to build better structures, the banks objected to the short duration of the lease from *their* point of view. Consequently, the initial lease period was increased to five years, during most of which the dwellings will be mortgaged in the names of the respective banks. Thus, in spite of relocation, the licensees still do not have security of tenure for more than an initial period of five years.

Even during that period, their property is mortgaged in the name of the bank who may take possession in the event of non-payment of loan instalments. As it is not possible to build the standard of structure required with the loan, licensees have to invest their own savings as well; but all that investment could be lost in the event of inability to repay the loan.

At the termination of a lease, either because it is not renewed or because the licensee is allotted a pucca tenement, he is entitled to compensation for the cost of construction of his dwelling as assessed by the Estate Office allowing for 'depreciation due to wear and tear'. Thus again he does not have the right to realize the exchange value of his investment and will be compensated on the basis of non-market criteria.

Finally, because of the 'temporary' nature of the transit camps, they are to be located outside the master plan boundaries, often far removed from existing development and sources of employment.

Initially, it is planned to relocate all the existing settlements. As the Housing Board starts functioning properly, the licensees of pucca tenements will be asked to apply for the Board's 'economically weaker section' housing units on a hire purchase basis. If any of the pucca tenements built under the resettlement scheme become vacant, transit site licensees will be allotted these. In turn the vacant transit site dwellings will be acquired by the Estate Office and allotted to new migrants to the city, who will be required to purchase these structures until they in turn become eligible for pucca tenements.

In addition to the administrative burden of managing such a complex process, it is based on the assumption that people can be moved around at will, irrespective of the impact on community networks, employment and costs. It also assumes, first, that the Administration and the Housing Board together will be able to continue a massive construction programme over a long period, and secondly, that with each move, each household will have economically improved its position as the costs will be greater each time.

Resettlement – The Limits of Autonomy

The construction of tenements began in 1974 and the Industrial Area labour colony was the first selected for resettlement. Not only was it the largest non-plan settlement in the city, with a population of 6446 in 1971 (Census of India, 1971a), but it was the most organized and was generally better off than other settlements. Its organization resulted from a large proportion of its residents being industrial workers and therefore belonging to trades unions. Among their demands was that they be granted either residential plots or pre-built dwellings on a hire purchase basis at prices prevailing in 1959, when they were originally moved to the labour colonies.

By the beginning of 1975, over 600 tenements were ready but no move was taking place. Enquiries revealed that the authorities had lost the nerve to enforce relocation. A visit by the Chief Commissioner along with some senior

Figure 7.8. The politics of 'participation'. Instead of demolition by force, a labour colony resident demolishes his house himself as *all* must move 'voluntarily'.

officers almost led to a riot. The residents protested about the treatment meted out to them and the conditions in which they were forced to live.

Although the tenements were ready, the Engineering Department was withholding completion certificates so that it might appear that this was the reason why they were not occupied. General elections were due the following year and the Administration knew that it could not rely on the support of the ruling Congress Party in moving the residents forcefully on the disadvantageous terms already described.

However the start of the Emergency in June 1975 changed the situation. By the beginning of August, resettlement of the Industrial Area labour colony was under way, entirely on the Administration's terms. Within the framework of the resettlement scheme, the operation was carried out efficiently. No physical force was used; all was done by 'persuasion'. The authorities worked out a detailed schedule of action. Dates for the termination of old leases were fixed block by block. A camp office was set up equipped with all the requisite forms and legal documents. Each household was dealt with there on the basis of individual merit, and allotment slips for pucca tenements or transit sites issued. A period for moving was granted and a date given by which the labour colony dwellings had to be vacated and demolished. The residents were 'encouraged' to do the demolition and arrange the disposal of the material themselves.

According to the Estate Officer, a lot of resistance was offered by the residents initially. But he felt it was a small proportion of the population, consisting of the local bosses, who were responsible for all the trouble, while the others were the genuine poor, amenable to any proposal. The authorities dealt with this situation by isolating the leaders, suggesting to the rest that they were misleading them and that they collected donations for themselves. The Administration refused to recognize any representatives of the residents, making it clear that it would negotiate only with individual households, and with them only in connection with their individual problems relating to the move.

Very soon, any organized resistance was totally destroyed, and collective efforts were fast converted into separate, individual demands. Once allotment had started, there was no possibility of collective negotiation; individuals scrambled for the best deal they could obtain. The vast majority preferred pucca tenements. Those unable to provide proof of residence before 1971 pleaded to be considered on the basis of their personal testimonies that they had indeed been resident since then. Those not eligible for tenements tried to invent evidence to the contrary. Long absent landlords returned to throw out their tenants to obtain allotments in their names.

The Power of Monologue

In the midst of all this, the terms on which resettlement was being carried out were pushed into the background. The Administration remained convinced of the merits of its scheme, seeing it as a means of taking people out of 'dingy hovels'. Any questioning of the scheme was labelled as trouble making, or simply that 'they did not know what was good for them' and that 'they needed to be educated to live better.' The 'voluntary' participation of the residents was taken as a clear indication of the 'popularity' and 'success' of the scheme.

Yet, the whole experience cannot be judged without reference to the context within which it took place. The Emergency had created a fear psychosis in the country. Several civil liberties and citizens' rights had been withdrawn. The normal restraints on the use of repressive State apparatus to enforce decisions were no longer in operation. Delhi was already experiencing indiscriminate use of brute force to carry out squatter clearance (Dayal and Bose, 1977). Arbitrary arrests were taking place everywhere, and public protest was threatened with severe treatment. Thus agreement from the residents under such circumstances can hardly be regarded as 'voluntary'.

Following resettlement, the land vacated was quickly allotted to the Industries Department at subsidized rates 'to prevent its being encroached upon again'. No immediate use is planned for the land vacated through subsequent relocation of another part of the same settlement.

Figure 7.9. The first transit camp outside the north-eastern corner of the master plan over two years after resettlement. The tent on the left in the background is the children's school.

In the Transit Camps

The first of the transit camps is little different from the original labour colonies. It is located outside the master plan area on the north-east corner. The quality of the dwellings clearly reflect the economic circumstances of the allottees. The better off have built pucca structures similar to those of the authorized lessees of the original labour colonies. The poorer have only been able to replace their old shacks, if even that. Although the school in the old colony was demolished, the transit camp did not have a school building for over two years, and the children were taught in two tents. Private doctors and quacks abound as before. The communal latrines are infrequently cleaned, and there are only a few more communal taps than before.

In the case of the second transit camp, located much further out beyond the south-east corner of the master plan, loans of Rs.1500 were made available to the allottees (recently increased to Rs.3000 for its second phase). The quality of structures is comparatively better than in the first camp, but that is because huts were not permitted. It is located next to a village and there is some pretence by the Administration that the camp is a village.

By October 1977, of the 500 loans given by one of the banks, 60 per cent were not being repaid*. In the case of the 17 per cent or more plots remaining

---

*Source: The manager, Punjab National Bank, Sector 28, Chandigarh.

unoccupied for two or three months after allotment, the Estate Office simply allotted them to other people. The lower income residents of the uncleared part of the settlement said that these people had either built huts elsewhere (as borne out by rapid growth of other unauthorized settlements) or simply returned to their villages as they could not afford to build better structures. In the case of those who were not repaying their loans, the bank had simply written to the Estate Office asking that strict action be taken against them or that their properties be taken over.

Democracy and the Freedom of Expression

Following the announcement of general elections and a relaxation of the Emergency in January 1977, the people felt free to express their demands again. One of the first demands of the transit camp residents was that they should be given permanent security of tenure there. The Administration had already decided not to remove these in the near future but to keep them as permanent 'reception centres' for newcomers. It also gave verbal assurances that the residents will not be forced to move 'at least for another 10 to 20 years'. At the same time, it was not prepared to legalize this assurance by changing the licensees' leases accordingly. The only concession to date has come in the form of the latest lease document saying that the five year lease is 'extendable to 20 years'. In the words of the officer in charge of resettlement, ninety-nine year leases are only given to those who pay auction prices. The same officer, when asked why the short leases and licensing were being used, replied that this was to enable the Administration to re-acquire the land 'should it need it for some other purpose in 10 to 15 years' time'. And asked about the likely costs and disturbance that being uprooted once again would mean for those being 'rehabilitated', he simply dismissed it as a consideration. Of course it was not going to mean any problems for those made to move.

When resettlement of the third part of the industrial Area colony started in June 1977, it was clear that the residents' participation was not all that voluntary. On the 5th June, the Chief Commissioner together with a troupe of senior officers, and preceded by a large contingent of police, arrived at the settlement to celebrate World Environment Day and to inaugurate the next stage of resettlement. After the senior officers had given their speeches, a local residents' leader stood up to put forward their demands. He wrongly assumed that he could use the microphone in the same way as the officers, but this was taken from his hand. He was told that he had asked to speak to the Chief Commissioner and not to the whole audience. Barely audible to the gathering, he read out the demands. The main one was that all residents should be allotted pucca tenements, but if this was not possible, those ineligible should be permitted to stay where they were and provided with improved services. The Chief Commissioner quickly snubbed him, saying that under Janata's rule there was no need to make 'demands'; it was only necessary for people to express their 'problems' so that the Administration could deal with them. He then abruptly walked away, quickly followed by the other officers. The unapplauding and silent crowd was rapidly dispersed by the police, who had stayed behind with their batons.

The residents' leaders then organized a strike to prevent the allotment continuing until their demands had been met. Allotment stopped for almost a month. In the meantime, the monsoons were approaching. Many of the settlement structures require extensive repairs before the onset of the rains. In the uncertainty of whether their leaders' demands would be met, the majority of the residents had not carried out the repairs. If they were going to have to move, it was not worth the cost and effort to do so. As roofs started collapsing, and as some of the people already allotted tenements started moving out, some of the women lost their nerve. Worried about their families' safety, they took a deputation to the Estate Office demanding that allotments should be continued immediately. Besides, the availability of two alternatives had created a division among the residents. Those eligible for tenements wanted to move irrespective of what happened to the others. The majority of those who demanded a continuation of allotment belonged to this group. *Their* demand was accepted as the legitimate one and used as a means of by-passing the leaders. Allotment was started again. In the general procedure for allotment, only one officer has the power to make the allocations. He seldom announces when he will be coming, and as most residents want to be present to support their cases, they have to take time off work, they frequently lose several working days. The argument for operating this system is that surprise visits avoid crowds and demonstrations and this enables more efficient working. Organized resistance under such circumstances is almost impossible.

When the resettlement scheme was first formulated in 1974, there were, as mentioned above, an estimated 8000 households living in non-plan settlements. By the middle of 1981, according to the officer-in-charge of resettlement, nearly 12,000 households had been resettled either in pucca tenements or transit sites, but over 6000 are still to be accommodated. With the problem continuing to grow despite attempts to rid the city of it, demolition of huts has again been resorted to at times, and now the Administration is planning to computerize the records of resettlement allotments to prevent wrong allotments and unauthorized transfers (*Sunday Tribune*, 1981).

In the course of this massive programme, some strange phenomena have occurred. During April 1979, over 700 huts were destroyed in six different incidents of fire in one of the larger unauthorized settlements near the Industrial Area. The Administration organized some immediate relief with the assistance of some voluntary agencies but made futher relief conditional on the affected families moving to one of the transit camps for 'rehabilitation'. The whole site was cleared during the process. During April 1980, a similar epidemic of mystery fires hit another unauthorized settlement in Sector 25. Again hundreds of families were rendered homeless, and after one of the fires there was almost a riot as some of the residents suspected the police and the firebrigade of having a hand in the matter. Even this time, provision of official relief was made conditional on the residents moving to one of the transit camps. In this case, as adequate serviced sites were not available, some households were moved to almost totally unserviced ones.

Back to the Underlying Issues

It is clear from the history of the growth of non-plan settlements in Chandigarh, that their status as defined by legal mechanisms and processes outside the control of the residents is a *dependent* one. The parameters on which the master plan is based further reinforces this dependence. Local autonomy, leaving aside the apparent autonomy which individual households have in devising dwellings to match their means and priorities, is meaningless as autonomy at the settlement level does not exist. Even their right to continued existence cannot be granted by the authorities as it would imply a challenge to far more than just the authorities' right to refuse to legitimize their existence. It would imply accepting non-plan developments as a viable settlement process which could repudiate the very objectives of planned development. There is a carefully considered evasion of setting any precedent which might become a means of challenging the provisions of the master plan.

It is also clear from the history of the Administration's policies towards the growth of non-plan settlements, that these have been derived from official responsibility towards maintaining and defending the existing structure of property relations. Within this structure, even if *dejure* security of tenure is granted to the settlements as a whole, it can *only* be a *post facto* act; and that too on an *ad hoc* basis, on consideration of individual merit. The price which low-income settlers have to pay for any recognition, whether *defacto* or *dejure*, is long years of insecurity, harassment, and suffering. *Defacto* security arises out of the authorities' fully understanding the function of the settlements as a supply of cheap labour for the rest of the city. It is far more convenient for them to pretend that they have nothing to do with the matter, that the conditions of insanitation, poverty and deprivation are simply a reflection of the 'inferior' and 'uneducated' people living there.

Further, the authorities will only convert *defacto* status into *dejure* when forced to do so. The recent policies to attempt to 'rehabilitate' settlement dwellers did not occur in a social vacuum. It was a response to changed socio-political conditions in the country. The underprivileged are no longer prepared to accept ruthless suppression of their demands or verbal promises of action in the future. The type of action which can arise out of this new consciousness, unless contained, can become a grave challenge to the *status quo*. The only means by which this can be contained are either through outright repression, or co-option. The Chandigarh authorities have chosen the second.

Co-option involves making those increasingly alienated from the structure of the *status quo* feel that they do have a place in society, that their needs are considered, and that they also are being offered something. However, with the little that is offered, frequently much more is taken away. In the process of the supposed 'rehabilitation' of Chandigarh's settlement dwellers, their collective organizations evolved over the years have been destroyed, the population dispersed and the better off amongst them segregated from the rest by being given pucca tenements.

Various means are used to make the residents feel that they themselves are to blame for their predicament. The ideological impact of this can be considerable. For example, the authorities have been explaining to the residents that the Administration is trying to do the most it can for the poor, implying that they ought to be grateful for its benevolence. It is seldom acknowledged that even the limited amount being done is not an act of charity, but a long overdue *right* of the settlers. The low monthly charge of the tenements compared with the market rents is cited as an example of this benevolence; why market rents are so high or what this has to do with the Administration's land sale policy is not discussed.

Experience of Other Third World Planned New Towns

In the majority of Third World new towns, planned either as administrative or industrial centres, the growth of non-plan settlements was neither anticipated nor acknowledged for extended periods after their emergence. The treatment meted out to them has been well documented in the cases of Brasilia (Epstein, 1973), Tema (Mitchell, 1972, 1975), Bhubaneswar (Grenell, 1972), and many others. In most instances, their destiny has included relocation, sometimes several times, always to make room for other more 'legitimate' or 'desirable' uses from the authorities' points of view. When their existence has eventually been 'recognized' and legalized, it has been in response to the resistance of the residents themselves to perpetual relocation, but almost always on terms and conditions defined by the authorities. In many cases, including those of Brasilia, Tema and recently Chandigarh, one of these terms has been their confinement outside the plan area, with the concomitant result that they are excluded from access to planned standards of infrastructure and services. In each of these cases, while the standards for the planned areas have not been lowered, but often maintained with the aid of public subsidy, the lowering of standards in non-plan settlements has been justified on the grounds of there not being sufficient resources available for subsidizing the needy.

At the same time, the commitment to provide basic infrastructure and services to all sections of the community through planned development has been used by the settlement residents to their advantage. The raised expectations of all sections of the community of what benefits planning was to bring has eventually forced the authorities to provide at least some services, albeit of lower standards, in the process of recognizing their existence.

In comparison to this, the example of Ciudad Guayana has been quite different. In what was considered a unique aspect of the city's planning, the team of 'experts' anticipated the need to permit lower standards of construction to accommodate the city's lower income residents. The need for allowing incremental improvement of dwellings was also acknowledged. However, in the process, and in line with what is being advocated by the World Bank and other agencies, right from the beginning the authorities withdrew from any real responsiblity towards enabling the lower income households to overcome their intrinsic handicaps. No aspirations were raised, few commitments were made, and benign tolerance for conditions of deprivation were implicitly included in the planning framework. The less well off were allowed the 'freedom' of managing within their limited resources.

A major factor which led to this decision by the planners was that under Venezuelan law, perpetual relocation of squatters can be an expensive business. Under this law, even when an unauthorized occupant of a piece of land is forceably removed, he has to be compensated for the current value of the improvements he has made on it. The development corporation calculated that on an average, expropriation of a *rancho* or squatter dwelling on a two-year-old site cost $310 while on a ten-year-old site it cost $890. These sums were much higher than the $47 cost of an undeveloped plot and $324 for a plot with minimum services (Corrado, 1969). It was therefore expedient for the corporation to 'plan' in advance to avoid such expropriation. It was thus decided to accept the inevitability of such developments but to localize them in the already low-income eastern end of the town.

Ciudad Guayana's state of development by the mid-1970s is revealing. As mentioned earlier as much as 78 per cent of the city's population had been 'localized' in the eastern end of the town. While 22.8 per cent of the city's housing stock had been developed within the 'progressive urban improvement' framework, an additional 38 per cent had developed totally outside it, leaving only 39.2 per cent of the city's housing conforming to higher standards (MacDonald and MacDonald, 1975). Although the higher standard housing areas have been provided with all modern services and amenities, again with considerable public subsidy, even the minimal commitment towards provision of services in the incremental improvement area has not been fulfilled. The 38 per cent of the city's non-plan housing remains almost without any services at all.

The influence of the technocratic planning approach on the socio-economic conditions of the city's population is self-evident from the following. Compared with Venezuelan cities of similar sizes (which have not received such massive State investment), Ciudad Guayana has a higher infant mortality rate, a lower literacy level, a lower ratio of hospital beds to population, and a higher proportion of people living in shanties. During the last ten to fifteen years, the skewed income distribution has not changed and the unemployment rate continues at between 10 and 13 per cent of the population. And all this in a city whose population in 1975 was 220,000 and which has been receiving as much as 10 per cent of the country's total investment, both public and private, but which only produced 4.5 per cent of its gross domestic product (MacDonald and MacDonald, 1977).

The flow of resources between Ashaiman, the non-plan part of Tema, and the planned part is equally revealing. One of the major functions of the development corporation within the planning framework is to provide land with industrial infrastructure on 'attractive terms' to industrial investors. In addition, most of the industrial employees live in housing subsidized by the government. Despite concerted efforts by the TDC to persuade private industrialists to house employees, they have not bothered to do so (Bauchie-Kessie, 1976; Glover-Akpey, 1976). With such legitimate mechanisms for the appropriation of social surplus, involving a heavy drain on public resources, the localization of the poor living standards and cheap labour in Ashaiman cannot be seen in isolation.

8

The People of the Non-Plan Settlements

The socio-economic circumstances of the people living in the non-plan settlements cannot be understood unless seen in relation to the dominant structure of the city's economy. The two are inextricably linked – one from a position of domination, and the other of subordination. In almost every sense, the residents of the non-plan settlements find themselves trapped in a position of unequal exchange. However, the city, itself, does not exist in isolation from the regional and national economies, and the circumstances of the non-plan settlements manifest the interaction between the city and the wider regional and national contexts in terms of the characteristics being produced locally by the national model of development.

The Fieldwork

The data presented here and in the following chapter are based on fieldwork carried out during 1973–75, whose objectives were to attempt to understand the role of the non-plan settlements in the urban structure of Chandigarh, and the process of their growth, by examining:

1. The socio-economic characteristics of their population compared to that in the planned part of the city.

2. The demographic characteristics of, and economic opportunities available to, the households living in them.

3. The occupational, income and employment structure of the heads of households and the extent of occupational mobility among them.

4. Their spatial distribution in the city and the significance of location for households in individual settlements.

5. The characteristics of the process of migration to, and settlement within, the city.

6. The process of housing in terms of investment, production and use evident in them.

7. The effects of the Administration's policies aimed at curbing, controlling and regulating their growth and their potential for being incorporated within the plan.

The fieldwork was carried out in two stages. Following a study of the 1971 Census data, the first consisted of a field survey of eight selected settlements comprising all four 'authorized labour colonies' and four totally unauthorized ones. These represented almost all the non-plan settlements in the city, only three 'unauthorized' ones – located, respectively, in Bajwada, Sector 26 adjoining the wholesale market, and one near the entrance to the city along the Ambala-Dehli road – being excluded (see figure 7.3).

In order to obtain sufficiently diversified and representative data, it was decided to cover a 5 per cent sample of households, keeping the household as the unit of investigation. A household was defined as a group of people, whether related or not, living together under the same roof. Selection was based on the location of individual dwellings, the head of the household of each twentieth dwelling being interviewed. The sample consisted of 293 households for which 286 interview schedules were completed. Of the seven schedules not completed, in two cases the residents were away on annual visits to their home communities, one dwelling had recently been vacated, and four respondents refused to answer after the initial questions, showing their feeling of insecurity which led to distrust of the interviewers.

The second stage of the investigation consisted of visiting a number of selected households with whom contact had been made during the main survey*. These visits took place over a period of almost a year in order to obtain the kind of information and understanding which is not possible from interview schedules. During this period, the forms of collective organization and leadership patterns existing in the settlements and their effective roles were studied.

Both here and in chapter 9, the terms 'head of household' and 'respondent' are used interchangeably. In the case of households consisting of a number of unrelated men sharing accommodation, where none could be termed the head of household, any one of the working members available was interviewed for the main survey.

Population Characteristics from the 1971 Census

Details of the distribution of population between the 'planned' part of Chandigarh and its non-plan settlements as recorded during the 1971 Census are shown in table 8.1 and, as is evident from this table, the population of the settlements had a number of outstanding differences from that of the planned part of the city.

1. The average household size was smaller than for the rest of the city.

---

*This was later supplemented through further visits and active involvement with the problems of the settlement residents during April 1977 to November 1978, after an absence of two years from the city.

Table 8.1. Population distribution in Chandigarh in 1971.

	Chandigarh city (total) 1	'Planned' part of city 2	'Non-plan' settlements 3	3 as percentage of 1 4
Number of households	51,554	45,510	6044	11.72
Household size	4.24	4.28	3.94	
Total population	218,743	194,879	23,864	10.91
Sex ratio (females per 1000 males)	752	765	655	
Scheduled caste population	21,487	12,272	9215	42.88
Literate population	145,048	138,594	6454	4.44
Literacy ratio	66.30	71.12	27.04	
Workers as a percentage of total population	33.34	32.27	42.09	

Distribution of workers into different economic activities

Agriculture, livestock, mining and quarrying	707	660	47	6.64
Industry (household)	293	267	26	8.87
Industry (other than household)	9028	6799	2229	24.69
Construction	3795	1112	2683	70.69
Transport, storage and communication	3095	2564	531	12.15
Trade and commerce	10,755	9674	1081	10.05
Other services	45,268	41,819	3449	7.61
Total	72,941	62,895	10,046	15.97

Source: *Census of India 1971*, Series 25 – Chandigarh, District Census Handbook, part X–B.

2. The sex ratio showed a much lower proportion of females per 1000 males compared to the whole city. Chandigarh, itself, had only 752 females per 1000 males compared to 930 for the country as a whole, but this is attributed to the high proportion of students in the city's educational institutions, and its being still at the development stage. But with only 655 females per 1000 males in the settlements, there is evidence of people being unable to afford to bring their dependents to the city.

3. Although their total population was only 10.9 per cent of the city's population, it represented as much as 43 per cent of those belonging to the 'scheduled' or backward castes* in the city. Thus while 40 per cent of their population was scheduled caste, the proportion in the planned part of the city was only 6 per cent.

4. Only 27 per cent of their population was recorded as literate compared to 71 per cent for the planned part. (During the 1971 Census, the Union Territory was found to have the highest literacy rate in the country.)

5. As much as 42 per cent of their population was working compared to 32 per cent in the planned part, there also being a slightly higher incidence of female workers in the settlements. However, the occupations of their working population were disproportionately concentrated in the categories of 'construction', 'other than household industry', and 'transport, storage and communications', the first representing 71 per cent of the city's construction workers. In the case of female workers, the difference was still further accentuated with as much as 88 per cent of the city's female construction workers being in the settlements.

Characteristics of the Non-Plan Settlement People

The households of the 286 respondents in the sample represented a total population of 1341, of which 531 (40 per cent) were working. Of these 424 were males, ninety-four females, and twelve children aged between six and fourteen. The proportion of female workers to the total was thus much higher than the 10 per cent recorded in the Census. 32.5 per cent were literate, a slightly higher proportion than indicated in the Census, while 57 per cent of the households belonged to 'scheduled' castes, a much higher proportion than the Census figure (table 8.1, column 4).

Some 80 per cent of the heads of households had come from rural backgrounds, the largest proportion from U.P., followed by Punjab, Haryana and Rajasthan, these four states being in the region surrounding Chandigarh.

All heads of households were males and 89 per cent were married, 5 per cent single and 6 per cent widowers or separated. Almost 80 per cent were aged between twenty-six and fifty-eight, and only 15 per cent were between fifteen and twenty-five.

Household sizes varied from single-person households to one case of a joint

*The officially listed 'scheduled' or backward castes generally represent those within the Hindu caste hierarchy recognized as suffering from historical social and economic deprivation and discrimination. Following Independence, a certain proportion of public jobs and seats in educational establishments were reserved by law for scheduled caste people, in addition to other privileges, to enable them to improve their conditions. The limited effectiveness of these measures after more than thirty years is evident from the concentration of such people in the settlements with the least remunerative jobs, a situation typical of Indian cities.

family of fifteen members, the average being 4.7 which is larger than the 4.2 for the whole city and 3.9 for the non-plan settlements, as recorded in the Census. This difference was probably because of an under-representation of single-person households in the sample, most of whom would have been living in the recent unauthorized settlements not covered by the survey.

Households predominantly consisted of nuclear or joint families or of close friends or relatives staying with another nuclear family. Nearly 20 per cent of the households had no female members, a typical characteristic of Indian male dominated migration. More than half of these were single-person households, the rest consisting of male friends or relatives sharing accommodation.

An interesting characteristic of one-person households was that a majority of them did not consist of unmarried men. The fact that they had acquired or built separate dwellings was possibly because of future plans to bring their dependents to the city.

In the case of almost half the total households, the respondents were the only working members, the rest having from two to one case of nine workers. The last was exceptional and consisted of eight recent male migrants from the same village who were staying temporarily with another, earlier migrant from their community.

As many as 38 per cent of the workers in the sample, other than the heads of households, were women. These working women were confined to a third of the 82 per cent of households with female members. Their work was almost totally restricted to unskilled manual occupations, such as sweepers, casual domestic helpers and construction labourers, with the accompanying low incomes. Eighty-six per cent of the households with women workers were those whose heads had incomes of Rs.250 per month or less (see figure 8.1) and all thirteen

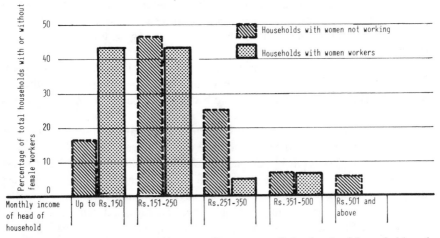

Figure 8.1. The relationship between the income of the head of household and whether working-age women were working or not.

working children in the sample belonged to similar households. Further, two-thirds of the heads of households with women workers were in unskilled occupations themselves. In many cases the households with two or more workers had a monthly household expenditure equal to or above their total incomes. Thus it is evident that the existence of more than one worker in a household, particularly where the additional workers were women, is more a product of economic necessity than an indication of well being or 'greed for higher incomes' as often assumed by some sections of the elite.

Households with their heads working on daily wages were the worst off. However, there were proportionately more workers, other than heads of households, in casual or daily wage employment, indicating the general low economic capacity of the work force (table 8.2).

Table 8.2. Distribution of forms of employment amongst workers in the sample.

	Self-employed	Casual	Daily wages	Salaried	Not recorded	Total
Heads of households	94 (32.9%)		66 (23.0%)	120 (41.9%)	6 (1.7%)	286
All workers including heads of households	145 (27.3%)	32 (6.0%)	133 (25.0%)	215 (40.5%)	6 (1.2%)	531

Source: Field survey 1974.

The constraints of parents' economic circumstances were inevitably reflected in the poor care of, and educational opportunities available to, their children. Forty per cent of the households with women workers were unable to send their children to school, compared to 33 per cent of those whose female members were not working. In terms of the occupational group of the head of household, 58 per cent of those in unskilled occupations were not sending their children to school. This is often interpreted as the backward attitudes of illiterate parents who, it is believed, need to be 'persuaded' about the value of education. Evidence collected during fieldwork suggested a totally different picture. A majority of the parents wished to educate their children, but could not do so because of their economic circumstances. While the mother was away at work, an elder child stayed at home to mind the younger children. Those who had lived in Chandigarh longer appeared to have overcome this problem either because there were no young children or because they had consolidated their economic status. Seventy-one per cent of the households who had been in Chandigarh for sixteen years or more were sending their children to school compared with 37 per cent who had come in the last five years.

Occupations, Incomes and Employment of Heads of Households

There was considerable diversity in the respondents' occupations, the range including those making a living by collecting scraps of paper and waste materials from rubbish heaps, to those in white collar employment such as bank clerks and class III government employees. For the sake of convenience all occupations have been classified into seven groups (see table 8.3).

The relationship between the respondents' occupations and their incomes is shown in table 8.4. Most occupation groups had incomes within Rs.150–250 range. Unskilled workers, the largest group, had the lowest incomes with a mean of only Rs.146 per month, while the mean for semi-skilled workers was Rs.208 per month. The widest income range was among those engaged in trade and commerce, indicating the importance of the scale of enterprise, with the

Table 8.3. Distribution of heads of household by occupation and authorized and unauthorized locations.

	Authorized locations	Unauthorized locations	Total	Percentage of total
1. *Unskilled manual*	56	57	113	39.0
construction labourer	28	14	42	
waste paper picker	1	1	2	
mali	3	6	9	
rickshaw puller	4	4	8	
sweeper	17	32	49	
boot polisher	3		3	
2. *Semi-skilled manual*	23	2	25	8.6
white washer	6		6	
lintol maker		1	1	
industrial worker	9	1	10	
cobbler	2		2	
cycle repairer	4		4	
clothes ironer	2		2	
3. *Skilled manual*	52	4	56	19.3
potter		1	1	
plumber	5		5	
welder	5	1	6	
mason	22		22	
carpenter	3		3	
tailor	10	1	11	
electrician	3		3	
painter/dyer	3	1	4	
concrete mixer operator	1		1	

Urban Planning in the Third World

Table 8.3. (Continued).

	Authorized locations	Unauthorized locations	Total	Percentage of total
4. *General services*	31	19	50	17.2
social worker/teacher	2		2	
government class IV employee	8	13	21	
government class III employee	12	3	15	
salesman/bank or poultry farm worker	4		4	
contractor	1		1	
scooter/taxi driver	4	2	6	
horse cart driver		1	1	
5. *Trade and commerce*	25	8	33	11.4
wholesale dealer	4	2	6	
small shopkeeper	5	3	8	
tea shop	2	1	3	
rehriwalla	12	1	13	
repairing and selling sacks		1	1	
mobile hawker	2		2	
6. *Livestock*	5	3	8	2.7
pig farming		1	1	
dairy	5	2	7	
7. *Unemployed/retired/ no response*	3	2	5	1.7
Total	195	95	290	

Source: Field survey 1974.

hawkers and *rehriwallas* at the bottom of the hierarchy and wholesale dealers in commodities such as fodder, waste materials (*kabadiwallas*) and timber at the top.

The general literacy level of the respondents was low, with almost 60 per cent totally illiterate. The distribution of illiteracy was further polarized among different occupational groups, 82 per cent of those in unskilled occupations being illiterate.

About 80 per cent of those in unskilled occupations belonged to scheduled and backward castes, while in the semi-skilled, skilled and general services groups there was a fairly even distribution between scheduled and non-scheduled castes. In the case of trade and commerce, and livestock farming, the

Table 8.4. Monthly incomes of heads of households by occupation groups 1 to 7 of table 8.3.

Rupees	1	2	3	4	5	6	7	Total	Percentage
Nil							3	3	1.0
150 and below	51	3	2	9	4		2	71	24.8
151–250	57	16	28	23	7			131	45.8
251–350	2	5	20	14	11	1		53	18.5
351–500	1		4	4	5	2		16	5.6
501–1000				1	2	4		7	2.4
Above 1000					3			3	1.0
No response/ don't know					1	1		2	0.7
Total	111	24	54	51	33	8	5	286	
Mean income in rupees	146.4	208.4	249.1	233.8	363.3	607.1	75.0		

Source: Field survey 1974.

occupations in which incomes were among the highest, there'was a much higher percentage of non-scheduled castes.

As already mentioned, 80 per cent of the respondents had migrated from rural areas. However, among those in unskilled occupations, the percentage was even higher, with 91 per cent from rural backgrounds. Thus there was a distinct relation between unskilled occupations, low incomes, almost total illiteracy, scheduled castes and rural backgrounds.

The main forms of employment among the respondents were self-employment, work on daily wages, and salaried employment. Incomes from the last two are limited, being totally fixed for salaried workers. In the case of those working on daily wages, the maximum monthly income can only be thirty times the daily wage, that also being dependent on work being available on all days of the month. Further, the manual nature of the work and the length of the working day do not leave time or energy for supplementing income from other sources. Thus the combination of daily wage employment and unskilled occupation with its low income produces the most insecure and undesirable situation. Government salaried employment for unskilled occupations offers the comparative advantage of a regular income, security of employment and a number of other benefits, and the respondents preference for this was evident as a high proportion (45 per cent) were government employees.

All those engaged in trade and commerce, and livestock farming were self-employed. A considerable variation of income is possible in self-employment, depending not only on the nature of the occupation but also the scale of the enterprise. Starting work as self-employed normally also requires a certain

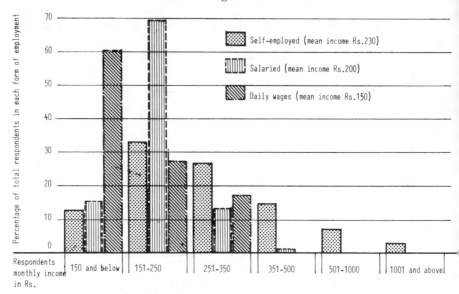

Figure 8.2. Distribution of heads of household by monthly income and form of employment.

amount of capital investment. The economic status of the self-employed respondents was evident from the fact that almost half of them had invested less than Rs.100. At the same time, 6 per cent had invested more than Rs.2000.

The distribution of respondents by their monthly income and forms of employment is shown in figure 8.2. More than 50 per cent of those working on daily wages had monthly incomes of Rs.150 and below. Salaried employees were comparatively better off, most being in the Rs.150–250 bracket, while the self-employed had a much wider range of incomes. In addition to their main work, 10 per cent of the households, other than the livestock farmers, were keeping one or two animals for milk or meat, either for themselves or to sell to supplement their incomes. The largest number of these were households whose heads were employed in general services or unskilled manual occupations.

The relationship between the respondents' employment and other variables such as caste, income, rural or urban background and state of origin displayed similar polarization as that between their occupational groups and these variables. Thus, there were proportionally more respondents belonging to scheduled castes or coming from rural backgrounds working on daily wages and in government salaried employment.

Occupational Mobility of the Heads of Households

Before migrating to Chandigarh nearly 60 per cent of the heads of household had unskilled manual occupations, but by the time of the survey this had dropped to less than 40 per cent. For the many rural migrants, occupational mobility was a necessity. Of the 165 respondents in unskilled occupations before migrating, 153 were either agricultural labourers or small cultivators with uneconomic holdings. Since coming to Chandigarh, they had become construction labourers, sweepers, obtained work in general services and factories, and so on. Some, such as cobblers and tailors, had reverted to their traditional caste occupations. Those who had been able to move into semi-skilled, general services and trading occupations had generally been able to improve their economic and social circumstances.

Another significant aspect of the post-migration change was the considerable decrease in the number who were unemployed; from 7.3 per cent before migration it had dropped to 1 per cent indicating the relatively greater employment opportunities in the city. As mentioned in chapter 2, much lower rates of unemployment among recent migrants have also been noted in other large cities in India. This could be a result of those not finding employment, returning to their places of origin or going somewhere else. It was not possible to discover the proportion of migrants who had done so, but clearly, few could afford to remain unemployed in urban areas.

Occupational mobility was not evenly distributed among the respondents. While 36 per cent of the non-scheduled caste respondents had changed from unskilled occupations to more skilled or better income ones, only 7 per cent of the scheduled caste ones had been able to do so. Similarly, the number of those with urban backgrounds working in trade and commerce had increased, while those with rural origins had, for the most part, only succeeded in improving their form of employment and had not been able to change to more skilled occupations. Those from the more distant states such as Rajasthan and Tamil Nadu had little or no occupational mobility. In particular, those from Tamil Nadu had all started with unskilled occupations on daily wages and had not changed from this situation despite twenty years sojourn in Chandigarh. Punjabis had improved the most, moving from unskilled to skilled occupations, trade and commerce or livestock farming.

There was slightly greater occupational mobility among older heads of households than the younger ones. Among the fifteen to twenty age group, the change was mainly from student or unemployed or from unskilled to semi-skilled or general service occupations, but the change in the twenty-six to fifty-eight age group was more even. Those older than this had mainly changed from unskilled manual occupations to petty trading or livestock farming, neither of which require much physical exertion. The relatively lesser mobility and general unskilled or semi-skilled occupations of the youngest age group is indicative of the slow process of acquisition of capital for trading, or skills for improving the exchange value of labour.

The respondents' occupations at the time of the survey were not necessarily their first in Chandigarh. Twenty-seven per cent had changed their occupations at least once, the maximum change being among those who had started as unskilled construction labourers. The largest proportion who had not been

able to change their occupations since coming to Chandigarh were those working on daily wages. However, of those who had changed the majority had
started as daily wage labourers, but had now become self-employed or salaried
employees. This was not only as a result of search for better employment, but as
a response to the changed demand for unskilled labour in the city.

With the city's development, the demand for unskilled construction
labourers had diminished. On the other hand, the growth of the higher income
population has generated its own demand for domestic workers and other
services. Many of the original construction workers who decided to
settle in the city changed their occupations to meet this demand. This change is
also evident in the changed pattern of employment among the respondents who
had migrated to the city more recently. While 40 per cent of those who
migrated fifteen or more years ago were still working on daily wages (almost
exclusively as construction workers), only 16 per cent of those who had come in
the last five years were doing so. At the same time, the proportion of salaried
employees had been showing a constant rise, most being employed in unskilled
or service government occupations.

Location and Characteristics of the Non-Plan Settlements

The major characteristic common to both the labour colonies and unauthorized
settlements was that both were confined to peripheral locations of the first
phase of the master plan area (see figure 7.3). This pattern is untypical of most
older Indian cities where such settlements tend to have a strong relationship
with high-density work areas and are often found in central locations. However,
as described in the last chapter the pattern in Chandigarh was enforced by the
Administration on the grounds that non-plan settlements represented a
violation of the master plan. A similar pattern is found in other Third World
new towns.

Labour Colonies on Authorized Sites

With the passage of time each of the four 'authorized' labour colonies (see
page 112) developed its own character, largely determined by the extent and
nature of the planned development in the vicinity. Socio-economic hierarchies
developed between and within them. For example, the labour colony just
behind the University in Sector 14 benefited considerably from the emergence
of a whole range of employment opportunities as a result of the growth of the
University and its resident population and the largest Post Graduate Medical
Research Institute in India in an adjoining sector. These advantages were
reflected in the occupations of the heads of households, 20 per cent of whom
were government employees and working not as sweepers, but as postmen,
clerks and *peons*. Women were able to supplement household incomes from
casual work in the neighbouring sectors. Evidently, even at the time of its

creation, a high proportion of the settlers in the colony were Punjabis engaged in relatively better occupations (D'Souza, 1968). Time had reinforced these characteristics. However, such relative prosperity had totally by-passed the south Indian community living in a part of the colony. Almost all its workers had remained in unskilled work on daily wages, despite being resident in the city from five to twenty years.

The Industrial Area labour colony, which as described in the last chapter was removed under the resettlement scheme, displayed similar characteristics. With the growth of industry in the area, there were increased opportunities for both skilled and unskilled workers in the area. At the time of the survey 40 per cent of the respondents were in skilled occupations and factory labour represented another 14 per cent of the sample. In 1965, Punjabis represented 60 per cent of the residents (D'Souza, 1968), and by 1974 they had increased to over 75 per cent. Further, while 57 per cent of the total survey sample were from scheduled castes, the proportion here was only 33 per cent.

The changes in the population of the Sector 14 and Industrial Area labour colonies were partly due to the integration of their better housing stock into the city's housing market. Many original allottees had either sold or sublet their dwellings to realize their increased exchange values. In addition, the locational advantages had led to the highest rates of unauthorized growth in them.

The Sector 25 and 26 labour colonies had not benefited to the same extent from the city's development. Their immediate surroundings remain either low density or totally undeveloped. Consequently, local opportunities for casual and unskilled work remained very limited. These disadvantages are clearly reflected in the occupations of the heads of households. For example, in the Sector 26 labour colony in 1965 more than half the heads of households were construction workers, and in 1974 almost half the sample still had unskilled manual occupations. In the case of the Sector 25 colony, all the respondents belonged to scheduled castes and 60 per cent were in unskilled manual occupations.

Settlements on Totally Unauthorized Sites

These settlements, while also mainly on the periphery of the master plan area, owed their locations to a process of 'natural evolution' in which their relationships with neighbouring areas had played a significant role. Because of the absence of official control or the demarcation of plots, their layouts did not have any formal pattern of streets and plots were undefined, varying considerably in size. Total uncertainty about the future and experiences of frequent demolition by the enforcement staff restricted dwellings to cheap structures with mud walls and thatch roofs.

The locations of the unauthorized settlements seemed to be influenced by two different factors. Two of the largest, the Kumhar colony in Sector 25 and the one spread over Sectors 32 and 33, started in locations not demarcated for planned development in the near future and where, consequently, preventive

Figure 8.3. A totally unauthorized settlement in Sector 25.

action was limited. The occupations of the heads of households were not necessarily dependent on being near other sources of activity. The Kumhar colony began when a number of potters settled in Sector 25 where they could carry on their potmaking with adequate space. Slowly, others settled there simply because a small settlement already existed. A survey in 1964–65 recorded only sixty dwellings (D'Souza, 1968), but by 1974 this had increased to about 1100. Part of this rapid growth was because the University, which owns the land, allowed some of its low-income staff to build their huts there. The origins of the Sectors 32 and 33 settlement lay in two or three sweepers having found cheap rental accommodation in a disused brick kiln. The history of its growth is described as part of the case history of one of the settlers (see page 155).

The respondents' occupations in these two settlements were much less diverse than those in the labour colonies, with 66 per cent of those in Sectors 32 and 33 and 60 per cent of those in the Kumhar colony being in unskilled manual occupations, well over half in both cases working as government salaried employees and therefore not dependent on being immediately adjacent to major centres for casual work.

The second factor, which had had a determining influence on the locations of the other two unauthorized settlements surveyed was their close proximity to centres with a high demand for cheap unskilled labour. The first, in Bajwada, was the smaller of the two as the enforcement staff had made greater attempts to prevent its growth. The second was on vacant land just behind the wholesale market in Sector 26.

Both Bajwada* and the wholesale market were centres requiring unskilled labour at short notice both day and night, to load and unload trucks and do other casual work. The growth of both settlements had been totally dependent on the availability of these employment opportunities in their immediate vicinity. For newly arrived rural migrants such settlements play an important role in enabling them to advertise their availability to those needing casual labour. They suffer greatly if totally removed from such locations, by such measures as the present resettlement scheme.

The striking feature of the four unauthorized settlements was that 93 per cent of their heads of households had rural backgrounds, 82 per cent of them belonged to scheduled castes and 83 per cent were from the two states of U.P. and Haryana.

Characteristics of Migration

The migration of new comers to the city represents the process of interaction between the local, regional and national contexts. By examining the process we can analyse not only the validity of the official assumptions regarding the motives for rural–urban migration, but also the viability of anticipating the nature and scale of such migration to the city, even if the apparently crude assumptions underlying Chandigarh's plan were replaced by more sophisticated ones. Only through such an examination can we estimate the actual possibility of total planning for any urban centre within the existing structure of the country's economy.

Here it is useful to note that, as mentioned earlier, the majority of residents in a new town such as Chandigarh are migrants. Within the existing parameters of the national society, no one is worried by over-migration of the wealthy, even if they are unemployed. The 'problem' arises only when sections of the impoverished majority attempt to do the same thing. That there might be a direct relationship between the city's well off minority and the increased demand for services which they generate, and the proportion of its poorer residents dependent on fulfilling such demand, seldom crosses the minds of the authorities.

In the early years there was a much higher proportion of migrants from urban backgrounds than more recently. A substantial number of people displaced from urban areas during Partition decided to settle in Chandigarh. Also the potential economic prospects in a new city attracted considerable numbers from smaller urban centres. With the growth of the city this attraction has declined. However, continuing social and economic pressures in the rural areas surrounding Chandigarh have produced an increase in rural migrants.

The earliest migration was predominantly from Punjab and Rajasthan. The

*The non-plan commercial centre at Bajwada was totally cleared during the Emergency (see page 185).

Punjabis included displaced persons, while the Rajasthanis were mainly rural migrants who came as construction labour. During the next five years, the influx was mostly from Haryana and U.P., changing to almost 60 per cent from U.P. alone in the five years, 1969–74.

This fluctuation in the number of migrants from different states during different periods, and also the proportions of their rural and urban backgrounds, is indicative of the different regional pressures triggering migration. Among Punjabis, the flow of largely urban migrants was a product of a search for better economic prospects. Their success in having achieved that objective is evident from their relative prosperity compared with other respondents.

In the case of rural migrants, however, the factors influencing migration were and are quite different. Within the national context of increasing unemployment, a high rate of population growth, and the destruction of several traditional modes of production in rural areas, there are considerable regional disparities. Following the 'Green Revolution' of the mid-1960s, Punjab and Haryana, already predominantly agricultural states, underwent considerable improvement in rural conditions. Punjab, particularly, had the lowest rate of urban population growth in India between 1961 and 1971 – 25.3 per cent against an average of 37.8 per cent for all states*. However, certain districts of these states, particularly of Haryana, remained outside the orbit of improvement. Conditions in other states are much worse. Some backward districts of U.P. and Rajasthan remain very vulnerable to natural disasters such as drought which can render large numbers of people incapable of finding work or food. At the same time, the towns and cities of these states offer very limited possibilities for absorbing surplus or destitute rural labour. As a consequence, there are periodic streams of temporary or seasonal migration into more developed regions of the country and their metropolitan urban areas, and many of the migrants never return.

In Chandigarh's non-plan settlements, the earlier movement of migrants from Rajasthan was caused by a drought in some districts. The respondents in the survey who had migrated at that time decided to settle in the city as there was little to return to; for them it was preferable to remain in the city even as daily wage labourers. The continuance of such migration from Rajasthan was evident in the summer of 1974 when a large number of families came to Chandigarh because the monsoons had failed there for two successive years. They had pitched tents in a peripheral sector and were surviving by doing unskilled work.

Similarly, the increasing numbers of rural migrants from U.P. (almost 80 per cent of the respondents from U.P. had rural backgrounds) came for reasons of

*Following analysis of 1971 Census data, D'Souza (1976b:349–65) concluded that the 'Green Revolution' had a negligible impact on the low rate of urbanization in Punjab during the period. On the contrary, this can only be understood in terms of the low manufacturing functions of most Punjab towns.

poverty or un(der)employment. U.P., besides being one of the most highly populated and backward states, is one of the most oppressive for those belonging to the lower castes. Thus, not surprisingly, a higher proportion of U.P. respondents (80 per cent) were from backward castes compared to respondents from other states. Although, even in cities like Chandigarh, those from scheduled or backward castes are only able to get the lowest paid, unskilled occupations, it is a considerable improvement on their conditions in rural areas. Urban conditions and forms of employment lessen traditional caste distinctions and enable them to escape feudal relationships, such as bonded labour, and to become a part of the country's wage economy.

In the context of a predominantly rural country, where the vast majority of the population has no urban experience, for a rural migrant the decision to leave the traditional place of residence must be a momentous one. Almost 80 per cent of the respondents had decided to migrate for economic reasons. They were almost equally divided between those who had been forced to consider migration because of poverty or unemployment and those who were dissatisfied with local economic prospects and had decided to move in search of better ones. Of the remaining 20 per cent, 6 per cent had been displaced by Partition, 6 per cent had been transferred, and the rest had moved for various reasons such as family quarrels or simply a spirit of adventure and a desire to see life in a modern city.

The chief reason for choosing Chandigarh was a perception of better income or employment opportunities in a new capital city, and this factor alone accounted for more than half the respondents. Other major considerations were associated with family, relatives, or friends in the city who could be relied upon for assistance in finding work and a place to live. In fact, some 25 per cent had decided to come to the city because a friend or relative had invited them. The vast majority had made the move with considerable caution on the basis of information received from friends, relatives or neighbours. This caution was further evident from the fact that two-thirds of the respondents, again predominantly from rural backgrounds, had first come alone to Chandigarh. Only after finding work and some kind of shelter had they brought their dependents along. More than half those who had come in the previous five years still had dependents in their places of origin, and a small proportion of even those who had come fifteen or more years ago still did so.

Further, the mere act of migration did not necessarily indicate a commitment to permanent residence in the city. Although two-thirds of the heads of households had decided to settle in Chandigarh, the rest were almost equally divided between those who were undecided and those who did not intend to stay permanently. The higher rate of uncertainty among those who had migrated in the last five years and the much greater commitment to stay among those who had been in the city for fifteen years and longer was again indicative of the slow and cautious process by which important decisions such as a permanent change to urban living are made. By the nature of the sampling method used, it was not possible to know what proportion of the total residents had returned, but the low rate of unemployment among the respondents would indicate the significance of employment in the decision-making process.

There appeared to be a significant correlation between a number of other factors, such as occupation, income, and caste, and the residents' commitment to stay in Chandigarh. A higher proportion with more desirable and secure occupations were sure about staying permanently than those with unskilled or semi-skilled occupations, and similarly a higher proportion with incomes above Rs.250 per month intended to stay than those with incomes below this. In the case of caste, three-quarters of the respondents from non-scheduled castes intended staying compared to three-fifths of the scheduled castes. This was probably because of the relatively greater inability of those belonging to backward castes to overcome their historical economic and social handicaps, even after migrating to the city.

It is significant that the Administration's policy to discourage further migration by demolishing new structures in the settlements had not affected the residents' decisions about staying in the city. There was no correlation between the number of times respondents had been forced to move and the decision to stay or not. This indicates the relatively low priority housing or housing conditions have compared to other factors such as income and employment, from the point of view of influencing the decision to make a permanent move from place of origin.

People of the Non-Plan Settlements and the National Context

For 60 per cent of the workers in unskilled occupations and working on daily wages or as self-employed (see table 8.2) there could be little benefit from any statuatory protection against fluctuations in the labour market. In comparison more than 60 per cent of the city's total work force is in government salaried employment, and although the majority have low, fixed salaries, they are protected against such fluctuations by security of employment and additional benefits such as health care, rent allowances and revisions in pay scales.

The high proportion of non-salaried workers in the settlements implies a concentration of unorganized labourers who have to fend for themselves and are in a weak position to negotiate for better returns for their labour. For example, in order to pay increased international oil prices, in 1973 the central government agreed to export a large proportion of the country's cement production to Iran. Some types of construction relying on cement were then banned with the result that large numbers of both unskilled and skilled daily wage labourers in the settlements were finding it difficult to find work for even half the days in a month. The terms on which they had obtained employment and the general absence of any effective collective organizations among them meant that they could derive little benefit from organized labour action. Strikes, if they could be organized, would be easily broken because of the workers' lack of resources to sustain themselves while not working.

Self-employment, romanticized and over-rated by many for the benefits it has to offer, means different things to different people as is evident from the sample. Those possessing some capital or skills change to self-employment as a means of bettering their economic status. However, for many it has few such benefits to offer. In the competitive environment for unskilled labour, at least 50 per cent of the self-employed found themselves condemned to self-employment. For a semi-skilled cobbler, self-employment does not necessarily mean an exercise of individual 'freedom', but merely a means of eking out a living by sitting and working on the pavement somewhere, unprotected from the elements or even by the law.

The migration of predominantly unskilled and impoverished rural migrants to the city is the clearest illustration of the way in which Chandigarh's structure is inextricably linked with the national context described in chapter 2. The circumstances of the migrants, themselves a product of the processes in operation in the wider society, are reproduced in urban areas as a result of population mobility. Clearly, this mobility is not a blind one. Evidence from Chandigarh's non-plan settlements substantiates the arguments concerning the urbanization process in India proposed by Bose (1973, 1977) and Sovani (1966), and introduced in chapter 2. The careful and cautious decision-making processes of the migrants, which underly this population movement, did not include direct consideration of the city's high environmental and design standards. Indirectly, however, these standards have been an attraction for them because of the demand for labour that both their implementation and maintenance suggest. The growth of non-plan settlements in the city has thus been dependent on the capital investment in the city, whether controlled by the public or private sector. The workers in the settlements are, however, by no means confined to the unorganized tertiary sectors of the economy. They include organized industrial workers, government employees and construction workers employed by both public and private agencies.

From the point of view of the residents already in the non-plan settlements, the continuing migration of unskilled labour lowers their ability to improve their bargaining power through organized collective action. From the point of view of the newcomers, even the low and uncertain standards of living in the city are *an improvement* on their circumstances in their places of origin, and it is this which determines their decision to move. The influence of the same factors on the migration of rural newcomers to Ciudad Guayana has been noted by MacDonald and MacDonald (1977) and to Brasilia by Epstein (1973). In this respect, regional disparities in the levels of economic development within the national economy, a characteristic of most capitalist countries, developed and underdeveloped, has important bearings on the ability of local urban authorities to 'plan' for, or anticipate the scale of such migration.

The settling of the migrants has been a positive act, undeterred by the prolonged hostility they encounter in the city. They have been expressing a determination to better their circumstances. Building their own shelter in the absence of any alternative also represents their will to transform their circumstances. Clearly it is the laws which have to be challenged, rather than their determination to climb out of the vicious circles of deprivation and poverty. It would indeed be tragic if millions of impoverished people stopped attempting to find means for survival simply because existing laws do not permit them to take the necessary action. In this respect, what is a 'problem' for the authorities is clearly a 'solution' for the migrants.

However, there are very severe limitations to the improvement which a majority of predominantly unskilled labourers can achieve. The constraints are defined by the existing social and economic relationships which produce an ever increasing concentration of power in the hands of a minority at the cost of decreasing opportunities for the majority. In this respect, what is a short-term solution today is almost certain to become a worse long-term problem within the existing framework of development.

The issues which this raises with regard to the potentials and limitations of urban planning in the Third World context are manifold. Total planning based on the parameters of only local control of the type attempted in Chandigarh and other Third World new towns is clearly not possible. No local planning framework, irrespective of its flexibility, can control or anticipate population movements resulting from national economic and social change, particularly when diverse aspects of national activities are unplanned.

The terms on which non-plan settlements might become integrated into urban planning systems, if the objectives are defined simply in terms of adapting planning norms to existing realities, implies an acceptance of 'no planning', which again is neither likely nor possible. The end result of a partial approach in this direction, as witnessed in Ciudad Guayana, is that of applying different norms to different sections of the community, confining non-plan and low-standard growth to locations deprived of the main benefits of public investment in infrastructure and services. A by-product of this approach is a lowering of the expectations for improvement among the deprived sections of the community.

To end this chapter, its more abstract and empirical content is supplemented by three case studies. They demonstrate nothing more nor less than the interaction of individuals or groups with the problems or constraints produced by factors beyond their control and the 'solutions' they have been forced to devise, some more successfully than others.

Case Histories

Group of Seasonal Migrants from Rajasthan
This group of between twenty-five and thirty households had pitched tents on a vacant piece of land between the authorized labour colony and the totally

Figure 8.4. The group of semi-nomadic families and their temporary shelter – remarkably adapted to suit their necessity for seasonal mobility.

unauthorized Kumhar colony in Sector 25 (see figure 7.3). Their small settlement had emerged suddenly during the summer of 1974 (see page 146). Their circumstances and seminomadic lifestyle are an illustration of the kind of factors which are forcing people to leave their places of origin.

At the time of first visiting them, a number of the men were just setting off on one of their trips to the mountainous district of Bilaspur in Himachal Pradesh. Each carried one or two heavy bundles of cheap crockery tied in pieces of cloth. Enquiries revealed that this was the beginning of one of several such trips to the district. After reaching their destination they would spend a week to ten days going from house to house collecting used clothing, shoes or other objects. In exchange they would give pieces of crockery, the exact number of pieces being bargained between the two parties. The average working day during such trips was from 6 am to about 4 pm.

When most of the crockery had been disposed of and sufficient articles collected, they would return to Chandigarh and sell the articles to wholesale *kabadi* dealers, a number of whom were working in the neighbouring settlements.

During these trips, the women and children stayed behind together with one or two men to look after them.

After resting for a day or two with their families the men would set off again on another trip.

A week later, on a second visit to the group, the men had not returned, but after the initial suspicion of strangers had been overcome, one of the more outspoken and elderly women described their reasons for being in Chandigarh and their intentions of only temporary residence in the city.

'We belong to the Churu district of Rajasthan. We migrate seasonally to other parts of the country to make a living for a few months. As our district falls in the desert zone, it is extremely sandy and dry there and therefore not very good for cultivation. Very little water is available. We own small pieces of land but very little grows on it. At the most, it is possible to cultivate it for only one of the two yearly agricultural seasons. For the rest of the time we have to devise other means of sustaining ourselves. So, we come here for three to four months during the summer, earn a little money, and then return to Rajasthan.

Our traditional occupation used to be making or mending shoes in villages. We started our present occupation of trading crockery for used articles, only a year ago.

The men are still away in Bilaspur. They chose that district for starting work because they had heard that there were good prospects in the region. When they return they will have earned a small amount of money. But, in the meantime, we women and children will have consumed most of it already. These days it is so difficult to save anything. During these months here we just manage to earn enough to survive and pay for our travelling expenses to and from home.

Shortly we will be returning to start sowing for the coming season. We have to wait for the rains before it can be done. Till the crop is ready, we will have to live by borrowing from the village moneylender. If there is a good harvest, we should be able to pay back the debt. If not, the new debt will get added to the old one. Occasionally, we have to pawn something or the other.

Why have we chosen this elaborate way of making a living?, it all has to be done for the sake of the stomach.'

When the site was visited again a month later, the group was no longer there. To cope with this semi-nomadic way of life, the households had devised an extremely functional and simple set of equipment. The tents consisted of a cheap or improvised tarpaulin which could be quickly assembled with the help of a couple of central bamboo supports, the corners of the tarpaulin being tied to pegs hammered into the ground. An earthen ledge was made round the covered space which was either filled with straw to provide a soft surface for sleeping or simply covered by pieces of cloth. This also kept the water out when it rained. For cooking, a portable earthenware stove had been devised. It could be taken either inside or outside the tent, depending on which was more convenient. When moving, all equipment could be easily dismantled and packed into fairly small bundles.

Scheduled Caste Mali from U.P.

The following is an edited version of an interview with a middle-aged man belonging to the *Valmiki* Hindu sect. *Valmikis* have traditionally been at the bottom of the Hindu caste hierarchy and are registered as a 'scheduled' caste by the government.

He was interviewed in the evening during the course of the preliminary survey of non-plan petty trading and services in Chandigarh. At the time, he was sitting on the pavement in front of the regular shops in a high-density residential sector selling potted plants with another relative. He had only ten or twelve plants lined up in front of him. Strictly speaking, he was indulging in the 'act of selling from a pavement', an activity theoretically not permitted in Chandigarh.

Although he and his successful career in the city cannot be taken as typical for those belonging to similar caste backgrounds (his personal charm, tactfulness, enterprising spirit and talent being exceptional), his narration has been included here because of his ability to articulate the experience of belonging to a backward community. This and his frankness were not easy to find among others from similar backgrounds. In addition, the story of his stay in Chandigarh over a period of fifteen to twenty years is a good demonstration of the role of both non-plan residential and commercial developments in urban areas in enabling some people to attain a certain degree of social and economic mobility.

'I belong to district Mainpuri in Uttar Pradesh and left home more than 20 years ago. Our traditional occupation is agriculture and my family owns two or three *bighas* of land there. I left home in search of work because the amount of land we had was insufficient for supporting the whole family and employment prospects in the area were bleak. Even today, landlords there pay only Rs.2 per day to agricultural labourers, who have to work 11 to 13 hours for this. Besides, if something goes wrong, they often deduct Rs.100 to 150 from our wages and can be extremely abusive. A shower of shoes on people like us for minor causes is not infrequent.

I first went to Saharanpur where I managed to find a factory job with a monthly salary of Rs.150. Eighteen to 20 years ago, the salary was good but one had to work under perilous conditions in the factory. There was a constant danger of accidents which could prove fatal. My mother was extremely unhappy about this and kept telling me to leave the job and look for something less dangerous even if it meant lower earnings.

Around that time, news about the construction of Chandigarh reached me. Others from our district who had come here sent back news of many employment opportunities and good prospects for starting a new life for people like us. I decided to come and examine the situation for myself. On the whole, my expectations were fulfilled and I have more or less settled down here.

When I first came, I got a job as a *mali* in a private school at a salary of Rs.50 per month. I started living in a *jhuggi* in the cluster of *jhuggis* built by persons belonging to my community next to the plants nursery in Sector 23. Soon I started looking around for a government job. It was not easy but I managed to make contact with a number of influential persons after having impressed them with my work. Pratap Singh Kairon was the Chief Minister of Punjab at that time and I worked for a number of other ministers and high officials privately. It was with Kairon's personal recommendation that I was given a government job as a *mali* in one of the government colleges where I've worked ever since.

When I first got the job I was allotted residential accommodation within the college premises but I was not too happy with the arrangement. The Principal of the college, who was also resident on the premises, used to keep me on my toes all the time with her instructions. I applied for a government quarter elsewhere and got one in this sector. I was really fortunate in having come in the early years as, since then, it has become extremely difficult for persons like me to get government accommodation. Those who came later are still on the waiting list despite having been in service for 10 to 15 years.

Now I have started growing plants on the small piece of land attached to my house for selling privately. I tried making a deal with a private nursery to get them to sell my plants on a 50 per cent basis. As I was going to be growing the plants and looking after them, I thought it was reasonable that I should get one rupee out of a plant sold by them for two, but they refused to accept my terms. They were prepared to give me only 25 paisas* out of Rs.2. So I decided against entering into an agreement with them. Instead, now I come here and sell the plants on my own every evening and can often make daily sales of Rs.12 to 15. At the moment I am training my relative in the work. When he has gained some experience we plan to set up a *rehri* of plants in the market round the corner. We hope to do good business because there aren't any plants *rehris* and there is a lot of demand for good plants.

I don't have many problems with the enforcement staff. I have worked for and supplied plants to some of the officers concerned and they are all sympathetic towards me. Two of them live in this very sector and I keep on good terms with them. At the most when there is a raid I allow the staff to take the plants they like the most and they are satisfied with that. The charm of plants is such that no one can resist them. I don't foresee any problems in getting a *rehri* licence or a

*One rupee has 100 paisas.

parking place in the *rehri* market either. It may be true that officially no more *rehri* licences are being issued, but with the help and patronage of 'people like you' all is possible.

Of course, the small piece of land attached to my house won't be sufficient for my plans of launching into business but we won't have any problems about that either. Recently, during his visit to Chandigarh, Jagjivan Ram [a prominent MP belonging to a 'scheduled' caste] got a site allotted to us *Valmikis* for a temple in this sector. Flowers and greenery, of course, are most welcome on temple premises. Besides looking after gardening, I hope to cultivate my own plants there too. I am sure that no one will object to that.

At the moment, I am head *mali* at the college. I have also won some prizes for Dahlias in competitions. My present pay, after all deductions for rent, provident fund, etc., is Rs.209. The monthly rent for the government house is only Rs.10.50.

All the family, including my parents are here now. We have no desire to return to our village although we go back every now and then for visits. Our house there remains locked. We still have our land which we often sublet to others for cultivation. Every year we get our share of 1 or 2 *maunds* of the produce. My sisters, who were married locally, are still there.

There are many reasons why we do not wish to go back. Having got used to the more sophisticated city life, village habits and customs appear unattractive to us. For instance, we have learnt to wear clean and nice clothes. In the village everyone still wears very dirty ones.

However, the main reason for our not wanting to return is the attitude of the high caste landlords towards us. They don't want us to make any progress. In fact they are hostile towards any of us wanting to live a better life. They want to retain their position of superiority and therefore cannot tolerate our desire for self improvement. Their authoritarianism, abusiveness, and economic exploitation of us is very oppressive. In the city, even we can at least have aspirations, as well as some chances, for our betterment.'

An Early Inhabitant of an Unauthorized Settlement

This man was one of the first 'squatters' in the totally unauthorized settlement in Sector 33. He had come to Chandigarh in 1961 and had initially stayed with relatives. In 1963 he obtained a job as a sweeper with the Air Force. When his wife and four children joined him, there was not enough room in the relative's house for everyone. He was the only earning member of the household, and had applied for a subsidized government house, but as none was available his name was put on the waiting list. Unable to afford the rent of even a single room on the private market, he decided to devise a more viable alternative.

There had been a brick kiln on the site of the settlement. However, by the early 1960s it was no longer in use and the owner had two or three sheds available. The man got one of these at a nominal rent and in 1964 he and his family moved in. The other sheds were similarly rented out.

Finding pieces of broken bricks lying around, he decided to build his own hut using mud mortar and a thatch roof. Slowly, other people began building huts and living there. The enforcement staff would come and demolish the huts, but they would be rebuilt. His own hut was demolished several times in the early years, but as the settlement grew in size the older huts became less vulnerable and only the new ones on the periphery would be demolished. (In the course of fieldwork, some households living on the outer edges were interviewed in the ruins of their demolished huts.)

By early 1974 his family had grown to nine. His wife could not work because of ill health. The eldest daughter who was eighteen had recently been married. She had not been able to go to school as she had to help her mother with the household work and the other children. Two of the younger sons were going to the government school in an adjoining sector. His net salary was Rs.195 per month, considerably more than he had earned ten years before, but because of inflation he was worse off. He could not afford to send the rest of the children to school because he could not pay for stationery, books and uniforms.

Two or three years earlier, because of the constant risk of fire with thatch and other problems of maintaining a mud hut, he had invested in building an improved single-roomed structure in which all members of the household lived. It had mud plastered walls made of burnt brick bats laid in mud mortar. The roof consisted of a layer of mud on timber boards obtained by taking packing cases apart. Although the whole family had helped in building, materials and hired labour had cost almost Rs.700, which he had borrowed from friends and relatives.

The house was kept scrupulously clean with frequent mud washes given to the floors and walls. In the summer, cooking and sleeping was done outdoors, but during the winter evenings and monsoons all activities had to take place inside when crowding was intense. To improve the family's living conditions, he wanted to add another room, but did not dare for fear of the additional investment of labour and painfully accumulated savings being destroyed by demolition. His name was still on the waiting list for government housing.

With resettlement, he must have been allotted a transit site 10 ft by 30 ft on which he and the family will have had to build again. Assuming that he took a loan of Rs.1500, his recurrent monthly cost for license fee and loan repayment will amount to Rs.42 for the next four years. This will be in addition to his debts from the building of the previous house. Even assuming his monthly salary is now Rs.250, his monthly housing costs will be almost 20 per cent of his income. With eight people to support on the rest, when prices of essential commodities have risen sharply, one can speculate about how household expediture might be cut – by stopping the schooling of even the two sons? And all this for a licensed site on a five-year lease.

9

Housing and Investment in Non-Plan Settlements

'Self-help', 'self-build', 'dweller control'; these are some of the expressions which have become prominent in discussions about the building process in Third World squatter or semi-legal settlements. A propagation of the advantages of self-help housing has accompanied the changing perceptions about such settlements discussed in chapters 1 and 7.

However there is nothing new either in the concept of self-help or in the content of the discussions about it. Self-help as a solution to the deteriorating living conditions of the working classes was not only discussed, but extensively practiced in nineteenth-century Europe, just as the assumptions on which it was justified were attacked by some contemporary writers*.

History has testified to the fact that even in industrialized countries, access to better housing for large sections of the working class was ensured not through self-help but major State intervention in terms of subsidized housing†. Even then their housing problem remains far from solved with a continuation of slums, inner city decay and homelessness. This intervention was made possible by the high economic growth rates and resulting affluence largely after the Second World War. Since the beginning of the present economic crisis there has again been an attempt to reverse, to some degree, the public commitment to provide subsidized housing to the deprived, low-income or unemployed sections of the community, by propagating the benefits of self-help or dweller control.

There could be some validity in the arguments against direct public sector intervention in housing in the Third World if it could be demonstrated that the reduced burden on the public exchequer would lead to higher standards, in the long term, for all sections of the population through an optimal use of public

*For a summary of contemporary literature supporting self-help solutions, see Sax (1869) and for a critique of it see Engels (1975, 40–74; originally published in 1872). For a twentieth-century critique of self-help housing, see Ward, P. (1982).
†For example, the percentage of mainly subsidized public housing to total housing in the UK increased from 1 per cent in 1914 to 33 per cent in 1974, while private rental housing decreased from 90 per cent to only 14 per cent. The change in owner-occupied housing during this period was from 9 per cent to 53 per cent.

resources. But, as shown in chapter 1, the present economic and political relationships within the global economy make the possibility of that course of development in the majority of Third World countries very dubious, and almost impossible.

The main argument presented against providing public subsidy for low-income housing in the Third World is that the governments of these countries simply do not have the necessary resources. Therefore, it is suggested that ways and means must be found to optimize existing resource availability at the household level by removing all obstacles in the way of its mobilization. A further argument used to support this view is that, in any case, the governments of most Third World countries have direct control over only a fraction of their national resources, the bulk being in the hands of the mass of the population.

While, undoubtedly, the latter argument is true as far as its first part goes, its second it is extremely misleading. Some aspects of the increasing maldistribution of incomes and wealth in the Indian case were considered in chapter 2. To continue with this example, in rural India 3.9 per cent of the total households own 39 per cent of the country's agricultural land, while 40 per cent of the poorest own only 2 per cent. Between 1961 and 1971, the top 15 per cent of rural households accounted for two-thirds of the total land value and absorbed two-thirds of the co-operative credit during that period. Not only that, the consolidation of economic power by the top 10 per cent of the population since Independence has made the position of the bottom 40 per cent more vulnerable. Agricultural mechanization and land owners' growing preference for permanent, technically trained farm workers has reduced even casual employment opportunities for the remaining landless labourers*.

The same applies in a more extreme form to the increasing concentration of private resources in the urban industrial sector. Between 1963 and 1973, tentative estimates suggest that the capital share of the top twenty groups in the corporate private sector rose from 32 to 38 per cent. Further, big business has made little effort to raise capital for its large projects; at least 50 per cent of their cost has been financed by public sector institutions (Oza, 1977:8–19). The critical point here is that at least 40 per cent of the urban population would not be below the poverty line if it controlled the bulk of national resources. The arguments about non-availibility of public resources for subsidizing low-income housing have to be seen in this context.

Self-help or self-build, by tackling the low-income housing problem in isolation from the dominant mechanisms prevailing in the rest of society, thus evades the relationship between the severe scarcity of resources at the household level and the structure of the total economy. The effects of this evasion and some of the myths surrounding the benefits of self-help housing to low-

---

*The data in this paragraph are taken from a public lecture given by the economist K. N. Raj at the India International Centre, New Dehli in August 1977.

income households are highlighted by the history of the housing process in Chandigarh's non-plan settlements over a period of fifteen or so years.

The Settlement Process and Residential Mobility

The major characteristic differentiating the residents of Chandigarh's non-plan settlements from those living in regular housing is that none owns the land on which his dwelling is built. Those allotted authorized plots in the labour colonies have the status of temporary lessees of the government, the rest are illegal squatters on public land, although the majority own the structures built on it. Land tenure status has a major effect on the residents' attitudes towards their housing situations and for this reason the terms 'authorized' and 'unauthorized' have been used here to denote tenure status of individual dwellings and not of whole settlements. In fact, in the survey nearly two-thirds of the households were living in unauthorized dwellings.

For more than 40 per cent of the respondents the settlements represented their first and only places of residence in the city. For a considerable number of the rest who had moved, some several times, the moves had been within non-plan settlements, either accompanied by a change of tenure status, or simply from one unauthorized dwelling to another. However, during the previous ten years a growing proportion (20 per cent or more) had moved into the settlements from regular housing (see figure 9.1).

Among the respondents who had managed to obtain immediate access to authorized plots in the labour colonies, a considerable number had migrated to

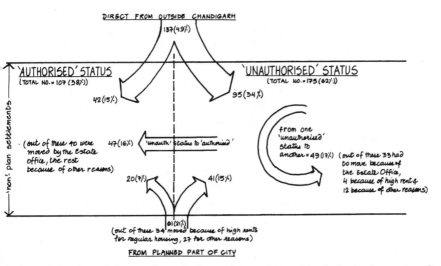

Figure 9.1. Distribution of respondents by authorized/unauthorized status of dwelling, previous places of residence and reasons for moving into or within the settlements.

the city during the period when plots were relatively easily available. The rest had either managed to buy tenure rights from original allottees or were tenants of authorized lessees. Some had managed to get the tenure status of their plots changed by persuasion or bribery of the staff collecting rents.

Most of those who had settled directly on unauthorized plots were living in unauthorized settlements and had come to the city during the last ten years. A small proportion of them had first lived in nearby villages or the neighbouring small town of Manimajra where the cost of living is much lower than in Chandigarh.

Of those whose moves had been from one unauthorized tenure status to another, the majority had done so because of Estate Office requirements. Most had had their dwellings demolished in one place and with no feasible alternative had simply built new unauthorized structures elsewhere.

Most respondents who had moved from planned residential areas into the settlements had done so because they could no longer afford the rising market rents for regular housing (see chapter 6). Others had moved because they had been living with relatives or friends in subsidized government housing, but after bringing their families to the city there was no longer room for them. Long waiting lists for government housing, high rents in the private sector or the inability to pay rent at all had forced them into the settlements.

Tenants and the Incidence of Subletting

Those allotted authorized plots are not allowed to sell or sublet either the land or their dwellings. The official arguments against selling or subletting are that authorized lessees were given the right to occupy government land for personal use only, and that its use for financial gain is an 'exploitation' of the privilege granted to them. The resulting restriction on the rights of the lessees to realize the exchange values of their investment has already been discussed in chapter 7.

Another argument offered against subletting is that some unscrupulous people have acquired several plots in the labour colonies and built minimal structures for rent, thus 'exploiting' poor tenants. It is seldom acknowledged that the same mechanism operates without restriction in the planned part of the city.

The implication of the official rules for those leaving the city for good or going on extended visits to their places of origin is that the authorized lessees should simply abandon their dwellings to the authorities. None of the original lessees was foolish enough to do this even when moving eleswhere within the city.

Thus both subletting and outright sales have been taking place more or less from the inception of the labour colonies. At the time of the survey, subletting, in particular, appeared to be on the increase owing to their increased integration with the city's housing market. However, only 13 per cent of the respondents were tenants compared with 80 per cent in the city as a whole, indicating that few were using their housing as a commodity.

This is not necessarily typical of non-plan settlements elsewhere. In Ashaiman, Mitchell (1975) investigated the considerable operation of entrepeneurial resident and non-resident landlords in building rental accommodation. In a study of a hutment settlement in Bombay (Desai and Pillai, 1972:83), it was found that 70 per cent of the households were tenants. A high degree of tenancy has been found in the squatter settlements of Dar es Salaam and Nairobi also. In a study of three settlements in Mexico City, Peter Ward (1976) noted the increase in tenancy with the age of the settlements and relatively increased security of tenure. In Chandigarh, the comparatively low degree of tenancy was partly a result of the recency of the settlements, the ready availibility of new land on which to build, and the minimal or nil paying ability of the lowest income households.

All except one of the tenants in the sample were living in the authorized labour colonies, and most of these were in authorized dwellings. Monthly rents varied from nothing to Rs.40, the mean being Rs.17 compared to about Rs.65 for a single room in regular private housing. More than two-thirds of the tenants had only one room per household and were living in conditions of greater overcrowding than the owners.

Compared with owners, there was a higher proportion of tenant households with only one or two members and no women, indicating that they were migrants in the initial exploratory stage. Further, a higher proportion either did not intend to stay in the city or had not made up their minds. That, as a group, tenants did not include the lowest income households, indicated the necessity for some rent-paying ability among them. The very low income levels of some households and the low cost of putting up minimal shelter were largely responsible for their resorting to self-building.

The Housing Process Among the Owners

Eighty-six per cent of the owners in the sample had built their own dwellings. Most of the rest had bought them semi-built and completed construction, and only 3 per cent had bought completed structures. Of the dwellings which had been bought, three-quarters were unauthorized which is significant in view of the authorities' allegation that 'unscrupulous people exploit the labour colonies by making large profits from subletting or selling the rights to authorized plots'.

The sums paid for complete or semi-built structures were generally in line with their market values at that time. These values were inevitably higher on authorized plots because of the greater security of tenure, and for some structures on unauthorized land the sale was only a token deal – one respondent having paid only Rs.10 for his hut. The majority of sales seemed to have been the result of natural mobility among the households, rather than attempts to realize increased exchange values for the structures. What

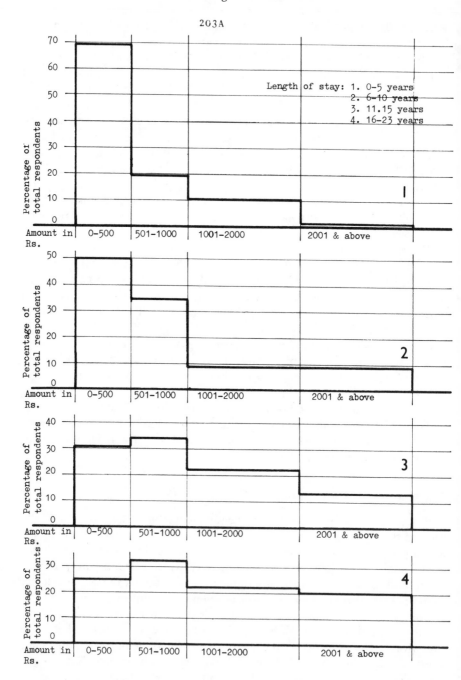

Figure 9.2. Distribution of respondents owning their dwelling by length of stay in Chandigarh and total amount spent on building or buying house.

integration there was into the main housing market of the city had remained minimal.

More than half those who had been wholly or partially responsible for building their dwellings had done so in stages, making additions or improvements over the years. Those who had built in one operation were primarily the owners of one-roomed thatched huts, which more or less have to be completed in one stage and require comparatively smaller investment.

The slow and gradual process of improvement and additional investment in housing was clearly evident from the length of residence of different respondents (see figure 9.2). More than two-thirds of those who had invested only up to Rs.500 had been in Chandigarh less than five years. However, even after sixteen to twenty-three years in the city, 25 per cent of the households in this group had not invested more than this, the poor quality of their dwellings reflecting the neglible amount of 'improvement' within their reach.

Monetary Investment in Housing

The range of monetary investment in dwellings varied from as little as the Rs. 10 one man had paid for his hut to as much as Rs.20,000 invested by one buffaloe owner in the Sector 14 labour colony. Three-quarters, however had invested Rs. 1000 or less.

One of the major factors affecting investment was the tenure status of the land. Because of the greater security of tenure of authorized plots and the longer time that these had existed, investment in dwellings on them was considerably higher than in those built on unauthorized land. This was apparent from the higher standards of building, a majority of the houses having at least $4\frac{1}{2}$ in burnt brick walls and flat roofs consisting of a thin layer of mud laid on cheap timber boarding. Most also had doors for safety and windows for lighting and ventilation, while a few even had cement floors, reinforced concrete roofs and private electricity connections. Such high building standards were, however, exceptional rather than typical even on authorized plots. Some of the older houses already had badly cracked walls and unstable roofs, showing a very real danger of collapse during a summer wind storm or monsoon downpour.

The typical dwelling built on unauthorized land consisted of a mud-walled hut with a thatch roof and mud floors. Few had doors or windows and often there were only pieces of cloth hung across openings or second-hand timber boards put across them at night. Small holes in the walls stuffed with rags were used for ventilation. Many of the structures had no natural lighting or ventilation and the atmosphere was made worse by the smoky fuels used for cooking. Not surprisingly, the health of the occupants suffers, particularly as these conditions are accompanied by poor diet and malnutrition. Inevitably outbreaks of malaria in the city are most severe in the non-plan settlements.

However, even in the case of unauthorized dwellings there was some

Figure 9.3. The myth of 'dweller control' for an impoverished household. A father and grandfather look on helplessly as the small child lies badly injured on the bed in the background because one of the hut walls had fallen on it following a monsoon downpour.

evidence of gradual improvement. Those who had the ability to do so were attempting to improve their dwellings, and to minimize the risks of fire and collapse. But, the generally low quality of the construction was an obvious reflection of the technical and financial limitations of the owners. No matter how much they are exhorted to make improvements through self-help, for the most deprived among them, there is little possibility of betterment through their own resources.

As would have been expected, heads of households who still had dependents in their places of origin, or who either did not intend to stay permanently or were undecided about staying had invested much less than those whose dependents were with them and had decided to settle in the city. Because of the high rate of 'turnover' migration (Bose, 1973:104) in the country as a whole, the number of migrant households in such circumstances of uncertainty must be considerable. The rigid and stringent rules of the present resettlement scheme excludes it from being a viable alternative for such households. Therefore the building of minimal unauthorized huts by such people, despite the heavy social and health costs, is going to remain an integral part of the urban landscape, irrespective of any amended 'planning' framework which might be introduced.

Solutions worked out simply on the basis of the computed incomes of households, and the assumption that a standard proportion of these is available for housing (and this includes typical World Bank projects) do not take into account the diversity of other commitments of those in the initial stages of migration, for example the additional travelling costs to and from places of origin, running houses in two places, and the uncertainties surrounding permanent urban residence.

The Use and Availability of Credit

It was clear from the survey that each owner household had had to invest *some* money, even if it were as little as Rs.50 to Rs.75. For an unskilled daily wage labourer, even such small amounts can be hard to accumulate. This can lead to heads of households having to borrow money from any available source. Institutional credit is almost inaccessible to the poor. Thus 21 per cent of the owner respondents in the survey had obtained credit from relatives, friends or moneylenders; only 1 per cent had received small government loans. Although informal credit can be obtained interest free or at neglible interest rates on the basis of kinship ties in some communities, those for whom this is impossible often have to pay exhorbitant rates. More than half the respondents who had had to borrow money informally were paying between 48 and 144 per cent on their borrowings, the rate from the banks being only 6–8 per cent. Of those who had received credit at the highest rates (120–140 per cent), almost all had the lowest incomes (Rs.250 and below). Such usurious practices are common in backward rural areas. The evidence of similar practices even in the residential areas of a 'modern' city such as Chandigarh reflects the continuing heavy social and economic odds against the rural migrant.

Non-Monetary Investment

The financial investment in housing discussed so far by no means represented the total investment made by households, and the generally low costs had been achieved in two additional ways. First, there was the use of second-hand or waste materials either acquired cheaply from wholesale *kabadi* (waste) dealers or simply picked up from rubbish heaps or building sites. Secondly, there was the considerable investment of the households' own labour.

The Acquisition of Building Materials

More than half the households had used at least some waste or second-hand materials, such as corrugated iron sheets, timber packing crates, bricks and brick bats, which they had obtained free of cost. The difficulty of acquiring even these materials free is reflected in the fact that only one respondent had been able to build his structure entirely from materials obtained free. This is significant in indicating that even the most rudimentary hut costs something in the monetarized urban economy. Thatch has to be paid for as it does not grow wild in the city and has to be transported from outside. Also the overall economy of scarcity has resulted in waste and used materials being drawn within the orbit of the market so that they have become difficult to obtain for those of limited means. Thus almost half the respondents had bought *all* their building materials. Those with the lowest incomes and unskilled occupations had resorted to greater use of waste and free materials, as had those not intending to stay in the city or who were undecided about staying.

Centres for Buying Building Materials

The widespread practice among the respondents of buying building materials from non-plan commercial markets and centres illustrated the strong relationship between non-plan residential and commercial developments in Chandigarh. Cheap and second-hand building materials and commodities such as bamboo, thatch and timber crates could more or less only be obtained in Bajwada (see page 186) or from the wholesale *kabadi* dealers working from some of the settlements. Other materials such as rough timber beams, although obtainable from the planned centres, tended to be cheaper in Bajwada because of the much lower overheads of the dealers there.

A third of the respondents had bought all their building materials from the non-plan commercial centres and 90 per cent had bought at least some there. Those with authorized plots had made greater use of the planned centres, but only 10 per cent of the total had bought all their materials there.

The Use of Self-Help Labour

More than 80 per cent of the builder respondents had used some household labour in building their dwellings, but two-thirds of the total households had made use of some hired labour. This is significant in so far as it is commonly assumed that dwellings in unauthorized settlements are constructed by the 'squatters' themselves.

The factors influencing the use of self-help construction appeared to be strongly linked to the households' economic status and stage in the slow process of expressing commitment to permanent residence in the city. Of the different occupational groups, unskilled manual workers had made the greatest use of self-help, followed by those in the general services category. The progressive decrease in the percentage of those who had used self-help with the increase in the income group of the head of household reflected its being largely a matter of economic compulsion. This was further reinforced by the fact that a significantly higher proportion of households with women workers had used only household labour. (The correlation between low economic status and women workers was noted in chapter 8.) Many other households who had used no hired labour consisted of recent and younger migrants, whose dependents were still in their places of origin. In their case the greater use of their own labour was largely an indication of their lesser commitment to permanent residence in the city and their uncertain economic circumstances.

Contrary to normal assumptions, making even simple thatch roofs requires

Table 9.1. Respondents by type of self-help labour used and preferred alternative if asked to move.

Type of labour	Own land on which to build	Pucca tenement on rent	Pucca tenement on hire purchase	No response or not applicable	Total	%
Only unskilled	15	0	47	6	68	38.8
Only skilled	5	0	7	2	14	8.0
Skilled and unskilled	35	8	47	3	93	53.1
Percentage	31.4	4.5	57.7	6.2		100

Respondents who were tenants, had bought their houses or had not contributed any of their own labour have been excluded.

considerable skill. Thus if self-help is divided into skilled labour (for example, carpentry, work with cement and making thatch roofs) and unskilled labour (for example, simple manual work such as lifting materials and making mud mortar), nearly 40 per cent of the owner households had been able to provide only unskilled labour and only 8 per cent totally skilled labour, while more than half had provided a combination of the two. Thus inevitably a large proportion of the unskilled and poorest builder respondents had had to hire skilled labour at least to make the thatch roofs for their huts. Their precarious economic circumstances, the frequent demolition of their huts or demands, as under the present resettlement scheme, that they move and build again, can result in some of the poorest households getting into debt on crippling terms of repayment. Many who prefer to avoid such debts try to rely on their own labour with the result that their dwellings are of very low standards and often positively dangerous.

When questioned about their preference if asked to move from the settlements by the authorities, more than half the respondents who had contributed some at least of their own labour preferred to be allotted government-built housing units on a hire purchase basis (emphasizing that the repayment instalments had to be within their means) (see table 9.1). The fact that only a little over 30 per cent showed a preference for being allotted land on which to build was a clear indication that the romanticized notion of 'dweller control' or a rejection of public housing was not a choice the respondents would have made had the option been available to them.

This conclusion was substantiated by the scramble for pucca tenements by the households in the Industrial Area labour colony under the present resettlement scheme, and this despite the fact that the tenements are on a monthly license basis when only 4.5 per cent of the respondents had indicated a preference for rental accomodation. As described in chapter 7, a difference in the security of tenure between the pucca tenements and the transit sites cannot be a major reason for the difference in demand for the two as in both cases the security is dubious and highly unfavourable for those being resettled.

The arguments put forward against the transit sites by those effected by the resettlement scheme were that, in addition to their limited financial means and technical capabilities, they simply did not have the time or energy to build their own houses. Even the older dwellings built on authorized plots reflect these limitations. The arguments interpreting the low standards of construction in typical non-plan settlements as reflecting the 'needs' and 'priorities' of the households living in them do not take into account the fact that no sane person 'needs' to live in a dwelling which leaks during the rains, or whose walls may collapse any time. People are *forced* to live in such circumstances.

Maintenance Costs

In addition to the costs of building, the quality of construction and the types of building material used entail disproportionately high recurring maintenance costs in relation to the total capital cost. Thatch needs replacing every second or third year. Rough timber beams or bamboo are eaten by white ants. Roofs blown off during wind storms or walls collapsing during the monsoons require reconstruction. The majority of households were spending between Rs.10 and Rs.200 per year on such maintenance, and such recurring costs can result in little incremental improvement despite incremental investment, because each new investment simply goes into replacing something rather than adding to the total capital accumulated in the dwelling.

According to a crude estimate, the total investment in the structures in all the non-plan settlements in Chandigarh*, housing about 15 per cent of the city's population, was about Rs.9.38 million. This has to be seen in relation to the estimated value of Rs.1023.3 million of just the private residential building in the planned part of the city where the number of dwellings was only two and a half times that in the non-plan settlements (Chandigarh Administration, 1974:59). Such difference in value demonstrates the absolute scarcity of investment surplus in the settlements.

Although it has frequently been argued that such non-plan housing investment represents very large sums in absolute terms, particularly in the relatively more affluent Latin American countries, the absolute figures can be very misleading by themselves. The relatively smaller investments made by large

---

*Total monetary investment in dwellings made by owner households in the survey was Rs.207,359. Adding 13 per cent for investment in rented houses gives a total of Rs.234,314 for 5 per cent of the total households in the settlements and thus Rs.4.68 million for the total. Allowing a further 100 per cent on this figure for inflation and self-help labour gives Rs.9.38 million at 1974 prices.

sections of Third World urban populations compared to those made by small proportions of their wealthy minorities, only serves to demonstrate that the vast majorities of their populations do not control the bulk of national resources. On the contrary, the poor quality of building materials and the technically inferior building methods and processes they are forced to adopt mean that they obtain extremely poor returns from their investment. The life spans of some of the older and better quality dwellings in the labour colonies had already reached their end at the time of the survey, leading to many households living in dangerous conditions.

Potential for Additional Investment

The extent of labour, time and capital invested in housing did not necessarily reflect the full potential of the households in the survey. As already mentioned, a major factor inhibiting greater investment was insecurity of land tenure. Nearly 90 per cent of the owners indicated that they would have improved their dwellings had they had greater security.

Asked what improvements they would have made had they had security of tenure, the majority indicated that they would have tried to improve the structures and to make them 'pucca' (see table 9.2). Their second priority was to increase covered space. The concern to improve the quality of their dwellings did not indicate any great ability to bring about spectacular changes but a desire to eliminate some of the recurring maintenance problems and the hazards of fire and collapse. For a household with limited means, even making a change from a thatch roof to one of mud on timber boarding can represent a major financial commitment.

Table 9.2. Respondents by improvements which would have been made if security of tenure were granted.

	Number	%
Would make dwelling pucca	67	27.8
Would add more rooms	25	10.4
Would try to make dwelling pucca and add more rooms	82	34
Would have improved dwelling generally	27*	11.2
Could not afford to make any improvements	33	13.7
Any other	7	2.9
Total	241 (72% of sample)	100

*Eight said that security of tenure would have enabled them to get a loan from the government with which they could have affected improvements.
Tenants have been excluded.

Space Standards

In terms of the number of rooms per dwelling the range of covered space available to households in the survey varied from one to a maximum of six rooms, with some three-quarters of the households living in one- or two-roomed dwellings. However, the picture was not much different in this respect from the planned part of the city (table 9.3) where there was only a slightly greater proportion of households with four or more rooms. Taking size of household into account, the settlement households were living in slightly greater conditions of overcrowding (2.1 persons per room in the whole city and 2.5 persons per room in the settlements). In the case of the settlements there was a more direct relationship between household size and the number of rooms per dwelling than in the whole city.

These relationships, however, have to be regarded with a degree of caution as they do not reflect the actual area available to different households. The average per household in the settlements was about 200 square feet and the average per person about 42.5 square feet; unfortunately comparable figures were not available for the city as a whole.

This picture of overcrowding does not depict the totality of the situation in the settlements. To a considerable degree, the discomfort was minimized by the widespread use of outdoor space for a variety of purposes, and almost 80 per cent of the households were using some outdoor space. The single-storeyed construction of dwellings allowed virtually every household to carry out at least some household activities outdoors, cultural factors and traditional living habits, as well as climatic conditions, facilitating this.

From the point of view of improving conditions of overcrowding, when covered space is inadequate, access to outdoor space is very significant. For those having to cope with desperately scarce resources, the function of covered

Table 9.3. Distribution of households by number of rooms per household for the whole city and for the non-plan settlements.

Number of rooms per household	Chandigarh city* (%)	Non-plan settlements† (%)
One	38	42.3
Two	34.6	32.5
Three	14.7	16.8
Four	6.4	5.9
Five and above	6.2	2.2
Unspecified	0.1	0.3

Source: *Census of India, 1971, Chandigarh: Housing Report and Tables.
         †Field survey 1974.

space is often reduced to that of providing a lockable store for household possessions and for activities demanding privacy. Particularly during the extrememly hot summers, the ability to sleep outdoors becomes a definite asset, and is much more comfortable and healthy than several people sleeping in an ill-ventilated room.

In this respect the residents of the settlements were probably better off than their counterparts renting cheap private accomodation in the planned residential areas as the latter is mainly available in two- or three-storeyed buildings. Those living on the ground floors can probably also make use of outdoor space, but those on the first and second floors have to live in far greater discomfort, particularly if without access to balconies or roof terraces.

Case Histories

To end this chapter, a number of selected case histories are presented to highlight the relationship between the solutions devised at the household level and the external constraints imposed on them by the structure of the wider society. The problem with individual case histories is that each one is unique and there is a danger of over generalization on the basis of individual circumstances. Further, almost invariably, the very fact of their willingness to tell their life histories made these people the exception rather than the rule. The most typical and underprivileged households are not represented as they were neither sufficiently articulate nor forthcoming in describing their experiences to outsiders.

Perhaps what comes through most clearly from these so-called housing 'solutions', in the short term, is their extreme vulnerability to changes in the general economy and, in the long term, to the State's policies towards them. Some of those whose experiences are described have already been moved under the present resettlement scheme. For others resettlement will come sometime in the near future. The case histories present not only the responses of the individuals concerning their housing problems but also the way these relate to the changing problems of their sources of income. As the occupations of all the individuals fall within the so-called 'informal' sector (see Chapters 10 and 11) the vulnerability of such occupations and its impact on housing problems comes through clearly in their histories. At the same time, the relationship between non-plan residential and commercial developments in the city is highlighted.

Tenant Cobbler from Rajasthan

This young cobbler was twenty-two years old and had first come to Chandigarh six or seven years before. His family belonged to the class of small land-owning cultivators and he had had to leave home in search of work as the family's income was insufficient to support the whole household. He was sending money home regularly.

On first arriving in Chandigarh he had no ideas about what he was going to do. A friend suggested working as a cobbler, and after working for five or six days with another cobbler, he had launched off on his own. Six years before all the equipment required – a chisel, a metal base for hammering and a couple of other instruments – had cost him only Rs.30. He had bought these from the Nehru-Shastri markets which were then in their heyday (see page 200). He was now buying his materials from the same supplier who had been moved to Sector 34. Because of the remoteness of the relocation site, the supplier made regular visits to the labour colony in Sector 26 as many cobblers were living there.

The young man had chosen the labour colony in Sector 26 because a lot of other Rajasthanis were living there. He had decided to rent accommodation as he was very uncertain about his future plans. After six years of residence in the city, he was still renting because he did not want to lose his independence by owning his own house. As he was unmarried he had been able to return home a number of times for periods ranging from three months to a year. Because of this, to build or buy his own dwelling would have been an unnecessary trouble to him. As it was, he was sharing, with four or five others, a 'pucca' room with a cement floor and roof in a dwelling on an author-ized plot. They were jointly paying a rent of Rs.20 per month and as he was earning between Rs.10 and Rs.15 a day he did not mind paying Rs.4–5 per month rent. It would have been impossible for him to find such cheap accommodation in regular housing anywhere in the city.

He liked living in Chandigarh because of its cleanliness and the better income opportunities it offered. He felt that he and others from his sort of background had improved their living habits by watching the affluent of the city, just as they had improved their economic situations from those prevailing in their rural homes. Although he was unhappy about the poor environmental standards of the labour colony and with living in one room with four others, he did not mind it too much because he spent most of the day walking around the higher income residential sectors.

He said that if he tried building even a 'kutcha' house for himself, it would cost him at least Rs.800–900 at current prices and a 'pucca' one of the type in which he was living would cost Rs.2000 (at 1974 prices). He had considered the possibility of buying the house as he could now probably afford it, but had not done so for fear of becoming tied to the city. He had not been home for two years and was not sure about how long he would stay there on his next visit.

He did not think any of the residents in his colony owned regular houses in the planned part of the city, although a few such as labour contractors and shop owners were quite well off.

His priorities can be seen as representing those of tenants in the settlements in general. An outright condemnation of subletting *per se* denies the existance of a group with such priorities. Some people simply choose to rent accommodation within their means and therefore avoid the problem of building and rebuilding for an uncertain period of time. However, it is important to point out that this cobbler was very fortunate in many respects. Being unmarried, his space requirements were limited, and he could save regularly. If with the same income, he had had four or five dependents, he might well have been forced to build because he could not afford to pay rent.

Sikh Carpenter Owning his Own House and Subletting One Room

This old man, aged somewhere between seventy and eighty, owned an authorized dwelling in the Industrial Area labour colony. His memory had deteriorated considerably and his real age was anyone's guess. In the winter of 1974 he was suffering severe rheumatic pains because of the cold and was virtually immobile. In better days he had been an extremely skilled carpenter and had worked in many places. He proudly showed some superb samples of his earlier work, which included intricate models for building and development work as well as suitcases made from plywood. Now, because of old age and ill health, he could barely make a living by doing odd jobs. He was using his house for both living and working. Of the three rooms on the ground floor, one was exclusively a workshop where he kept his tools and raw materials. His house was one of only two or three in the colony with a first floor.

He was living alone in Chandigarh because his family had deserted him. His neighbours said that his wife and children used to show up occasionally when they needed money or assistance from him, but now that he was in a precarious situation, they had not been seen for a long time. He did not even know of their whereabouts.

With the ability to work fast disappearing, he had been trying to get a government pension for old persons with no sources of income. Months of trying and several trips to various government offices had got him nowhere except to have collected a large number of intricate application forms and instructions for obtaining documents such as birth certificates, affidavits, medical certificates, etc. He could neither fill in the forms nor produce any of the other documents, particularly the birth certificate, which he had never possessed. His story is an edited version of his own words.

'I have led an active and eventful life and worked for several important persons and organizations. Originally, I belonged to West Punjab where I used to work for the Railways. I was displaced during Partition and whatever I had in Pakistan was left behind. As a refugee, I first went to Delhi where I got a job as a carpenter with Delhi Cloth Mills. Thirteen or fourteen years ago, I decided to come to Chandigarh because it was going to be the new capital of Punjab. Here I only worked on a daily wage basis. I could earn more money that way. I even used to go to other towns like Solan and Simla if any work was available there. Sometimes, I used to stay there for months at a time. It was relatively easy to get residential accommodation in these towns at a monthly rent of Rs.15–20 which I could easily afford. Now, I cannot take much physical exertion. I do whatever little work I can find at home only. I have been working like this for the last two or three years.

I used to be able to make good money here in the early years. Having started from a scratch after Partition, I managed to save quite a lot from my job in Delhi. Most of that got spent in marrying my daughters. Then they deserted me. I came to Chandigarh alone and have been living on my own ever since. Whatever money I made here, I spent in building this house and getting myself established for working on my own. Now, sometimes, I can still get work for Rs.60 to 100. That can keep me going for a month or so. Normally, I just get work for Rs.2 or 4 and that too after a gap of several days. At times, I cannot even afford a cup of tea.

When I first came to Chandigarh, I used to live in Bajwada. When they evicted us from there, I got a room on rent in this colony. I did not like paying rent for the kind of accommodation I could easily build myself. In any case, the owner was paying only Rs.1.50 to the government and charging me ten times as much. The plot of land on which my house is built was lying vacant. All the houses on both sides, and in front of it now, were built afterwards. They are all unauthorized. Even I could not get a plot

Figure 9.4. The sikh carpenter looks at his house proudly despite the cracks in the wall indicating its precarious condition.

allotted in my name because the Government had stopped new allotments. Fed up with paying rent, I decided to build my own house anyway.

I bought a truckload of 2000 bricks. At that time they used to cost only Rs.20 a thousand. With them, I first built the back room. I did most of the construction myself and hired only one unskilled labourer to help me with carrying and lifting materials. Being a carpenter, I did all the joinery work myself too. I used mud for mortar and the walls are only 4½ inches thick. Now they are beginning to look unstable. The roof is made of a layer of earth on bamboos.

Then I started pleading with the government clerk who used to come to collect rent from the authorized plot holders to accept it from me as well. After three years of persistant requesting, he agreed to start doing so and included my name on the official list of authorized lessees.

Slowly, I added the two rooms in the front. Three or four years ago, I built the room on the first floor which I have sublet to another carpenter for the last three months. He pays me Rs.25 per month for it. With no surety of income from my own work, his rent is my only regular income now.

In all, I must have spent about Rs.500 to 600 on the whole house besides my own labour. Materials used to be cheap before. These days, it is as if everything is on fire. Inflation has made life miserable.

There are rumours that the Government is planning to demolish this colony in the near future. Some other development seems to have been planned on this land as a lot of bricks and other building materials are being deposited on the vacant land adjacent to us. The last two or three lines of houses, including mine, are likely to be the first ones to be demolished.

I do not know what I will do if my house is demolished. All residents of the colony are trying to pressurize the Government to give us alternative accommodation if we are evicted. They say that the small tenements under construction in Sector 30 are for people evicted from here. But those are double storeyed which is of no use for persons like me. A carpenter has to cut and chop timber, hammer nails, etc. How can that be done on the first floor? Besides I need space for storing my raw materials and equipment. One small room just won't be sufficient for my requirements.

Besides, the rents are likely to be much higher. There are some here who cannot afford to pay Rs.1.50 per month. When the rent collector does not come for six months and then demands Rs.9 in one go, many simply cannot pay. If they start charging Rs.30 or 40 per month, I will be doomed. I am not even capable of building another house like this one any more.'

As feared by this carpenter, his house was among the first to be affected by the resettlement scheme. If he was allotted a pucca tenement at Rs.30 per month plus service charges, it is difficult to know how he would be surviving. The change would have also deprived him of his rental income. The government pension, which he had finally succeeded in getting in 1975, was only Rs.40 per month. He could not have chosen the transit site option, as he was in no condition to build another house. At the same time, even his old house in the labour colony had reached a precarious condition. It was a frightening experience to climb to his first floor with the badly cracked walls and shaky roof. It was unlikely that the house would have lasted another two or three years without major reconstruction, which he was not in a position to undertake. Thus neither 'dweller control' nor the government's subsidized resettlement scheme really offered a 'solution' to his housing problem. For people like him, there really is no housing solution possible within the existing structure of society except through a State welfare scheme. Perhaps he was destined to die on the pavement, homeless, like thousands of others in the country?

Buffaloe Keeper in the Unauthorized Kumhar Colony

'Originally we belonged to West Punjab. Displaced during partition, we first went to the Karnal district in Haryana. Since the government paid compensation only to those refugees who had property in Pakistan, we received nothing. We belonged to the class of petty traders in livestock who live by their labour. We did not own any property. With the small savings between four or five households, we managed to buy 10 or 11 acres of land in Haryana. As it was insufficient to support all households' members, many of us had to work as agricultural labourers. Wages were low and work terribly hard.

My father-in-law had some contacts in U.P. where he managed to make a deal for 200 or 250 acres of land and asked us all to join him there. So we sold our land in Karnal and first came to Chandigarh because a couple of my relations were here. Unfortunately the deal made by my father-in-law never came off. Having sold off our land in Karnal at Rs.1200 per acre we have ended up remaining landless because since then land prices have been increasing continuously. Now that same land is not available for even Rs.12,000 per acre.

When we first came to Chandigarh eight or nine years ago, we had a thatch hut here. Some of the houses surrounding ours were already there. A few years later we replaced

Figure 9.5. The buffaloe keeper and his school-going son replacing the timber and mud roof of their house with one supported by metal girders.

Figure 9.6. His wife and daughter-in-law assist with the mud plastering.

the hut with a flat-roofed structure built from second-hand bricks, as the hut was about to collapse. Then we added the second hut in which my eldest son and his wife now live. When I started keeping buffaloes, we built the third hut. Now the main structure in which myself, my wife and our younger children live needs to have its roof replaced. We must do that before the monsoons as it is sure to collapse during the rains. The two flat-roofed huts cost me Rs.300 each. The main structure has walls made of pucca bricks which is why it is still standing. We built it four years ago and it cost us Rs.500 then. Now I have another truckload of brick bats for rebuilding it. The rough timber beams have been eaten by white ants although we had coated them with coal tar. The thatch roofs cannot survive for more than two years without the white ants getting at them too. This time I intend to get rid of the problem for good by replacing timber with iron girders at least in the main structure. The three girders I will need will cost me Rs.120 each. I can get them from the Industrial Area. All the other materials like timber boarding and small timber rafters for supporting it, I will be able to get from *kabadiwallas*. I expect the whole rebuilding operation will cost about Rs.650 excluding the family labour.

Of my four sons, the three older ones work. The fourth one goes to school. I am not sending any of my three younger daughters to school. I do not think education will be particularly useful for them and in any case, what is the use of having children if they are not playing around the house. My eldest son is twenty years old now. He and the next son were working already when we first came to Chandigarh around 1965. One worked as an employee in a *dhaba* for a year and a half. The second used to ply a *rehri*. In the beginning even I worked as a *rehriwalla*, selling roasted peanuts and other snacks in front of the colleges. Later I gave it up and started keeping buffaloes for selling milk. Now I stay at home and only my sons go out to work. Recently we had to sell one of our two *rehris* because it had become quite dilapidated. So now the third son has started working as a *rickshaw* puller. You can get an old *rickshaw* on hire for Rs.2 per day and a new one for Rs.2.50.

I could not educate my elder sons because both in Pakistan and in Haryana, we lived in rural areas where either there were no schools at all or, if there were any, they were far away. It is difficult to send a small child 3 or 4 miles away on his own.

Chandigarh was our first experience of living in a city. Because there are many educational facilities available here, I decided to educate at least one of my sons to find out what education is all about. If I live long enough I will try and give him the highest education possible but that will depend on his *karma* and fate as well*.

City life suits us well. Agricultural work is really tough. Even after a whole day of hard manual work one only earns Rs.5 or 6. In the city it is much easier because one just buys and sells fruit and can do reasonably well on that. There would be no problem at all if the enforcement staff would not harass us. The trouble is we do not have a license for my son's *rehri*.

In the early years, we had a *rehri* license because the Estate Office used to issue them easily. But business was not very good so we sold the *rehri* along with the license. Then

---

*Just a couple of months after this interview, the son going to school fractured his right femur in an accident. As this resulted in his losing a year, he refused to go back to school. He said he felt ashamed of being left behind by his classmates. Instead, the parents decided to marry him off, although he was still only sixteen or seventeen years old. Now he has a twelve or thirteen year old bride and works as an unlicensed *rehri* plier.

we improvised our present cycle *rehri* from second-hand parts bought from *kabadiwallas*. This type of *rehri* is more convenient because one can cover longer distances. The other type has to be pushed on foot all the time which is slow and tiring. The real problem is the danger of getting caught without a *rehri* licence. Both my sons and those of my relatives living nearby have a lot of trouble on this account. The other day my sons had brought watermelons from the wholesale market and unloaded them for selling near the entrance to the settlement. The enforcement staff not only took away all the melons but also the plank they use for displaying the melons. To recover the *rehri* a fine of Rs.30 has to be paid each time. Last month one of my relative's sons had to pay Rs.300 to 400 in fines alone. Now he has managed to get a licence by paying a bribe of Rs.150 to someone in the Estate Office.

When they confiscate a *rehri*, it cannot be brought back on the same day. You can go and reclaim it the following day by paying Rs.30. I think they have raised it to Rs.50 now. If one is unable to pay the fine within a week, the impounded *rehris* are auctioned by the authorities. The day before yesterday, the *kabadiwalla* in this settlement bought three *rehris* in the auction. He even bought chairs, boxes and tables because they seize whatever they can lay their hands on. The persons who cannot collect enough money to pay the fines in time are done for.

The people are really fed up with the enforcement staff now. The other day a lot of *rehriwallas* beat up one of the inspectors. They auction *rehris* worth Rs.1000 for Rs.100. Anyone who cannot pay the fine of Rs.50 loses his *rehri*. We have a rehri workers' union but what can it do? It can only help those who have licences but the Estate Office has stopped issuing new licences. You either have to pay bribes or have 'approach'. Someone who cannot do either has no way out. I am prepared to pay a bribe of Rs.50 to Rs.100 if 'you' can get me a licence. The Estate Office's reasoning that there will be too many *rehris* if they continue issuing new licences does not make sense. How can even a government employee who cannot make both ends meet on his salary survive if he is not allowed to ply a *rehri*? For illiterate persons like us it is impossible to even get salaried jobs except the most low paid ones. We have to do this type of work to lead a reasonable life. In any case, they have other interests. To you and me they say that they have stopped issuing licences but in reality they have done no such thing. Once I got a licence myself by taking gifts of fruit to one of the officers concerned. Whoever gives them a bribe or feeds them can get a licence any day.

Even with regard to housing, the point is that if one has a reasonable sized plot one can make do modestly. If the government offers us anything at all for moving from here it is only extremely small plots like the ones in the labour colonies. That makes life extremely difficult for us. Even here we will need more space in the near future. After all, I have four sons and three of them are married already. Even the buffaloes need a shelter. It would be ideal if we could get houses built according to our requirements and pay for them in instalments. If it is more economical for us to build houses individually, then the government should give us plots at fixed prices and loans for house construction. We can pay back in a number of years.

I think there must be several persons in this settlement who could build houses in this way provided the government sells them plots at low prices. A few of those doing commercial work could probably afford to pay market rents but they do not want to live in rented accommodation. I do not know about those who own land in rural areas. They might eventually return there as they keep going back, frequently. The ones having fixed jobs are fairly settled. Most people here prefer salaried jobs because they bring both security and a regular income. For us they are no good as at the most we could get jobs as *chowkidars* or *malis* which is hopeless.

The trouble is that we cannot have a strong organization to fight collectively. We have a 'panchayat' in the settlement but it cannot work very effectively because it has no funds. Also the status of the whole settlement is unauthorized. The most it can do is to resist the demolition of huts or other harassment of colony dwellers by the enforcement staff. In fact the only strength we have is of our votes. Till now we have always supported the Congress but it has never kept its promises. During the last elections I personally organized a lot of support among our community for the Congress candidate. When he got elected as an MP, and we went to see him, we were not allowed to go near his house. He keeps guard dogs to protect himself. In the next election we might support the *Jan Sangh*. Their members have been doing quite a lot for us recently. A few months ago, they arranged for the settlement behind the wholesale market to be burnt down during a raid by the enforcement staff and later got the government to pay compensation to all the hut owners for the damage. Those people have been able to rebuild much better huts now.'*

Tailor from U.P. in Kumhar Colony

This tailor was working full time in the settlement itself. He was among the most enterprising of the residents and was extremely proud of his achievements through sheer hard work since coming to Chandigarh five years earlier. He had built himself two rooms to start with and had slowly added three more on the sides. One of these he was using as his work place, one he had rented out to a small shopkeeper and the third he offered to persons in difficulty but meant to use for keeping his buffaloe when he got one. He belonged to a small group of articulate people in the settlement who were its 'intellectual' leaders, and his 6 ft × 7 ft tailoring shop was the centre where everyone gathered to discuss daily events and philosophize on the predicament of settlement residents. His story and some of his own and his friends views are presented in his own words.

'When I first came to Chandigarh I had a debt of Rs.500 or 600 to pay off in the village. Seeing what little many persons in this settlement, even those who have been here for fifteen or twenty years have achieved, I have not done badly at all in five years. I have paid off all my debts, I have built five rooms, I own three sewing machines instead of one now and I also have two cycle *rickshaws* which I have rented out. Recently, I have also started stocking small amounts of cloth to sell to my clients and if it works, I will have a small side business of selling cloth.

I get a rent of Rs.20 per month for the shop and Rs.2 per day for each of my two *rickshaws*. It is good that I invested my savings in buying them sometime back. They cost me Rs.600 each. Now they cost Rs.900. I rent them out to whoever wants them. Sometimes people do not pay me the rent but what difference does it make to me if a poor man does not pay even for ten days. Here you will find a lot of consideration for the poor. My work from tailoring is also very good. I am the only full time tailor in the

---

*Several hundred huts in this settlement were burnt down in a spate of mysterious fires in April 1980. Perhaps the buffaloe keeper was amongst the victims and has been 'rehabilitated' in a one-and-a-half room tenement or a 10 ft by 40 ft transit site.

Figure 9.7. The tailor and two of his friends in his shop.

whole settlement. A few others work as tailors part time to supplement their incomes from salaried employment. On a good day, I can work from 6.00 a.m. to 6.00 p.m. and earn up to Rs.30 in one day. But that is only when there is so much work. I enjoy being my own boss and like working hard. It is only through hard work that one can achieve anything.

The same work in the village had left me in debt. Actually, even now, were it possible for me to make a reasonable living in the village, I would prefer to stay there. After all, one does not leave one's home except when all other paths are closed. My village is 150 miles from here. We do not own any land there and income opportunities are extremely limited. My elder brother, his family and my mother are still there. Actually I came here because one of our relatives had run away with someone else's woman. I hoped to bring him back to his senses and save the family's reputation. I never succeeded in persuading him to go back, but in the process ended up staying here myself.

I learnt my tailoring skills as people learn in the villages; working here for six months, there for six months and so on. Acquiring a skill is a difficult job. It is just like studying where you have to start from learning the alphabet. Actually learning never ends. You can always learn more but it is necessary to acquire at least sufficient skill to be able to earn a living.

You ask me why I stay in this settlement when I could afford to rent regular accommodation? You see, if it were not for about ten persons like me this colony could not have survived till now. One of my friends has just returned after going round several offices. He does not belong to the 'panchayat' here but he goes round government offices for the sake of the settlement residents. When an appropriate law does not exist, it has to be framed from a scratch. We see our work as getting new laws framed and put into force. The government simply says no to everything. Don't do this, don't do that, and so on. But for us it is a necessity to do something. We are sitting on this land by force. We have no rights within the existing legal framework.

As things stand, we have two possible predicaments facing us in the future. One is that as and when we are moved from here, the government will give us some alternative accommodation. The other, which is equally possible is that we will be simply kicked out. What will we do in the second case? Go over to Pakistan? As we are Indians, the government *has* to give us some place to live. After all we are not birds who can live on trees if the government refuses to give us land.

We are not asking for houses in return for nothing. We are prepared to pay for them, but in accordance with our means and abilities. We feel that the government should make three alternatives available. The first should be for those who can afford to pay between Rs.5000 to even Rs.10,000 for building houses but in instalments spread over a number of years. There are several households in this settlement who would be prepared to save Rs.50 per month for the purpose.

The second case would be that of government salaried employees: a monthly deduction from their salaries could be made at source for repayment.

The third alternative has to be for the daily wage labourers who cannot afford either of the first two. To them the government should give plots provided with foundations. They can slowly build the structures themselves. It is inevitable that a majority of them will only be able to build huts. If the government does not like seeing huts, it should count the number of such persons and provide them with proper houses instead of demolishing the little they are able to do for themselves. How can they be expected to build much else when they earn so little?'

10

The Growth of Non-Plan Employment

This part of the book deals with another typical characteristic of Third World cities – the widespread phenomenon of hyper-tertiarization of their urban economies, particularly the expansion of petty trading and service activities.

The Problem of Third World Un(der)employment

As in the case of squatter or semi-legal settlements, during recent years attitudes towards petty commodity production and petty trading and services in Third World cities have changed. They are now seen as a potential means for sustaining autonomous economic growth with the help of public policies especially framed to support them. The concern with the accelerating rates of un(der)employment in these countries has led to this change in focus. The inadequacies of development models proposed for Third World countries in the early 1950s, formulated in terms of achieving accelerated rates of economic growth, without considering employment, have become increasingly clear. Then it was simply assumed that economic growth would take care of the employment problem by its 'filter down effect'.

By the late 1960s it was realized that 'accelerated growth' strategies, based on maximizing gross national product, were neither leading to the desired level of income redistribution nor solving the problems of poverty and unemployment in the Third World. As pointed out by Chenery *et al.* (1974:xiii)

> It is now clear that more than a decade of rapid growth in underdeveloped countries has been of little or no benefit to perhaps a third of their population. Although the average per capita income in the Third World has increased by 50% since 1960, the growth has been very unequally distributed among countries, regions within countries and socio-economic groups.

The increasing preoccupation with Third World poverty and unemployment, and the clarification that economic growth *per se* would not alleviate poverty within a given time, was also a consequence of increasing political and economic crises in many underdeveloped countries. As the problem of unemployment worsened, it was increasingly the subject of international debate. In 1964, the ILO adopted the Employment Policy Convention (No. 122) and in 1969 launched its World Employment Programme (WEP). A series of country studies was undertaken to evolve 'employment-orientated strategies of development'. In all these studies the emphasis shifted from the formulation of development strategies based only on economic growth to policies focusing on employment as a major objective (see Thorbecke, 1973).

The ILO country studies were accompanied by a number of city studies followed by a number of sector studies, showing a tendency in development models focusing on lower and lower levels of generality. It was the ILO Kenya study, completed in 1972 (ILO, 1972), which led to the identification of the so-called 'informal sector' (see p. 6) as a target area for increasing income and employment opportunities. The 'informal sector' was defined as comprising those economic activities largely escaping recognition, enumeration, regulation and protection by the government. The Kenya study reported that employment in the informal sector, although often regarded as unproductive and stagnant, was in fact competitive, labour intensive, using locally-produced inputs, developing its own skills and technology, and family or locally owned. In Kenya's urban centres this accounted for 28–33 per cent of all those employed, and the study placed the greatest emphasis on its productive role, advocating a positive attitude on the part of government towards its promotion*.

The 'informal sector' concept has developed from earlier dualist models (see p. 6). The definitions of the sectors have varied depending on the criteria used. For instance, they have been seen as two juxtaposed systems of production – one derived from capitalist production, the other from the peasant system (McGee, 1973b:138); as two types of economy: a 'firm centred economy' and a 'bazaar type of economy' (Geertz, 1963:28); as two circuits: the 'upper' and 'lower' circuits (Santos, 1971); and as two sectors: 'a high-profit/high-wage international oligopistic sector and a low-profit/low-wage competitive capitalistic sector' (Brown, 1974).

The significant difference between the informal/formal sector concept (Hart, 1973) and earlier dualist approaches was the distinction it made between different types of income opportunities, i.e. between wage employment and casual or self-employment. It was this aspect of Hart's formulation of the informal sector which led to reappraisals of the role and function of small-scale activities in Third World cities and a reassessment of employment strategies and proposals such that,

> from being the Cinderalla of underdevelopment, the 'informal sector' could thus become a major source of economic growth. (Leys, 1975:266)

The view that the informal sector has a positive role in employment generation and economic growth has led to a wide range of policy proposals such as recommending government support and recognition of it through granting contracts to small enterprises, making credit available to them, and strengthening the links between the informal and formal sectors.

*For a criticism of the ILO Kenya report, see Leys (1975).

The informal/formal sectors model, like all earlier dualist models, evades the question of the relationship between different production and distribution systems within the structure of national and international economies. As in the case of non-plan settlements, reform and improvement is sought through independent policies for the informal sector irrespective of its interaction with the formal sector.

By focusing on the 'relationship between different elements of the productive ensemble' rather than on defining 'two sectors', Gerry (1974, 1977), Bienefeld (1975) and others have challenged the validity of the sectoral analysis based on the outward characteristics of different types of activities. As pointed out by Gerry (1974:5)

> it is probably this preoccupation with characteristics and the refining of definitions which has caused such studies to neglect the fact that, to an important extent, it is the relations between these different systems or sub-systems of production which determine those phenomena which will characterise each of the elements of the ensemble, and will lay the foundations for the functioning of the whole.

In a number of studies examination of the 'relations of production' of the petty commodity sector, which includes artisan production and trading within the urban economy, showed that the growth of petty commodity production was involutionary*. Writing about the 'pettiness' or the smallness of the majority of informal activities, Gerry (1974:13) has pointed out that

> Their present situation is one of mere reproduction, in the majority of cases, of their conditions of existence. Certain among them do make the transition, through a process of accumulation and often with outside financial assistance, to small capitalist enterprises; however, the majority are characteristically stunted in terms of individual and global development and growth by a structural imbalance at the local, regional, national and international levels. The clearest phenomenon of imbalance is that between the growth of industrial wage employment [the 'formal' sector] and that of the [urban] population of working age. Hence when [it] is stated that the 'informal' sector's growth of employment in a majority of Third World countries probably outstrips that of the 'formal' sector's, it must be made clear that this is a necessary response to extremely unfavourable conditions, and not necessarily an indication that the petty producers and traders, artisans and labourers are teetering on the edge of a technical and employment revolution.

The objective here is not to go into the intricacies of the various levels of the current theoretical debates†, but to examine the status of one particular category of the so-called informal sector's activities which have emerged in

---

*See Gerry (1974), Bose (1974) and King (1974).

†For a comprehensive review of the literature on the subject see Moser (1976).

Chandigarh. The potential for achieving a benign relationship between petty trading and service activities and the State, within the existing parameters of the national economy – a major policy recommendation arising out of the informal/formal sector analysis – can thus be investigated.

As mentioned in chapter 5, by 1975 over 50 per cent of the total trading and service enterprises in the city had emerged in non-plan forms and locations. The city's planning framework gave no consideration to the income and employment problems of large sections of the population. Persistent attempts have been made to curb or even prevent the functioning of non-plan enterprises. According to the protagonists of the employment and economic growth potential of the informal sector, the Chandigarh authorities are 'misguided' in their negative attitude towards such activities and ought to change to a policy of support and promotion rather than harassment. In one of the few detailed studies of the functioning of hawkers within an urban economy McGee (1973a) arrived at similar conclusions, making a plea for more appropriate planning and administrative policies for Third World cities rather than a continued reliance on inappropriate ones derived from Western experience.

What is proposed here is that the underlying conflicts are far more fundamental and that there are very severe constraints on the changes of policy which the authorities themselves can affect, because of their role in maintaining the *status quo*. Thus as in the case of Chandigarh's non-plan settlements the city's plan has had a major impact on the status of non-plan commercial and service activities.

The shift of emphasis towards generating employment opportunities as an explicit component of economic growth and development strategies has tended to place employment on a pedestal in its own right. The questions to be asked are: employment in what and leading to what kinds of improvement for those employed in the typical labour-intensive and resource-starved, self-employment activities? Employment of *any* form for the majority of the Third World's low-income population may be acceptable in the short-term if in the long-term it is going to lead to a significant improvement for them. However, employment for the sake of employment, for example in low-productivity occupations with insecure and irregular incomes, cannot be seen as the main objective of long-term development strategies. Neither can employment in labour-intensive, small-scale and low-capital investment activities be labelled 'desirable' by itself.

The First Non-Plan Commercial Centre in Chandigarh

Non-plan commercial developments in Chandigarh started even before construction of the city began. Among the first migrants to the site were many refugees still on the look out for better opportunities to make a fresh start in life. The demand for basic goods and services by the technical staff and construction

Figure 10.1. A street in Bajwada.

labour living on the site offered bright prospects for starting small enterprises requiring little investment. From the very beginning, there was a clear inter-dependence between the low subsistance wages of the building labour and the cheap goods and services being provided by the first non-plan commercial enterprises in the city.

Bajwada, the village south of Sector 22 (see figure 7.3) and adjoining the temporary bus terminal for the site, began to attract pioneers who had pinned their hopes on a bright future in the new city. As construction started and building contractors, thousands of labourers and technical and government staff moved to the site, Bajwada responded by catering for their needs. Besides supplying essential commodities, one of its major characteristics from the beginning was the production of traditional items such as *charpoys* and tin trunks, ginning cotton for quilts, and making furniture at short notice. Because of the availability of basic necessities, a large settlement of construction workers grew up in its vicinity.

Initially, the newcomers either bought or rented land or buildings from local villagers. Later, the village was acquired by the CPO. The Estate Office demarcated temporary sites nearby and leased them to the petty shopkeepers and producers at nominal monthly rents. Eight or nine years later, when considerable planned development had taken place, it was decided to clear Bajwada. When the official 'Bajwada Liquidation Scheme' was formulated in 1959, there were 242 authorized lessees. The actual number of enterprises operating was much greater, although exact records had not been kept.

Under the scheme, alternative sites on the shopping streets of residential sectors were offered to the lessees. These were sold at the concessional rate of

Figure 10.2. A small tin-trunk manufacturer in Bajwada.

75 per cent of the price fetched by similar plots at the last auction. Payment had to be made in four equal annual instalments.

All occupants were informed of the government's decision by individual notice and by the beat of drum.

Among those not considered eligible for alternative accommodation were (i) persons who had not been 'recognized' as authorized occupants of sites in Bajwada; (ii) 'squatters'; and (iii) *kabadis* and *bharpunjas*, because no sites were available in the new city for these trades.

Of 278 applicants, 181 were allotted sites or built shops in nine or ten different sectors. At that time all these sectors, with the exception of three or four, were hardly developed and business prospects were extremely poor. Twenty-two people who could not afford to purchase sites in planned sectors were given temporary shop sites in the labour colonies. The rest were found ineligible for allotment.

In 1975, fifteen years later, Bajwada remained 'unliquidated'. Those who were allotted alternative sites or built shops accepted them but did not necessarily move there. Some of them filed appeals in the High Court on the grounds that the alternative accomodation was unsuitable for their requirements. These included a man who was running a bus transport company and another owning a flour mill, both of whom had been allotted small 'booths' in residential sectors. While their cases remained pending in the High Court for several years, these people could not be evicted by force. In spite of several eviction attempts, the *kabadis* and *bharpunjas*, for whom there was no accommodation planned in the new city, continued working from Bajwada. Most of the others who had not been considered 'eligible' for rehabilitation also stayed on.

The main argument for clearing Bajwada was that its location and form violated the master plan. It was tolerated only as long as planned facilities were not available. This in itself defined its status in relation to the plan. However, the real reason for its clearance was that those working there had not acquired commercial land-use rights by the rules specified for planned development. It was important for the authorities to allow no precedent to be set by which their official procedures might be challenged. Further, those who had paid auctioned prices for commercial plots expected the authorities to prevent others paying only nominal lease rents or no land-use charges at all from benefiting from this unfair competition.

The concept of 'unfair competition' of this type is valid only when the competing parties are doing so from positions of equal strength. Whereas all the planned category traders and entrepreneurs, by virtue of their ability to pay the high entry costs for planned development, *had* to be above a certain economic status, Bajwada housed a far wider spectrum of economic circumstances. Certainly, it included trade, service and production enterprises which could easily conform to the economic demands of planned facilities. At the same time, it had a large number of those who were financially incapable of sustaining high costs of land and buildings. In some cases the low capital resources of the owners of enterprises resulted in this. In others, the nature of the commodities or services being provided in relation to the purchasing power of the customers demanded a reduction of overheads to the minimum. Quilts, *charpoys,* earthen-ware pots, all commodities used by even the poorest citizens, belonged to this category.

Furthermore, the official clearance scheme gave no consideration to the importance of location and the concentration of a wide range of activities in the same place, to the enterprises concerned. Bajwada was essentially drawing its customers from the whole city and not catering simply for a local market. Being in the vicinity of a high-density residential sector and on the road linking the city to other areas, further added to its locational advantages. The official scheme attempted to disperse eligible lessees mainly into unattractive locations, designed to cater for local markets. It did not even consider what was to be the fate of the smaller enterprises, the so-called 'squatter' category in the main, and those most dependent on being in the vicinity of a thriving commercial centre. Thus, not surprisingly, the Bajwada clearance scheme was far from successful.

In 1975, the Administration had another list of 231 'recognized' squatters in Bajwada. Again it was not comprehensive. The definition of what constituted Bajwada remained arbitrary. Just across the road there was a long line of one- or two-person enterprises engaged in shoe repairs, selling second-hand shoes and earthenware pots, and barbering and dyeing. The group of recognized squatters had made an agreement with the Administration that no newcomers would be allowed to join them and, therefore, the number considered for rehabilitation remained the same. In effect, it merely amounted to the newcomers sitting on the other side of the road. The increase in numbers had not stopped.

The Growth of Other Non-Plan Modes of Operation

Alongside Bajwada, other forms of non-plan commercial and service activities had been growing in the city. Many hawkers on foot or bicycle, and *rehriwallas* had appeared on the scene. They provided daily necessities such as fresh fruit and vegetables, popular snacks, and sweets at the doorsteps of the early settlers. They had to go on long rounds to serve their dispersed customers. Slowly, as the low-income population of Sectors 22 and 23 grew, many of them started congregating either near the rapidly developing shopping streets of these sectors, or on open spaces adjacent to high-density residential areas. Some only worked as *pattriwallas* without being mobile during any part of the day. Others, particularly fruit and vegetable *rehriwallas*, spent most of the day going from one area to another and came to the higher density locations only in the evenings. Such locations started functioning as non-plan markets with all the

Figure 10.3. A mobile *rehriwalla* 'doing the rounds'.

Figure 10.4. *Pattriwallas* selling used clothing.

characteristics of a bazaar-type economy (Geertz, 1963) and became focal points for attracting large numbers of both customers and sellers, particularly in the evenings.

In addition to such markets, groups of *dhabas* selling cheap cooked meals, tea shops, and hot and cold snack sellers grew up in the vicinity of building sites where there were large numbers of construction labourers, or adjoining other busy locations such as the points where buses connecting Chandigarh to other towns stopped. In such locations some people had built *khokhas*, others had *rehris* and many simply worked from the ground as *pattriwallas*.

Similarly to the case of non-plan settlements, as the pace of planned development increased, the continued growth in the numbers of *rehris*, *pattris* and *khokhas* became a cause of alarm for the CPO. The unauthorized use of land, particularly by the non-plan markets, was interpreted as an 'enforcement' problem. The enforcement staff were instructed to prevent such non-plan enterprises from being stationary anywhere. This resulted in frequent confiscation of the goods of *rehri-* and *pattriwallas*. Some of them escaped this persecution by bribing the enforcement staff, but generally it caused a lot of resentment among the petty traders.

From the beginning, retail distribution of fruit and vegetables was almost totally monopolized by *rehri-* and *pattriwallas*. They were among the first of the petty traders to form an association for collective action to defend their interests. In 1957, the Fruit and Vegetable Sellers' Association had already organized a strike to resist wholesale traders raising their commission rates. In

Figure 10.5. A *dhaba* with charpoys and tables laid out for serving meals.

1959, it took up the issue of working conditions and rights of fruit and vegetable sellers and made a representation to the Estate Office demanding the demarcation of a number of sites from which they could function without constant harassment.

According to an official document, 'The entire problem was examined in detail in the year 1959, and the Capital Project Authorities earmarked certain places in the city for the parking of *rehris*. Simultaneously, hand-cart bye-laws were framed under the Punjab Municipal Act, 1911, and notified in November 1959.'

However, by defining the specially earmarked areas as '*rehri* parking sites', no consideration was given to *pattriwallas* or *khokhas*. They remained totally unprotected. Owing to the relative security the possession of a *rehri* began to signify, many *pattriwallas* who could afford it acquired *rehris*. Some *khokha* enterprises also replaced their minimal structures by *rehris*. But in these cases *rehris* were only useful as a passport to some legal protection; they did not need them for their work. These enterprises mainly retailed commodities such as provisions, cloth and general mechandise, or provided services such as cycle and shoe repairs. The majority, unless extremely small scale, were incompatible with mobility, a characteristic considered essential for *rehris* by the Administration.

With the first hand-cart byelaws, a system of issuing licences for *rehris* at nominal annual fees was also introduced, and the parking of *rehris anywhere* but the authorized sites was forbidden.

Figure 10.6. An immobile *rehriwalla* using additional ground space.

Figure 10.7. Impounded *rehris* and rickshaws standing outside the Estate Office.

The authorities' attempt to enforce mobility among the non-plan enterprises did not arise simply out of a stereotype notion about their mode of operation, although such stereotypes do exist. In the different context of Hong Kong, McGee (1973a:22) has overemphasized the importance of the colonial stereotype of the native hawker among British planners and administrators in similarly insisting on mobility among hawkers. The preoccupation of Chandigarh Administration, as of most urban authorities elsewhere, was to prevent permanent land occupation, particularly for commercial purposes, by means other than paying the market value.

Experiments with Different Rules

With the available strength of the enforcement staff, enforcement of the rules proved impossible. In mid-1961, unable to control the growth of *rehris* by other means, the authorities fixed the maximum number of hand-carts permitted in the city at 956 on the basis of licences already issued.

Enforcement continued to prove difficult. The problems created by 'unauthorized' parking were discussed in a meeting of the local Advisory Committee at the end of 1965. It was decided to constitute a sub-committee to study the matter and as a result new hand-cart byelaws were issued early in 1967. In these:

(a) Provision was made to fix the maximum number of *rehris* from time to time.

(b) The licence fee was increased from Rs.12 to Rs.50.

(c) Provision was made requiring special 'designs' for *rehris* for specific trades.

(d) Driving licences for *rehri* pullers were introduced.

These byelaws were assailed in a writ petition filed by the Rehri Workers' Union in the Punjab and Haryana High Court. The court held that restriction could not be placed on the number of *rehris* and it reversed the decision to increase licence fees. It further ruled that the Administration might modify, delete or amend the byelaws and develop them in accordance with the law and the Constitution. Restrictions on *rehri* parking times as suggested by the sub-committee could not be enforced until made law.

Another sub-committee was constituted in 1969 to study the problem again. This sub-committee unanimously decided to *abolish* the plying of *rehris* altogether. It also recommended that the Senior Town Planner and Chief Architect should find suitable areas in various sectors where cheap sheds could be built and leased to the already licensed *rehriwallas*. However, the legal adviser to the Administration commented that the

imposition of an absolute ban on the plying of hand-carts in the Union Territory of Chandigarh is not legally permissible. Partial restraint, restricting their entry into specific sectors can, however, be imposed in the public interest.

The recommendation of constructing 1500 sheds for the existing *rehri* pullers was accepted by the Officers' Committee in 1970. It was also decided that no restriction be imposed on the trades being followed by *rehriwallas*, which had been another proposal of the first sub-committee. Accordingly, forty-eight sheds were constructed in Sector 23 on an experimental basis.

However, the experiment did not prove successful. After the first sheds had been built, the waiting list of those wanting them grew at an accelerating rate and the Administration decided that it would be extremely difficult, if not impossible, to provide sheds for all the *rehriwallas*.

The 'Problem' of the Pattriwallas

In the meantime, the enforcement staff continued confiscating the goods and equipment of the *pattriwallas*. In the mid-1960s the *pattriwallas* formed an association, *Pattri Beopar Mandal*, to take collective action against the on-slaughts of the enforcement staff. Initially, the association made representations to the authorities demanding authorized sites from which to work without harassment. It received no sympathy and was told that there was no room in the new city for *pattriwallas*.

However, by skilful manipulation of timing and political factors, the group then set itself up as a non-plan market under the name of the Prime Minister, Lal Bahadur Shastri. Within two years, having moved twice to different locations and having attracted the members of a *rehri* union, who called them-selves Nehru Market, the Nehru-Shastri Markets were well established as a throbbing and vital centre of commercial activity, offering a whole range of goods and services at highly competitive prices (see page 200). They became extremely popular, attracting customers from all over the city and were the closest to a typical Indian bazaar that Chandigarh ever had. Their final non-plan location was on a piece of land reserved for commercial development along the road between Sectors 21 and 22 (figure 10.8).

By 1971–72, it had been decided to remove these markets. The Administration considered forceful eviction, but legal and political factors militated against this. After prolonged negotiations, meetings and political interventions, it was agreed to resettle the petty traders in the local shopping centres of different sectors. A majority of the 'booths' allotted to them were dispersed in relatively undeveloped sectors (see figure 10.9). The price of land was fixed at 75 per cent of the average amount fetched by similar plots in open auction during the previous three years, and the buildings were charged at cost price. The allottees were given the additional concession of buying the booths on a hire purchase basis over a period of twelve years.

The method used for screening those eligible for allotment was similar to that adopted thirteen years earlier for Bajwada. Under the scheme 224 'eligible' people were allotted booths. Another 164, which included those considered 'ineligible' as well as some who felt that they could not afford a booth, were provided temporary sites in Sector 34 on a rental basis (this sector was virtually undeveloped at that time). All the rest, particularly the many *pattriwallas* and *rehriwallas* who were not members of the Nehru and Shastri Markets Federation, were provided no alternative. All stalls of the markets were razed to the ground in one operation and the site cleared.

The relocation of Nehru-Shastri Markets is useful for highlighting some of the underlying conflicts involved in government support or encouragement of 'informal sector' activities. In this case, about 400 small traders were removed from a central location which, even in the master plan, was reserved for commercial use. The markets were thus not violating the plan's land-use provisions. The only difference was that the master plan had visualized large showrooms on the site instead of small shops. Arguably, if the welfare of over 400 small traders had been the central concern of the authorities, the markets could have remained there and the plan provisions modified accordingly.

However the effect of resettlement on the small traders did not figure in the authorities' preoccupation with getting the site cleared as soon as possible. Following the removal of the non-plan markets, the land lay unused for four or five years and only recently have some large showrooms been built there. In fact, had the Nehru-Shastri Markets not been well organized, they would not have been 'rehabilitated', but simply evicted.

The main preoccupation of the authorities was to avoid setting any precedent by which sheer occupation of commercial land could be legalized or 'recognized'. The repercussions of this on the Administration's land sale policy would have been grave indeed. The regular shopkeepers had protested several times about the Nehru-Shastri Markets, and in the final analysis, the Administration had to give greater consideration to *their* demands than to those of the smaller traders. It is not possible for the authorities to support two totally opposing systems of acquiring land-use rights: one based on an individual's economic power, and the other on literal physical occupation of land.

As in the case of the status of non-plan settlements, the impact of urban planning on the circumstances of small enterprises in the city is quite clear. They must ultimately make way for their more powerful competitors when the land they are forced to use through physical occupation acquires a sufficiently high value to make it attractive for bigger enterprises to invest in it. The role of the public authority within the existing societal framework is predefined as that of ensuring the operation of these mechanisms. Urban planning only plays the function of defusing the direct social conflicts involved by becoming an intermediary.

The Framing of New Byelaws

The phenomenon of Nehru-Shastri Markets occurred during the phase when the Administration was considering the possibility of abolishing the plying of *rehris* althogether. *Rehri* and *pattri* markets continued to spring up in locations from which they had been removed. Standing instructions were issued to the enforcement staff to remove goods placed on the ground in various *rehri* parking sites so that these might not be converted into markets like the Nehru-Shastri ones.

In April 1972, the Estate Officer suggested that all approved parking sites should be paved with cement, and water and electricity provided. Some officers believed that certain goods such as provisions and cloth should be banned on *rehris* as these tended to lead to *rehris* taking up fixed locations. Some felt that permanent occupation of land could be prevented by allowing parking on approved sites only during fixed hours. As a result new byelaws were brought into force in May 1975.

Their main features include the following:

1. Cooking and serving meals is prohibited unless the stove and all other equipment are on the rehri itself.

2. The Chief Administrator may specify not only the total number of licences, but also the number of specific parking places.

3. Each licencee will have a specific authorized parking site.

4. Parking on the authorized site is permitted only during specified hours. Standing on any other road or public place is forbidden at any time.

5. No hand-cart may be taken to the Capitol complex, the Leisure Valley, the city centre or sub-city centre in Sector 34.

6. Breach of any of the provisions is punishable with a fine of up to Rs.200 and if continued with a further fine of Rs.20 per day.

7. All hand-carts must be changed to conform to one of the approved standard designs.

The fate of these bylaws in practice remained suspect. The Administration found it extremely difficult to implement any of its legal restrictions as the following incident shows.

An Experiment with Enforcement by Force

Despite the restrictions a group of *rehriwallas* selling snacks and cheap cooked meals was operating in the city centre, close to one of the cinemas. Because of the popularity of the cinema, they did a brisk business and the lower paid office workers obtained their lunches from them.

The authorities alleged that this group was supported by 'vested' interests with political contacts, who exploited the petty traders by charging them 'protection' money. One Estate Officer decided to try and dislodge the so-called vested interest. Without giving any warning (which is not permitted by law even to government authorities dealing with unauthorized occupants of land) a large contingent of police suddenly descended on the group one morning. The whole site was encircled, a barbed wire fence put up, the goods and equipment thrown out and the site levelled by a bulldozer. Directly after the site was turned into a parking lot, as prescribed in the master plan.

The traders organized protests and circulated a leaflet with the morning newspapers distributed throughout the city, informing the population what had been done to them. They accused the Estate Officer of kicking the poor in the back while having amassed a fortune for himself and his relatives during his tenure in office*. Failing to get any sympathy from local authorities, they sent a deputation to New Dehli which spent a month lobbying MPs and Ministers, not returning to Chandigarh until it had succeeded in getting instructions sent to Chandigarh Administration to demarcate an authorized parking site to the evicted traders, in the city centre itself.

A major reason for the success of the traders' deputation was that the general elections were due in the following year and the party in power was looking for grass roots support. Knowing that *rehriwallas* and their dependents constituted a considerable proportion of the vote, political parties could not afford to alienate them even if it meant a loss of face for the bureaucracy.

Thus, although the Administration had parliamentary approval for its byelaws, their real value remained in great doubt. Markets in the city had become organized and militant and the enforcement staff did not have the courage to enter them to enforce the regulation.

The Emergency and the Stifling of Collective Action

The start of the Emergency in June 1975 proved a heyday for the authorities from the point of view of their ability to enforce much that they had failed to do before. The first victim was Bajwada. Barely a month after the declaration of the Emergency, it was forceably cleared. Writs filed in the High Court to obtain stay orders proved meaningless as the authorities moved too fast and presented the court with a *fait accompli*. No compensation was paid to those evicted, and while some were capable of conforming to the planning regulations, others were far more vulnerable and their fate remains unknown. Those at the bottom of the hierarchy, such as shoe repairers and barbers, were given verbal permission to continue working from an adjoining authorized site.

Another major target was the clearance of non-plan enterprises functioning from totally unauthorized locations. These included three of the most lucrative locations: the city centre, the Capitol complex, and between the University and the Post Graduate Medical Institute. The achievement of the city centre non-plan traders, of getting an authorized parking site there, was thus soon annulled.

*When interviewed soon after this incident, the officer spoke of the low level to which the non-plan workers could stoop to be vindictive. Whatever the pros and cons of this argument, he did not seem to be particularly concerned about the disruption in the livelihoods of the scores of people that his action had caused.

A dozen or more authorized *rehri* sites were totally cleared, provided with cement paving, a water tap and toilet, and exact locations for individual *rehris* chalked out, in accordance with the byelaws. All the other provisions of the byelaws were also strictly enforced. There was an intensive *campaign* for confiscating unlicenced *rehris*, and in a short period the number operating in the city was considerably reduced.

Fear of prosecution, increased penalties for default and the inability to resort to protest at this time, led many non-plan enterprises to stop functioning altogether and traders to leave the city. As an indication of this, while up to mid-1973 2179 licences had been issued, by 1977 the number was reduced to only 1775. This reduction was achieved by only renewing the licences of those owning *rehris* and ensuring that no licensee had more than one licence. This policy was based on the premise that those owning a number of *rehris* exploited others by employing them as *rehriwallas*. The superficiality of this argument is evident when wage labour is seen as a totally legitimate form of activity in all other fields.

The effects of this policy on employment are not considered by the authorities. And certainly little consideration is given to the factors which lead to people taking up such occupations in spite of severe official restrictions and harassment or that the pattern emerging in Chandigarh only reflects the pattern of an enlarged tertiary sector in most urban areas in the country, and in other parts of the Third World.

Internal Conflicts, Official Attitudes and 'Planning'

Since the end of the Emergency, non-plan enterprises have been on the increase again. Although the enforcement staff keeps the unauthorized ones on their toes, such action is having a much reduced effect. Some of the older cleared sites are once more attracting traders. The *rehriwallas* granted authorized parking sites and licenses are demanding sheds on their sites. The *pattriwallas* not given legal protection before are demanding authorized working sites. The regular shopkeepers are protesting about the *pattriwallas* depriving them of business by working just outside their shops. The whole range of non-plan commercial and service enterprises, simply placed under the umbrella of the 'informal sector', is riddled with conflicts and contradictions.

A majority of the senior officials view non-plan enterprises as an under-world of anti-social elements, exploitation by political and economic vested interests, protection rackets, tax evasion, profiteering and adulteration. Although it is recognized that many resort to such occupations because of poverty and a lack of alternative opportunities, there is a strong impression that a majority have high incomes and are actually very rich.

However, in addition to these stereotype notions about non-plan workers, as is clear from the history of the interaction of Chandigarh's non-plan enterprises with the planning framework, the problem is not simply one of 'misunderstanding'. The underlying conflicts are more fundamental. The authorities, by virtue of their responsibility towards maintaining the existing pattern of property relations, must subordinate the interests of the smaller enterprises to those of commercial property owners. Thus, while unable to prevent non-plan enterprises entirely, they harass them to the point where they are unable to consolidate in any one location, particularly a 'desirable' one, where the economic returns are the highest.

The planning framework, by determining land use in advance, further accentuates this situation. As no consideration was given to such enterprises, and no land-use allocation made for them, they have been forced to 'fit into' the interstices left unused by others. Further, as they are dependent on being in areas of high residential density or intense traffic movement, many inevitably come into conflict with the functioning of the city's infrastructure required by the so-called formal sector. Thus they must constantly be removed from traffic junctions and shopping centre pavements, as other sections of the community protest against their disrupting other activities.

And still more, given the highly competitive environment in which non-plan enterprises must survive, sub-groups within them have conflicting interests. Few want to continue working in the totally free market situation into which they are forced. Thus, as and when the opportunity arises, sub-groups attempt to obtain legal protection and benefit at the cost of others. Inevitably, in the end, the worst sufferers are the most vulnerable and underprivileged. For them, within the existing hierarchy of socio-economic relations, there would appear to be few opportunities of betterment, either in the short- or long-term, irrespective of changes in official policy.

Nehru-Shastri Markets: a Case History

The story of the markets already discussed on page 196, is presented here in an edited form as narrated by the man largely responsible for organizing the whole venture. It illustrates very clearly the nature of the underlying conflicts between the needs of the petty traders and the priorities of the authorities in the modern, planned city.

'I used to run a tea-stall in Samrala. In 1960, I came to Chandigarh with the intention of building a house here. Soon I began to notice the many *pattriwallas* who made a living by selling their wares from the pavements. They were frequently harassed by the enforcement staff who used to take their goods away. I decided to join them as a *pattriwalla* to find out more about their situation. In the process, I forgot about building my house.

I set up a *pattri* in front of the jeweller's shop in the shopping centre in Sector 22 where many of them used to sit. At that time, there were about thirteen or fourteen of us. Besides us, there were another twenty-five to thirty others working in this way in the open space in front of the Punjab National Bank in the same sector (figure 10.8). I realized that nothing would be done to change the situation unless we made an effort ourselves. First I went to see the Chief Secretary to complain about our harassment. Instead of receiving any sympathy, I was told that the enforcement staff was doing the right thing because *pattriwallas* spoilt the beauty of the city by making it look disorganized and dirty. Then I decided to call a meeting of everyone in the trade to work out a joint plan of action. In all, we were about forty at that time. The meeting resulted in the formation of a union and we started collecting a small subscription for meeting union expenses.

Then the union made a representation to the Chief Secretarty demanding an authorized site from where we could work in peace. Again he told us that no provision had been made in the capital for *pattriwallas* and no laws had been framed for them. I realized that we would get nowhere through regular channels and that some other means would have to be devised.

After getting the assurance of a good local journalist's support, I organized our members to make a crucial move. I instructed each of them to buy a few bamboos and a tarpaulin. After carefully studying the calendar, I picked a time when there were three or four public holidays in a row. Late in the evening of the last working day, all of us got together in the park in front of the Punjab National Bank, quickly put up temporary stalls with the bamboos and tarpaulins, and started selling our goods from them.

We had got a large number of posters printed which were posted all round the city. These announced the inauguration of 'Shastri Market' of petty traders with the blessings of the Estate Officer, the Capital Minister, etc., thanking them for their support and letting us name the market in honour of our beloved Prime Minister Shastriji*. To add to the fanfare, we had invited a band to celebrate the market's inauguration.

This was in 1965 when Punjab was still undivided and the campaign for a separate Sikh state was at its height. I worked out a clever plan to exploit the political situation. Some members of our union were Akalis (Sikhs). So we arranged the holding of an *Akhand Path* (recital from the sacred book of the Sikhs) for the auspicious occasion of the market's inauguration.

At the end of the public holidays, there was an *Akhand Path* going on in one corner of the market, a recital of the *Gita* in another, and at night *Jagrata* was being held. When the enforcement staff arrived, all these ceremonies were in progress. Our Sikh members reacted strongly saying that they would not tolerate an insult to their holy *Guru Granth Sahib* which an interruption of the *Akhand Path* would have implied. They started shouting slogans asserting that they would be cut to pieces before allowing such an act to take place. Unnerved by the situation, the enforcement staff sought the advice of the Estate Officer who instructed them not to take any action for the time being.

This event was closely followed by Prime Minister Shastri's death in January 1966. While everyone was mourning his death, I realized what a boon it could prove for our cause. I told the others to stop mourning and be grateful.

We decided to close the market for a whole week and launched another series of religious recitals and ceremonies as an expression of respect for the dead leader. Black flags were hung over all the stalls. Shastriji's ashes were brought to

*At that time, Lal Bahadur Shastri was the Prime Minister of India.

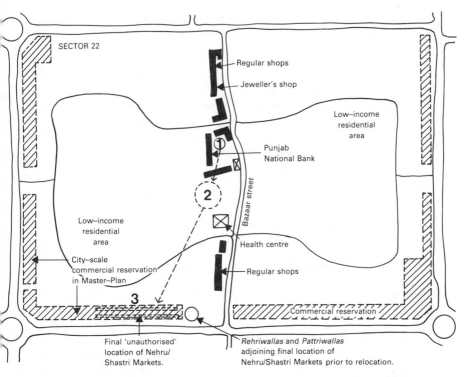

Figure 10.8. The different locations of Nehru-Shastri Markets in Sector 22 prior to rehabilitation in planned shopping centres.

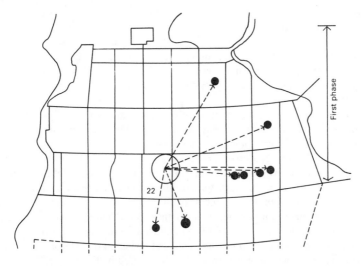

Figure 10.9. Relocation of the Nehru-Shastri Markets into regular shopping centres.

Chandigarh to be taken round in a procession to enable people to pay their last respects. Our market happened to fall on the route chosen for the purpose. When the procession reached us, many of us stopped it by lying across the road insisting that the ashes be brought inside the market named after him for his blessings. Our demands were met and we managed to place an enormous wreath around the urn containing the ashes. The wreath, besides having a large photograph of the dead Minister, had a board attached to it saying that it was an expression of respect of the members of Shastri Market. The urn was later placed in Nehru park where large numbers of people came to pay homage. In this way we managed to get a lot of publicity for the market.

A few months went by without further developments. Then we received a request from the Capital Minister to vacate the space we were occupying. We asked him to tell us where we could go. After some hesitation he advised us to move to the undeveloped piece of land between the health centre and the rear of the shops (figure 10.8). We took our stalls apart and rebuilt them in a more organized way at the new location.

Around this time, a number of *rehriwallas* had formed a union called Milaap Rehri Union. They had been watching how we, having started as *pattriwallas*, had managed to get established in a big way without paying anything to the government. They decided to follow our example and set up a number of stalls adjoining ours, and named themselves Nehru Market. With this kind of influx, the combined strength of the market went up to almost 900 stalls at one point, but then slowly stabilized at about 400 to 450.

We had to remain constantly alert to the government's plans against us. By moving us to a disadvantageous location behind the regular shops, the Capital Minister had reckoned that most of our businesses would fail and the market disintegrate slowly. On the contrary, we were doing extremely well. We organized a lot of lucky draws, gift schemes, etc. to attract customers and people flocked to our market because of the general cheapness and variety of goods available. Seeing that we were unlikely to go of our own accord, the government decided to evict us by force. We found this out in advance.

We filed a writ in the High Court against the Estate Office on the grounds that the government itself had allowed us to use the vacant land and could not simply evict us without providing any alternative. The Capital Minister requested us to withdraw the petition on the understanding that our case would be given due consideration, and we complied.

Following this event, Punjab was reorganized into the new states of Punjab and Haryana and Chandigarh was brought under the central government in November 1966. A new Chief Commissioner was appointed who got the whole city surveyed. In his report he recommended that all unauthorized encroachments on government land should be removed immediately excepting our markets, which were to be left undisturbed till some solution could be devised.

A local Advisory Committee for the city, consisting of a number of private individuals and government officials, with the Chief Commissioner as its chairman, had been formed. Our case reached this committee for discussion. Although the Chief Commissioner had earlier recommended special consideration for our case, he agreed now with the other members that we should be evicted by force. Again we got hold of this confidential information.

We filed another writ in the High Court. A notice was issued to the Estate Office to show cause for its plan of eviction. The government counsel argued that we had illegally occupied government land. Our counsel replied that we neither denied this nor intended to assert any rights on the land. However, giving the example of a person whose house had been occupied by another, he pointed out that the former still had to take refuge in a court of law to get his grievance redressed and could not simply resort to the use of force. The Estate Office agreed not to evict us by force.

Things went on like this for some time. We maintained contact with influential people to keep our plight publicized. Then we were asked to move once again. This was in 1967/68. We were told that the present site was unsuitable for a market because it caused tremendous disturbance for the health centre and the adjoining residential areas. The Chief Commissioner said that this time we were being moved to a site which was reserved for commercial use even in the master plan and that the Administration would eventually build small shops or booths for us there and not ask us to move again. Again we built the stalls in a systematic way with each person getting a standard plot. All these moves cost each of us a considerable amount of money.

During this period we sought the assistance of the Congress MP from Chandigarh. It was with his support that it was eventually decided that each of us should be allotted pucca booths in regular shopping centres in different sectors on a hire purchase basis.

The Administration got different numbers of booths built in five sectors (figure 10.9) Their size was the same as our stalls. During the long period of negotiations preceding the move, we raised several issues. Firstly, we were concerned that the shopping centres of residential sectors were designed to cater to the daily needs of resident populations whereas our market predominantly consisted of general merchants, cloth dealers, furniture makers, traditional restaurants, waste material dealers and sellers of fancy goods. We requested that the general character of our market was not destroyed. We also pointed out that furniture makers, waste material dealers and eating houses could not function from 8 ft by 16 ft booths as their space requirements were greater. It was decided to allot double units for these particular trades.

The process of preparing lists of those who were legitimate members of the markets proved to be tedious, leading to many undesirable developments. We prepared lists of our members on the basis of our records and pointed out names of those who had recently infiltrated the markets by buying off smaller traders who could not compete. We demanded their exclusion from those selected for allotment.

What actually took place was that the names of a large number of people who had never even worked in the markets crept into the official lists. From the most junior inspector to the highest official, bribes were being accepted. We complained that if the lists prepared by us on the basis of our records were not going to be accepted, why had they been asked for in the first place. The discrepancies between our lists and the official ones created a situation of confusion among our members who started losing confidence in the leadership. The land did not belong to any of us or our fathers, but the fraudulant means by which official lists were finalized led to a lot of rich traders, who had nothing to do with the market, getting their names on them.

Another issue we raised was the fate of the *rehris* and *pattriwallas* functioning from the area adjoining our market. Were they going to be allowed to continue at the same location while our members were sent to less developed sectors where business was sure to decrease, possibly leading to the bankruptcy of many? We felt that they should also be resettled in small sheds or some other form acceptable to the Administration. I even suggested that allottees should be photographed and issued with identity cards so that any illegal subletting or transferring of rights at a later date could be easily detected. All I was given were verbal assurances but no action was taken.

As a result of all this, whatever malpractices could get into our markets, crept in. The rich shopkeepers who had managed to get in were able to evade sales and incomes taxes to their hearts' content. They did extremely well because they could afford to offer a greater variety of goods to attract more customers. Earlier, even the small traders had started getting goods on credit from wholesalers owing to the success of the market. But they could not compete with the bigger ones and success for them was limited from the beginning. The rich ones started making a fortune whereas the poorer ones remained as poor as before. They neither had the brains nor the capital to do well besides being afraid of breaking the law.

Since resettlement in planned shopping centres, many of them have been almost bankrupted, having sold all their assets. Because of the lack of business, even wholesalers are not prepared to give them goods on credit any longer. We neither got the benefit of being on popular bus routes nor of having much local demand to cater for. Many of our members have had to lock up the *pucca* booths and go back to the old location as *rehriwallas* simply for the sake of economic survival.

At the same time, the *rehriwallas* working at the old location in Sector 22 have remained there inspite of the government's promises to the contrary. Their sales have shot up and so has the extent of new unauthorized development there. They have been telling our old customers that the new markets have failed and that they constitute Shastri Market now. Whereas we had manintained a certain discipline in conforming to standard stall sizes, now there is a free for all. One person with one *rehri* license is doing business of thousands of Rupees using 5 to 10 *rehris* put together. Some have stocks worth Rs.50,000 each. Many whose stalls were well known have gone back there. Many have sold the *pucca* booths allotted to them on concessional terms, but no action has been taken against them. Others have sublet, which is not permitted either.

Those of us who chose to abide by the law and wanted to make something of our lives are still fighting it out but our financial situation is precarious. Take my example. When we moved to the new shops in 1972, they just consisted of bare shells. An average of Rs.4000 had to be spent by each person on shop fitting. Then, I've paid approximtely Rs2500 in monthly hire purchase instalments by now. On top of that, I've been sitting virtually idle for two years with hardly any income. There are not many of us who can bear this kind of a financial strain. Besides, now we can neither get goods on credit from wholesalers nor invest much in our undertakings ourselves. What can people be expected to do under the circumstances?

I had been the General Secretary of the market from the beginning and for the last five years, I have remained the President. Everything was made with my hands. Most of our customers belonged to the lower income groups. Some even came from higher income backgrounds but they were not many. The general quality of our goods did not cater for their requirements. Our market had become really famous for the cheapness of its goods. Although many persons used to evade the payment of sales tax, the market still used to pay approximately Rs.10,000 per month. Now we don't even pay Rs.2000 because sales have dropped so much. There was a good spirit of participation among the members and donations were frequently collected for charitable purposes. We used to start work at 6 or 7 a.m. and come home around 9 or 10 p.m. In the evenings every-thing used to be tied up and *chowkidars* used to watch the place at night. Later on we had even made the stalls lockable. There were no thefts or damage. Few used to have incomes of less than Rs.1000 per month. Now it isn't even Rs.200. It is difficult even to pay the monthly hire purchase instalments. It's all my fault. I got everyone in this plight and now they blame me for their predicament. But how was I to know that the government would not keep its word. It did not stop further unauthorized encroachment. Most of us were small businessmen who could not sustain the financial implications of the changed situation'*.

*Source: personal interview, June 1974.

11

Employment in Non-Plan Enterprises

This chapter examines the characteristics of non-plan enterprises and attempts to identify the causes which produce these characteristics and their relationship to the conditions in the wider society. By doing so we can explore the degree to which either these can be changed so as to become compatible with the planning framework, or the extent to which the planning framework can be modified to accommodate non-plan enterprises.

Methodology and Definitions

The data presented here were obtained from the 1971 Census and from fieldwork, which was carried out in two stages during 1974–75. The first stage consisted of a preliminary survey of all non-plan enterprises in the planned part of Chandigarh, and the second of a detailed study of a selected market. During both stages, the following definitions were used:

1. An 'enterprise' or 'establishment' was defined as a functionally-independent unit, irrespective of its size. For example, one man working as a tailor from a pavement was counted as one operational unit just as a *dhaba* or traditional restaurant making use of considerable space and employing five or six people was also counted as one unit.

2. The activities of all enterprises were divided into three broad groups: trading, service and petty production, and recorded in detail.

3. All non-plan enterprises were further divided into seven categories on the basis of their mode of operation:

Category 1. Mobile hawkers on foot or bicycle who take their goods or services to customers rather than being attached to a fixed location. Typical examples included balloon and paper-flower sellers and knife sharpeners.

Category 2. Pattri– or *thariwallas* offering goods or services from pavements or other ground space. Both *pattri* and *thari* belong to a range of descriptive colloquial terms reflecting common retailing forms. Typical examples included petty traders selling cheap cloth and household goods, and services such as tailoring, shoe repairs and cycle repairs.

Category 3. *Mobile rehris.* The term *rehri* denotes a four-wheeled barrow which *can* be pushed. Typical examples were fruit and vegetable sellers. (As discussed in chapter 10, this category is the only one qualifying for the Administration's approval *providing* the *rehris* maintain mobility.)

Category 4. *Immobile rehris.* These were enterprises making use of *rehris* which were obviously immobile as the tyres were deflated or wheels sunk into the ground or removed altogether, but were not using any space other than that on which the *rehri* was parked. Typical examples were fruit or vegetable traders and tobacconists.

Category 5. *Immobile rehris making use of additional ground space.* The criterion used for placing enterprises in this group was the use of ground space in addition to that taken up by the *rehri*. Typical examples were petty cloth retailers using *rehri* tops mainly for storing goods, but who spread rugs on the ground to display their merchandise while transacting a sale.

Category 6. *Immobile units, with or without rehris, but making use of additional furniture* such as benches and *charpoys* and fixed *tandoors* (traditional earthen ovens) and occupying considerably more space than most of the other categories. Typical examples were *dhabas* serving cooked meals.

Category 7. *Khokhas*, which in colloquial language denote cheap improvized structures used as shops, which are fixed in location.

City-wide Significance of Non-plan Enterprises

A preliminary survey recorded 2663 non-plan enterprises using 2008 *rehris* and employing 3491 people. Eighty-three per cent were engaged in retail trading, 15 per cent in repairing and services and only 2 per cent in petty production. The distribution of all non-plan enterprises by their type of activity and mode of operation is shown in table 11.1. Numerically, they represented 48.8 per cent of the total enterprises in planned residential sectors. Four-fifths were operating from groups of more than ten units, the rest being dispersed in smaller groups or single units along main and secondary roads in the city.

Assessment of the relationship between employment in non-plan and planned enterprises had to be restricted to retail trading only, as comparable data for other planned enterprises were not available. The 1971 Census recorded 5065 people employed in 1880 retail establishments in the city. As this excluded most non-plan enterprises, the figures can be taken as representing employment within the planned framework. On this basis, the comparative distribution of 'planned' and 'non-plan' establishments by type of trade and numbers employed is shown in table 11.2.

The first aspect evident from the table is that the total number of non-plan establishments was greater than the planned ones, the former representing 54 per cent of the total. The fact that this proportion changes considerably when considered in terms of the number of persons employed (36.3 per cent by the

Table 11.1. Distribution of non-plan enterprises by type of activity, mode of operation and number of persons employed.

| Type of activity | Number per category | | | | | | | |
	1	2	3	4	5	6	7	Total
Trading								
Fruit and vegetables	1	87	619	123	9	6	9	854
Provisions	1	8	13	31	35		10	98
Dhabas and hot snacks		22	25	44	7	124	13	235
General snacks and drinks	12	63	137	71	17	31	12	343
Household goods	13	72	11	66	49	3	20	234
Cloth and clothing		45	8	30	137		16	236
Tobacconists		18	1	57			7	83
Footwear		2		8	27		6	43
Hardware, paint and electrical goods							21	21
Miscellaneous (earthenware pots, fodder, *kabadis,* etc.)	5	16		1	5	10	21	58
Sub-total	32	333	814	431	286	174	135	2205
Services								
Cobblers, cycle repairs, barbers and dyers	5	238			10	1	12	226
Tailors, blacksmiths stove repairs, etc.		18		12	16		31	77
Miscellaneous (shoeshine, clothes ironing, knife sharpening, etc	2	51		1				54
Sub-total	7	307		13	26	1	43	397
Small manufacturing								
Furniture, stoves, tin trunks, etc		4		2	3	12	40	61
Total	39	644	814	446	315	187	218	2663
Total number of persons employed in each category	39	723	821	565	513	498	332	3491
Percentage of total	1.1	20.7	23.5	16.2	14.7	14.3	9.5	

Table 11.2. Comparative distribution of planned and non-plan retail trading establishments by type of trade and size of employment.

Type of trade	Planned* no. of units	no. of persons employed	Non-plan† no. of units	no. of persons employed
Food, beverages, tobacco and alcohol	636	1152	1378	1544
Textiles	211	637	236	355
General merchandise and others	800	2045	356	456
Restaurants and hotels	233	1231	235	529
Total	1880	5065	2205	2884
Percentage	46.0	63.7	54.0	36.3

*Source: Census of India, 1971, Establishment Report and Tables, Part III, Series 25: Chandigarh, Table E-111.
†Field survey, 1974

Note: Although the net figures for planned and non-plan establishments are not strictly comparable because of the different years to which they relate, they can be taken to reflect the situation in 1974 fairly closely. The Nehru-Shastri markets were moved from the non-plan to the planned sector after 1971. Any increase in the latter may be considered to be more than offset by the decrease effected in the former by the change.

Table 11.3. Distribution of planned and non-plan retail trading establishments by number of persons per establishment.

No. of persons per establishment	Planned	Non-plan
1	834	1695
2–4	804	499
5–9	175	11
10–19	47	
20–49	15	
50–99	2	
Unspecified	3	
Percentage	63.7	36.3

Sources: As table 11.2.

non-plan and 63.7 per cent by the planned) is indicative of the predominance of small enterprises in the non-plan group (table 11.3). While 77 per cent of the non-plan enterprises were employing one person, only 44 per cent of the planned ones were doing so.

The retail distribution pattern for the city as a whole is also evident from the table. Over 90 per cent of all establishments were employing a maximum of four people, indicating the predominance of small enterprises in handling retail trading. Large chains of supermarkets remain conspicuous by their absence, which is typical of urban centres throughout India.

Here it is useful to note that 'smallness' of scale, a characteristic considered typical of 'informal' sector activities, is by no means confined exclusively to non-plan enterprises, at least in retail trading. McGee (1973a) has noted the late entry of big capital into retail distribution even in developed countries and that the majority of Third World urban economies continue to be dominated by small enterprises. In the rather special case of Hong Kong, where the transformation of a predominantly underdeveloped economy into an industrial one took place very rapidly between the mid-1960s and early 1970s, the relationship between the increased attractiveness of the distributive sector for big business following an increase in the purchasing power of a large section of the population comes through clearly. From this case it would appear that the growth of the equivalent of non-plan (or informal) trading enterprises is likely to be a continuing feature of Third World cities until large capital finds it sufficiently attractive to take over retail distribution. In Hong Kong this takeover is apparently taking place already and the authorities have begun to attack hawking activities structurally by preventing inheritance and increasing licence payments. From this it would seem that the growth potential for non-plan enterprises is dependent on the reluctance of big capital to take over retail distribution. Once this situation has changed, non-plan enterprises are likely to lose large proportions of their normal markets, irrespective of what impact this might have on the employment opportunities in the 'informal' sector.

The second aspect revealed by table 11.2 is the significant contribution of non-plan enterprises in retailing foods, beverages and tobacco. Nearly 70 per cent of all establishments and nearly 60 per cent of those employed in handling these commodities belonged to non-plan enterprises in Chandigarh. This was largely because the distribution of fresh fruit and vegetables had been almost monopolized by non-plan traders.

The other two trades in which non-plan establishments accounted for more than half the total were textiles and 'restaurants'. Generally, the quality of textiles handled by them is inferior to that available in regular shops, and planned and non-plan 'restaurants' are not strictly comparable. *Dhabas* (the non-plan restaurants) are eating places where a restricted variety of cheap traditional meals are prepared and served. In contrast 'modern' restaurants offer a diverse range of food. The non-plan enterprises grouped under the category of restaurants and hotels in table 11.2 include not only *dhabas* in the strict sense of the term, but also units selling typical north Indian cooked snacks and tea, which are frequently eaten by low-income sections of the population instead of meals. Thus, half of all cooked food establishments in the city were in the non-plan group and employed 30 per cent of the total engaged in this activity.

The concentration of essential commodities such as foods and lower quality textiles in the non-plan group is indicative of the strong relationship between the low purchasing power of a large section of the population and the low over-heads which non-plan modes of operation entail. These negligible overheads are obtained by evading permanent placement in buildings, and the real estate market altogether. As already mentioned, the majority of non-plan settlement residents use non-plan markets and enterprises for obtaining most of their goods. Thus, while non-plan enterprises represent a form of employment for those engaged in them, low-income sections of the population are dependent on them for obtaining lower cost goods and services.

Characteristics of Different Modes of Operation

The characteristics of each of the seven modes of operation in terms of predominant type of trade, service or petty production, and sizes of enterprises in terms of number of *rehris* and persons per enterprise are described below.

Category 1. Only 1.5 per cent of the total enterprises fell within this group, although the number could not be recorded accurately as coming across mobile hawkers is dependent on chance. As they do not use a fixed location, they are not considered 'a problem' by the authorities.

Category 2. The hardening of the Administration's attitude towards this group, particularly after the development of the Nehru-Shastri Markets was discussed in the last chapter. However, in the last few years, cycle repairers, cobblers, dyers (those dyeing and starching turbans and saris), and barbers in this category have been slowly granted recognition. This partial security remains a verbal one with the attached condition that they do not put up any form of shelter. It is also highly selective as only 20 per cent of the enterprises in this category were eligible.

Pattri– and *thariwallas* represented almost a quarter of the total non-plan enterprises in the city. More than 90 per cent of them had only one person working, the rest two.

Category 3. All the 814 units in this category were engaged in trading, 97.5 per cent of them handling food, mostly fresh fruit and vegetables. All the units were using only one *rehri* each and 99 per cent were one-person enterprises.

As this mode of operation is the only one with legal recognition it is significant that it represented only a little over 30 per cent of the total non-plan enterprises and less than a quarter of the total non-plan workers.

Category 4. Seventeen per cent of the total enterprises were in this category. Ninety-six per cent of them were engaged in trading, fresh fruit and vegetables again being the main commodities.

There was much greater variation in the size of enterprises in this category compared with the first three. About 75 per cent of the 446 units had one *rehri* and employed one person, while 20 per cent had two and employed two people. The rest had three or more *rehris* and correspondingly three or more employees.

Category 5. The majority of the 315 enterprises in this category, which represented 12 per cent of the total non-plan enterprises, were engaged in trading. Almost half were selling cloth and clothing, and they comprised nearly 60 per cent of those selling these commodities. Sixty-two per cent were using one *rehri*, 30 per cent two and the rest three or more. Almost one-half were one-person units, two-fifths two-person, and the rest three or more.

Category 6. This category accounted for only 7 per cent of the total non-plan units. Almost 70 per cent were *dhabas* and the extensive use of furniture and other equipment was necessitated by the need for customers to be able to sit down while eating. Thirty per cent of the enterprises were not using *rehris* at all, while more than half the rest used only one and the majority of the remainder only two.

Although enterprises in this category represented such a small proportion of the total, because of the larger sizes of the individual units they constituted 14 per cent of the total number of people employed in non-plan enterprises. Only 16 per cent of the 187 units were one-person enterprises, while 40 per cent employed two, 26 per cent three, and 18 per cent four or more.

Category 7. There were 218 units in this category (8 per cent of the total). About 60 per cent were engaged in trading, 20 per cent in services and 20 per cent in petty production. The 332 persons employed represented 20 per cent of the total. Nearly 40 per cent were working in one-person units, about 20 per cent in two-person ones, and the rest three or more.

These enterprises were almost totally confined to two locations in the city: 92 per cent were either in Bajwada or on the road bordering the Industrial Area labour colony. The rest were dispersed in a number of residential sectors.

Since the survey was carried out in late 1974, and following the enforcement of the latest byelaws, some of these modes of operation have been severely restricted or eliminated altogether (at least temporarily). Categories 5 to 7 have been the worst sufferers.

In fact the present official policy only accepts non-plan modes of operation for people below a certain economic level and consolidation and improvement beyond it is not permitted. According to official arguments, if a *rehriwalla* wants or is able to expand his business he must do so within the framework of planned development, i.e. either pay the market rents for the smallest shop or buy commercial premises at auctioned prices. Implicit in the type of proposals emanating from the informal/formal sectoral analysis (see chapter 10), there is a similar assumption of a clear cut separation between the two sectors. In reality, of course, no such division exists and the slow process of accumulation taking place in some enterprises, as is demonstrated by the case histories later in this chapter, is seriously hindered by such official restrictions.

Sector number	Gross residential density per acre	No. of informal enterprises per 1000 persons
1	2	3
2	7.4	6.6
3	5.8	4.8
4	7.8	10.7
5	6.0	10.7
6	0.2	12.4
7	26.3	7.5
8	22.4	15.6
9	8.9	8.5
10	11.3	6.0
11	15.4	47.1
14	28.0	5.4
15	48.8	2.0
16	18.0	27.0
18	29.0	7.0
19	44.5	3.3
20	106.6	3.3
21	50.7	0.7
22	97.2	1.2
23	67.4	2.4
24	26.7	116.6
27	66.0	
28	34.0	
29	17.2	
30	13.4	
35	9.7	

A: Location of selected market

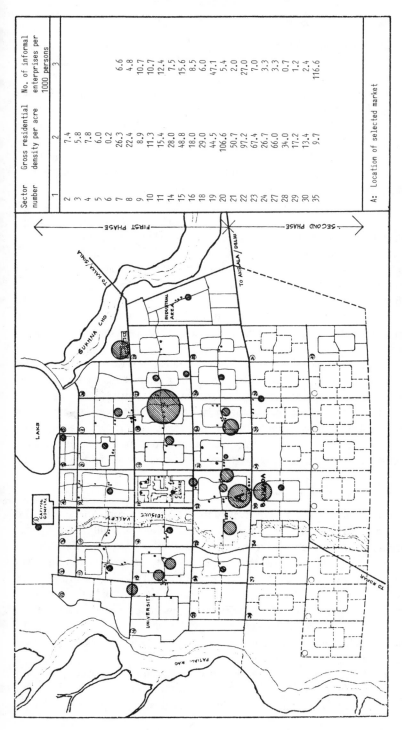

Figure 11.1. Spatial distribution of non-plan enterprises in planned sectors relative to gross residential densities and number of informal enterprises per 1000 persons in 1971–1974.

Location of Non-Plan Enterprises

The spatial distribution of non-plan enterprises in the city is shown in figure 11.1. Eighty per cent of them formed part of market concentrations. The largest single market, consisting of 503 enterprises, was located in Sector 19, followed by one on the south-western edge of Sector 22 adjoining Bajwada which had 339 units.

As is evident from the figure, the distribution was fairly uneven in the master plan area. Just over half the total enterprises were located in only five residential sectors, 15, 19, 20, 22, and 23, which housed 40 per cent of the city's population. Generally the number of non-plan enterprises per 1000 persons in different sectors bore a strong relationship to the stage of development of the sector, and the size and income levels of its population. The northern, low-density and higher-incomes sectors, with comparatively more planned shops per 1000 persons, had fewer non-plan enterprises (figure 11.1). On the other hand, sectors located in the middle of the southern belt of the first phase area, which had already exceeded planned target populations, had a much higher number of non-plan enterprises.

Another characteristic of the distribution of non-plan markets is that they were not directly related to the populations of individual sectors but to those of up to three or four surrounding ones. In fact some attracted customers from all over the city.

The enterprises functioning from dispersed locations were spread along a number of major and minor roads. Services along main roads (V3s) consisted mainly of cycle repairs with a number of associated enterprises catering for the needs of the traffic. Along the smaller roads within sectors, they comprised cobblers, barbers, clothes ironers, dyers and *tandoors*, providing services to residents of surrounding areas. Small concentrations were frequent in the vicinity of road junctions where larger numbers of customers could be reached.

The Case of a Selected Market

The market selected for detailed investigation was located on the south-west side of Sector 22 (figure 11.2) on a piece of land zoned as a public open space in the master plan. A recent addition to it had spilled over to the other side of a private housing block, on to an area reserved for commercial development along the V2 on one side of the sector (figures 11.2 and 11.3). According to the 1971 Census, Sector 22 had the second highest density of any residential sector, predominantly comprising low-income residents. On one side of the market there is low-income housing for government employees, and on the other side housing blocks built on some of the smallest private residential plots. Bajwada was across the V2.

The market contained about 340 enterprises, the number varying not only from day to day, but considerably between mornings and evenings. Its stable core consisted largely of immobile trading units dealing in provisions, cloth,

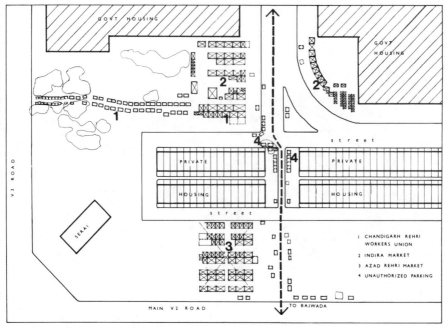

Figure 11.2. Sector 22 market: land use and location of the four market sub-groups at the time of the survey.

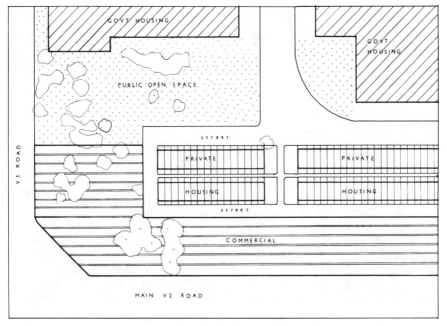

Figure 11.3. Sector 22 market: planned land use for the site and surrounding areas.

Figure 11.4. View of the market from its busiest end with the immobile CRWU units and Indira Market in the foreground and the mobile CRWU *rehriwallas* stretching in two lines into the distance.

Figure 11.5. A closer view of the Indira Market. Provision enterprises and a part of a *dhaba* in the right foreground.

Figure 11.6. One of the nuclear family units selling repaired second-hand clothing within the Indira Market. They are at the bottom of the economic hierarchy.

Figure 11.7. A row of vegetable *patriwallas* situated at the furthest end of the market.

ready-made garments, footwear, general merchandise, *dhabas*, and services such as tailors, barbers, cobblers and stove repairers. In the evenings it was reinforced by a large number of *rehri*– and *pattriwallas*. These were mainly fruit and vegetable sellers, with a few providing snacks. The market started bustling with activity from about 5 pm with office workers shopping on their way home, and continued like that up until 10 or 11 pm. In the morning, work started early to catch customers before they went to work.

The survey consisted of completing seventy-seven interview schedules covering about 25 per cent of those working in the market in different categories of trading and service enterprises. Before this, the market was surveyed generally and leaders of the four sub-groups within it were interviewed to obtain historical background and their views on the prevailing situation. The leaders' statements were crosschecked against the views of ordinary members to eliminate elements of exaggeration. Leaders of various other markets in the city were also interviewed to place the selected market in the general context. Official attitudes were obtained from discussions with a number of senior officials responsible for policy decisions and enforcement.

The Occupations of Market Workers

Ninety-one percent of the market enterprises in the sample were engaged in trading and 9 per cent in services. More than half the traders were selling fruit and vegetables. The next largest group was cloth and clothing sellers, and of these nineteen, two were selling cheap shop-soiled garments referred to as 'rags' and five, secondhand clothing. The other commodities being handled were provisions, snacks, household goods, tobacco and *paan*, footwear, crockery, and cooked meals. Four of the seven service enterprises were tailors, the others being a cobbler, a stove repairer and a picture framer.

For 90 per cent of the respondents work in the market was their *sole* and *full-time* occupation. Four were doing it part-time, the remaining four resorting to it only seasonally. The seasonal workers were all selling fruit or vegetables and were dependent on finding alternative employment during the lean work periods of the agricultural cycle. Two of them came from villages on Chandigarh's periphery.

For 70 per cent of the respondents their present occupations were their first in the city. The majority of the rest had changed from initial, extremely low-investment trading and service occupations to comparatively better ones in similar categories. Except for three government employees and two unskilled daily wage labourers, the rest had been self-employed previously.

Choice of occupation among the respondents was based on two major considerations. First, the lack of alternative employment opportunities or access to capital resources for starting any other enterprise, and secondly, the availability of retailing experience through family, relatives or friends. It is generally believed that starting a small retailing enterprise is easy. However, evidence of frequent cases of bankruptcy and losses even among the smallest enterprises in the market indicated why experience is such an important consideration, as is the significant role of friends and relatives in aiding a newcomer to join the game.

The continuity of traditional occupational patterns was also evident from the castes of the respondents. Of seventy-seven traders, thirteen were *Banyas* which is a major trading caste within the Hindu caste system. Of the *Banyas,* only one was selling fruit and vegetables, which are comparatively easier to handle; the others were retailing provisions, general merchandise, crockery and textiles. Within the market the *Banyas* were obviously doing better than most of the others in spite of having started from almost nothing.

Organizational Characteristics of the Enterprises

Over half the respondents were self-employed in one-person enterprises, while a further third or so were in family enterprises. The family enterprises included several fruit and vegetable *rehriwallas* who jointly acquired stock and used separate *rehris* for selling. In this way transportation costs can be reduced and established family members can support newcomers by cushioning the impact of initial losses due to inexperience or other blunders. Even in the case of one-person enterprises, considerable casual assistance from school-age sons was in evidence in the evenings. Only four respondents were employing five assistants between them. There were three partnerships, two employing one paid employee each. In all, seventy-seven enterprises represented 125 full-time workers, of which only seven were paid employees.

The distribution of different modes of operation between the enterprises when they started had changed considerably by the time of the survey. There had been no change in the number of mobile hawkers. The number of *pattriwallas* had decreased from eleven to seven, and the four who had changed had done so because of the need to have a *rehri* to avoid harassment by the enforcement staff.

Of thirty-two enterprises which had started as mobile *rehris*, four had become immobile. One had given up mobile work because of the greater vulnerability to harassment on the roads. The other three had become immobile as a result of gradual expansion of business or because they found that there was no difference in income whether mobile or working from the same location and because mobility was very tiring.

The most significant change was in the increase in enterprises in category 5. Category 7 did not exist in the market at the time of the survey as all *khokhas* in the city had been demolished. All seven respondents who had started with *khokhas* had acquired *rehris* and changed to category 5.

Rehris and their Use

Three-quarters of the enterprises were making use of *rehris* in some form or other. Since starting operation the number of *rehris* had increased in total as had the number per enterprise. Nearly 60 per cent of the respondents using *rehris* owned all their *rehris*; 25 per cent were using only rented ones and the rest both owned and rented. Over 45 per cent of those owning at least one *rehri* had started with rented ones and 43 per cent were owners from the beginning. Of those who were renting, almost half were doing so because they could not afford to buy, while nearly 40 per cent were doing so because they could not get a *rehri* licence as the Administration had stopped issuing them.

The average monthly rent per *rehri* was Rs.28.50, the range varying between Rs.15 and Rs.40. The price of an ordinary *rehri* was between Rs.200 and Rs.400, specialized ones costing much more. That almost half of those renting could not afford to buy is indicative of their poor financial status. Unable to invest a sum of Rs.200–400 they had to incur monthly overheads of Rs.15–40. The Administration's 'freeze' on new licences was forcing even those who could afford to buy their own *rehris* to rent them. The artificial scarcity created by this policy had created a black market in licences, some of the respondents having paid up to Rs.250 for a licence alone. Only four of the 101 *rehris* in the sample were unlicenced and all were owned by their users. All four had been working as *rehriwallas* for three or four years but had been unable to get a licence.

Investment, Turnover, Incomes and Credit

The range of the value of goods in stock in different enterprises showed a variation from as much as Rs.15,000 to as little as Rs.12 (figure 11.8). Those providing services have been excluded here as in their case this criterion was not comparable with the trading ones. More than 60 per cent of the trading enterprises had goods worth less than Rs.500 in stock.

The monthly turnover of goods also fell within the range of stock values, but according to this criterion the largest number of enterprises fell in the range Rs.1500 and Rs.10,000, which accounted for more than 60 per cent of the total.

This variation was mainly due to the difference in the type of commodities being handled. Fruit and vegetable sellers have to get fresh stock in small quantities on a daily basis. The quantity of goods in stock is therefore not an accurate indicator of the turnover of the enterprise. Traders handling goods such as cloth or crockery, on the other hand, need to keep larger stocks on display to be able to offer some variety to their customers and do not have to buy at short intervals.

Similarly, the range of daily incomes of individual enterprises was fairly wide, varying from Rs.100 to only Rs.5. Figure 11.9 shows a fairly even distribution between enterprises earning Rs.5–10 to Rs.21–30 per day, with 14 per cent earning Rs.35 and above. However, when these figures are converted into incomes per full-time worker there is a significant shift to the lower end of the range with 65 per cent earning from Rs.15 to below Rs.5 per day. It should be noted that most of the respondents did not have any accurate idea either of their incomes or their profit. This was particularly evident in the case of fruit and vegetable sellers. There is a high degree of bargaining associated with sales in

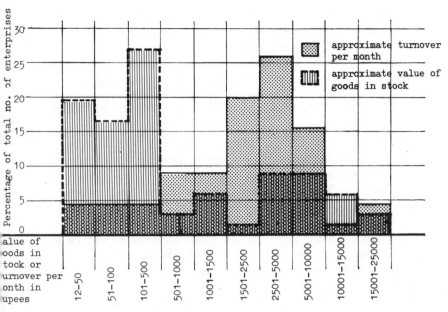

Figure 11.8. Distribution of enterprises by approximate value of goods in stock and turnover per month.

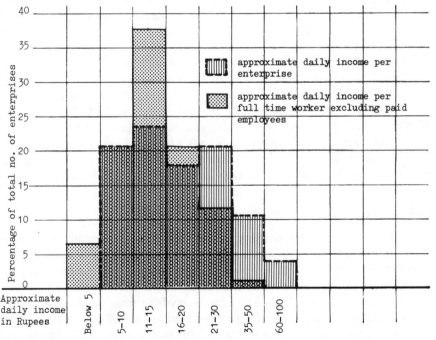

Figure 11.9. Distribution of enterprises by approximate daily income per enterprise and per full-time member.

such markets and that is one of the attractions for their customers. The traders work with approximate notions of the prices they must charge and instinct plays a considerable role in surviving in business.

Market traders had strong links with wholesale dealers. The strongest ties are related to the terms on which the wholesalers supply goods to the retailers. Only 20 per cent were in a position to purchase wholesale goods for cash; 24 per cent were using a combination of cash and credit; and 51 per cent were obtaining all their goods on credit, the majority paying a daily commission. The commission system is used exclusively by fruit and vegetable wholesalers. It involves the following procedure: early in the morning when fresh stocks have arrived, wholesalers auction goods to the highest bidders. Retail distributors who can pay cash do so on the spot. Others receive goods without *any* cash payment on the condition that at the end of the day an agent of the wholesaler will come and collect the auctioned price plus a commission of 4–5 per cent for the credit facilities given for the day. In the evenings these agents could be seen walking round the market with fat account books. No security other than an introduction by another retailer who has already proved his trustworthiness to the commission agents is demanded.

Thus non-plan enterprises had strong links with the so-called 'formal' sector of the city. Interviews with wholesalers revealed that non-plan enterprises were responsible for the retail distribution of 75–80 per cent of fresh fruit and vegetables, 50–60 per cent of provisions and 20–25 per cent of general merchandise. This link, however, works most unfavourably for the smallest non-plan units. An individual with no capital resources, selling fruit and vegetables finds it very difficult to get out of the clutches of wholesalers. First, profit margins in these commodities are the lowest. Secondly, if he is using a *rehri*, it is bound to be rented with recurrent monthly overheads. Thirdly, as a newcomer he is unlikely to be able to acquire a licenced one which can mean heavy fines each time he is caught by the enforcement staff. And fourthly, he must pay a high daily commission to his wholesale supplier. The end result is that accumulation of any kind is very difficult. On the other hand, those in such situations increase the profits of the formal sector suppliers as well as making fruit and vegetables available cheaply to almost all sections of the population.

Daily Work Patterns and Working Hours

The average day for market workers was long and arduous, particularly for fruit and vegetable sellers. Daily auctions in the wholesale market, located in one corner of the city, take place between 5.30 and 6.30 am. Mobile *rehriwallas* had to walk there pushing their *rehris*, and some who had rented cheap accommodation in surrounding villages had to walk anything from two to four miles. Thus 29 per cent of the respondents started work between 4 and 6 am; another 41 per cent did so between 7 and 8 am, not stopping until equally late in the evening. Again, fruit and vegetable sellers had to work late to try to dispose of their left over goods. Because of the constraints of these work patterns, 40 per cent of the respondents worked between fourteen and seventeen hours a day. Only 5 per cent worked seven to eight hours, the normal for regular wage employment.

In addition, 50 per cent took no holidays except a few religious festivals or when other essential duties had to be attended to. Thirty-five per cent took off one day on the last Monday of each month because it coincided with the monthly closing of the wholesale market.

Here it is useful to note that frequently occupations such as those of market traders are thought of as labour intensive. One of the positive characteristics of 'informal' sector activities has also been given as their labour intensiveness. However, observation of the market operations made it clear that for large parts of the working day they were labour 'extensive' and not intensive. Except for the evenings, when business was brisk, a majority of the workers simply had to wait for potential customers. At the same time, their labour could not easily be available for any other activity. From this it can be seen that an extension of employment in such activities, as proposed by supporters of a growth of the informal sector, so long as the demand for which they cater remains unaltered, would simply place more people in the work situation without any increase in the amount of work involved. The consequence of this is likely to be the division of the same total income among a greater number of people, leading to a fall in average individual incomes. An increase of such labour-intensive activities cannot be seen as an answer to the problems of low productivity of labour, low incomes or high rates of un(der)employment.

Mobility and Work

Sixty per cent of the market enterprises were not mobile at all, while the rest were mobile to varying degrees. However, given the option 75 per cent preferred working from a fixed location for reasons varying from functional requirements, the exhausting nature of mobility, to avoid harassment by the enforcement staff, better sales and notions of greater 'respectability' associated with working from a fixed location compared with 'doing the rounds'. The rest preferred a combination of mobility and working from a fixed location.

The authorities' insistence on mobility has to be seen in this context. In the case of Hong Kong, McGee (1973a:51) came to the conclusion that a majority of hawkers had moved from being mobile to being static in response to a rapid increase in urban density in the Colony between 1950 and the early 1970s. In Chandigarh, too, the same appears to have been the case. In the early years, when the resident population was dispersed over a large area, a majority of the non-plan enterprises had to go out in search of customers. With increased residential densities, this is no longer necessary. Indeed, in this particular market, a considerable proportion of the enterprises had built up strong links with the adjoining areas and were extremely reluctant to move.

Asked if they would be prepared to move to another location if the government offered them small shops or sheds there, only 17 per cent said yes without any qualification. Thirty per cent said that they would move only if the whole market was relocated; 20 per cent said that they would move if there was sufficient business at the new location; 21 per cent were totally against moving because they had established businesses at the existing location and were not prepared to face the risks of moving even if offered shops on easy terms. This was the response of those who had been working in the market for many years.

The Workers' Views about their Occupations

Nearly two-thirds of the respondents were not trying to change their occupations. Some were genuinely satisfied and would have chosen to continue even if alternatives were available, whereas others were resigned to continue because there were no alternatives. The majority of the remaining 30 per cent or more did not like their occupations, but could do nothing to change. However, some were looking for other jobs and intended to give up their non-plan enterprises. Thus a sizeable proportion of the total found themselves condemned to non-plan self-employment.

In this context, it is important to note that the social status of non-plan occupations is low, and beset by prejudices and social stigmas. Compared with the incomes of non-plan settlement residents, those working in the market had comparatively high incomes. Yet, to overcome social barriers, many of the respondents were prepared to change to more 'desirable' occupations if these became available, even at the cost of reduced incomes.

Socio-economic, Demographic and Migrational Characteristics of the Workers

A significant proportion (31 per cent) of the respondents were displaced during Partition. Another 31 per cent had come from Punjab, Haryana and Himachal Pradesh, the three states immediately surrounding Chandigarh, and a further 31 per cent had come from further afield. The remaining 7 per cent came from neighhouring villages. For more than half the respondents, Chandigarh had been their first experience of urban life. Another 12 per cent were first generation urban dwellers, their fathers having rural backgrounds; and 30 per cent had lived in urban areas for at least two generations.

Table 11.4 shows the reasons why the respondents had migrated to Chandigarh. The first four reasons, accounting for half the total, are related to economic pressures; the third being specifically related to problems resulting from small land holdings and businesses, and the fourth reflecting the impact of land reforms introduced by the government.

It is important to note that nearly 30 per cent were either students or unemployed before migrating to Chandigarh, highlighting the role of urban employment opportunities in attracting them to the city. The chief reason for

Table 11.4. Factors leading to respondents' decision to migrate to Chandigarh

Reason	Number
Had to leave in search of employment	12
No local business prospects or because suffered a loss	11
Family was too large to support on small land holding or on the amount of work available	11
Could not get land as a tenant because of land reforms, or was afraid of loosing land to tenants so sold it, or because lost land in litigation	4
Had a quarrel with family or employer	7
Wanted to see new city, wanted to be independent from family, tired of village life, did not want to work on the land	12
Any other (Bad health caused by previous occupation, retirement, transfer, due to war with Pakistan, drought, etc.)	8
NA/DK (belong to surrounding villages, was born here, parent migrated when was a child)	12

Source: Field survey 1974.

choosing Chandigarh was the presence of friends or relatives already there. Over 40 per cent of the respondents chose the city on the basis of this consideration alone; 23 per cent chose it thinking that as a new city it would offer better prospects than elsewhere.

The high percentage who had come on the basis of having contacts in the city was indicative, as in the case of the non-plan settlement residents, of the general caution with which such decisions are taken. The importance of family and community support was further reflected in the help received by newcomers on first arriving in the city. Fifty-four per cent of the respondents had received assistance from relatives or friends in starting work. Assistance did not necessarily imply direct financial support. It varied from staying with friends or relatives on arrival, to getting information about work prospects and goods and services likely to be in demand, to information about the workings of the city and introductions to wholesalers from whom credit could be obtained. The 45 per cent who did not receive any assistance were either those who came when there were few other settlers, or were the poorest and most underprivileged. The latter also belonged to the lowest castes.

Four-fifths of the respondents were literate. In relation to the low literacy rate of the Indian population generally, this was very high particularly when compared with that of the non-plan settlement residents (see page 134). However, only 8 per cent had education above matriculation and thus could not easily make use of their education in finding alternative employment.

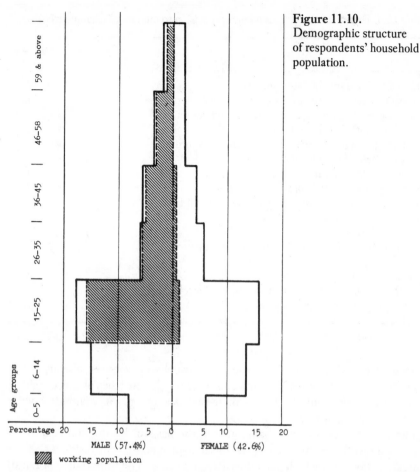

Figure 11.10.
Demographic structure
of respondents' household
population.

Nearly 70 per cent of the respondents were under thirty-six years old, and more than 70 per cent were married. Of the 26 per cent who were unmarried, almost all were in the fifteen to twenty-five year old age group. What was significant was that even in this age group, 46 per cent were married. This combined with the fact that the respondents were almost exclusively men (there was only one woman in the sample) was indicative of the prevalence of early marriages among the section of the population represented by the market workers. These factors are significant in another respect. They not only indicate the existence of social and economic pressures which necessitate becoming economically productive at an early age, but also the early imposition of the additional burden of supporting dependents.

The demographic structure and distribution of workers by age and sex among the respondents' households is shown in figure 11.10. The percentage of workers to total household population was a little less than the 33.5 per cent for Chandigarh as a whole. As in the case of non-plan settlements, it is generally believed that those in non-plan occupations have a larger number of workers per household which compensates for lower incomes. This was evidently not so in the case of the households represented in the sample. Some 40 per cent of the respondents were the only workers in their households. In addition, 26 per cent had dependents outside Chandigarh to whom varying sums were sent as and when possible. Because of this the respondents' incomes within the city did not truly reflect their saving or paying abilities. Only 8 per cent periodically received money from home.

Housing and Residential Mobility

The location and type of residential accommodation of the respondents is an important indicator of their economic status. Over the years, the availability of cheap residential accommodation had become more and more difficult. In spite of this 74 per cent of the respondents were living in regular housing in the planned part of the city, 54 per cent of them in Sector 22 itself or in one of the neighbouring sectors. Proximity to work place was obviously an important consideration. Thirteen per cent owned regular houses and 57 per cent rented them. In all cases except one, the respondents from households owning planned houses had been living in Chandigarh for not less than eight years and some for more than twenty years. Twenty-six per cent were living in non-plan areas such as Bajwada or in adjoining villages, 6.5 per cent of them being indigenous inhabitants of the villages. Only one respondent lived in a labour colony.

Tenants were paying rents varying from Rs.20 to Rs.200 per month; the higher rents being paid for accommodation in regular houses.

The distribution of the respondents' places of residence between planned, non-plan and village locations when they first came to Chandigarh and at the time of the survey showed that while 36 per cent had started living outside the planned framework of the city, by the time of the survey the percentage had dropped to 19.5. While this decrease in those living in non-plan accommodation was certainly partly due to an improvement in the economic circumstances of some, others had felt compelled to rent regular accommodation because of persistent harassment by the enforcement staff.

However it is important to point out that the relative well being compared, for example, with the residents of non-plan settlements, of this market's workers was not necessarily typical of the conditions of those working in non-plan enterprises. The highly advantageous location of the market and the length of time it had been established made it exceptional in many ways. Those in the non-plan settlement sample with similar occupations were generally worse off and represented the more disadvantaged among those working in non-plan enterprises. This was partly because of the restricted social surplus available among the majority of their much lower income customers. The market workers had access to a comparatively more diverse range of customers with similarly diverse incomes.

The Evolution of the Market Ensemble

As with the non-plan settlements, the limited potential of local autonomy for non-plan enterprises becomes very clear from an examination of the market ensemble. Their apparent security through the granting of *de facto* official recognition during certain periods of the market's history, and the withdrawal of this recognition with changes in the socio-political environment (for example during the Emergency of 1975–77) is a useful illustration of the subordinate status of non-plan activities *vis à vis* the dominating core of society. While *de facto* recognition brings illusory short-term benefits, it is a useful means for the authorities to keep their long-term options open and to limit or restrict non-plan activities when they are seen as threatening the interests of the so-called formal sector.

The issue here is *not* that the authorities are unaware of the negative impact of their policies on the income and employment opportunities of the under-privileged, but that considerations about employment opportunities must, *of necessity*, be subordinated to other demands. This fact in itself defines the limited and dependent potential for autonomous growth for the so-called informal sector activities.

While presenting a variety of histories of individuals working in the market, the following sections also examine the role of collective organizations as perhaps the only effective means available to non-plan workers to achieve at least temporary improvements in their working conditions. The vulnerability of even these organizations when faced with repression by the State is evident from their fate during the Emergency.

At the time of the field survey (the end of 1974) the market ensemble consisted of four sub-groups which had evolved around separate group interests within the market as a whole. This had produced a situation of mutual inter-dependence, no group interferring with another providing the market was not threatened in any way. The sub-groups may be classified as follows (table 11.5 and figure 11.2).

1. Those belonging to the Chandigarh Rehri Workers' Union (CRWU) and representing the oldest and largest group in the market.

2. Members of a group which had called itself Indira Market after the Prime Minister. This was the second largest group and was formed in 1971–72 before the general elections.

3. Azad Rehri Market which emerged as a group with a separate name and identity in August or September 1974.

4. A less defined group of market workers without a separate organization or name, but all functioning from 'unauthorized' locations within the market ensemble.

Although most enterprises fell into one of the four groups, there were no

Table 11.5. Types of activity and modes of operation in the four market sub-groups.

Type of activity	CRWU total	NI†	Indira Market total	NI†	Azad Rehri Market total	NI†	Diffused Group total	NI†
Trade								
Fruit and vegetables	160*	35					5*	1
Provisions	2	1	16	4			2	
Dhabas and hot snacks			7	2	2		2	
Snacks and drinks	1*						2*	1
General merchandise			7	2	3	1		
Mill and handloom cloth			5	1	28	7		
Ready made garments			5	1	4	1		
Shop-soiled garments							8*	2
Second-hand clothing			22*	5	2	1		
Tobacco and *paan*	1	1	3					
Footwear			3	1	5	1		
Crockery	2*	1			4	1		
Sub-total	166	38	68	16	48	12	19	4
Services								
Tailors			9	2	7	2		
Cobblers			1				1	1
Stove repairs			3	1				
Photo frames			3	1				
Barbers, dentist			5					
Sub-total			21	4	7	2	1	1
Total	166	38	89	20	55	14	20	5
Mode of operation								
Category 1	24	5	22*	5	2		2*	
Category 2			15*	2	15*	4	1	1
Category 3	133*	26					12*	3
Category 4	5	3	2		3	1		
Category 5	4	1	43	11	35	9	1	1
Category 6			6	2				
Category 7								
Others		3						
Total	166	38	89	20	55	14	20	5

*The total numbers of these tended to vary from day to day, therefore the figures are approximate.

†*NI* = number interviewed.

sharp boundaries between them. Some enterprises could be classified in either of two groups, while many of those working from unauthorized locations also belonged to one of the other three. Whereas identification with one group could be suitable for an enterprise at one stage in its development, at another it could become irrelevant leading to change from one group to another.

Chandigarh Rehri Workers' Union

The origins of the market lay in the demarcation of an area reserved in the master plan as public open space as an authorized *rehri* parking site in 1959. As described in chapter 10, the initiative for obtaining authorized parking sites came from the Fruit and Vegetable Sellers' Association. The CRWU had evolved from this association. It was the only registered union in the market and was the largest *rehriwallas'* union with membership throughout the city. Although now its name suggested representation of different trades, its members were still predominantly fruit and vegetable sellers.

Its organization comprised a central elected body supplemented by elected representatives from each authorized parking site, who were responsible for dealing with the problems of the individual sites. Meetings of 'officers' were held every month and elections took place annually when all members were invited to participate. It was one of the most democratic unions of petty traders and the only one not openly exploiting political patronage.

The union had a legal advisor, and had been responsible for taking several disputes with the Administration to the High Court. It was the only union of non-plan enterprises which after negotiating agreements with the Administration on codes of conduct had attempted to comply with them. As a matter of policy, no attempt was made to defend those members who openly defied such agreements, particularly regarding working from unauthorized locations. Members had to pay Rs.2 per month to finance union work.

Because of its organizational structure, the CRWU had several internal limitations. For example, it did not defend the rights of unlicensed *rehriwallas* who had to work 'illegally' simply because no new licences were being issued. Also it did not cater for the needs of newcomers to non-plan occupations although their needs were often the most pressing. Because of its general emphasis on compromise and negotiation with the authorities, the CRWU also remained aloof from the struggle of those demanding the right to work from some of the totally unauthorized yet most lucrative locations in the city. Despite these limitations, it was the only organization capable of mobilizing large numbers of people when the working conditions of existing *rehriwallas* were threatened by the most restrictive of the handcart byelaws.

In the market, CRWU members worked in a line stretching from one end of the authorized site to the other (figure 11.2). At the end, which was the busiest part of the market, there was a stable core of immobile *rehris* selling fruit and vegetables. A little further down, a number of *rehris* were parked in the late mornings and remained there until the evenings. Beyond them, from about 2 pm onwards, other mobile *rehris* collected. At the end of the line there were *thariwallas* selling vegetables. Apart from the immobile units at the top of the line, there were no fixed parking sites. Those who arrived first had the greatest choice of location. The distribution of different sized enterprises from one end of the line to the other reflected the social and economic hierarchy within the group.

The local union leadership had organized the collection of Rs.1 per month from each person using the site, whether or not a CRWU member, to pay for daily cleaning. Contrary to common allegations against union bosses of charging newcomers for the right to work in such markets, no respondent in the group had had to pay anything.

The group's members consisted of people of diverse backgrounds and ages, although the majority had rural origins. Compared to other groups, fewer CRWU members were from traditional trading occupations and castes.

Chandigarh Rehri Workers' Union: Case Histories

Chairman of the Union

At forty-five years old, the chairman of the CRWU had one of the longest associations with the market, and had been active in the union throughout.

Displaced during Partition, he had initially settled in a small town in Haryana. Unable to make a success of running a canteen there, after selling the small piece of land he had bought in the district, he had moved to Chandigarh twenty years before in the hope of finding better prospects. In Pakistan he had worked with his father in running a shop. In Chandigarh he decided to return to retailing and started selling vegetables as a *pattriwalla*. The small capital he had acquired through the sale of the land in Haryana was invested by his joint family in a residential plot in the city. The choice of working as a *pattriwalla* was dictated by the very small investment necessary for starting business.

When the first handcart bylaws were introduced in 1959 and the persecution of *pattriwallas* increased, he obtained a *rehri* 'to avoid trouble'. During his twenty years in the market, he had *never* done mobile work as he considered it beneath his dignity. At the time of the survey he was using three immobile *rehris* and had put up a tarpaulin shelter as protection against the weather.

He was one of two workers in a joint household of twelve, consisting of his own and his brother's families. His brother was working in the same way in another market. With their combined income, the two had been able to repay the loan for building their house and were sending all seven of their children to school. Asked about his aspirations for the children, he replied that he was hoping that by giving them education, they would have better opportunities in life than he and his brother had had.

He was adamant about not being prepared to move from the existing location because after twenty years, as he said, 'every child knows me here, and I have established a good business by winning regular customers'.

Rural Migrant who came to Chandigarh Eighteen Years Ago

This man had come to Chandigarh as an adventurous youth wanting to see the new city. He had had virtually nothing in his pocket and came on the strength of 'knowing a couple of people in town'. To support himself, he worked as a *chabriwalla*, hawking roasted chick peas while exploring different areas. One of his friends, who was a wholesaler, enabled him to acquire chick peas on credit without having to make any payment and also put him up in his house.

After some years he married and decided to settle in Chandigarh. To improve his income and support his wife, he invested his small savings from working as a *charbriwalla* in starting a vegetable *rehri*. The *rehri* was rented for Rs.10–15 a month as he could not afford to buy one.

By 1974, his household had seven members with five children below twelve years old, and the two of school age were going to school. He was illiterate and at thirty-three was the only worker in the household. He said he had learnt to manage basic accounts orally. He wanted to buy his own *rehri* but had not been able to do so as no new licences were being issued. Instead he was forced to rent one at a much higher rent (Rs.30 per month) from a wealthy private teacher who owned about fifty *rehris*.

He did mobile work for five to six hours every second day on his way back from the wholesale market because he had to walk back anyway. Otherwise he preferred working from the market because of the greater security from the enforcement staff.

Figure 11.11. Rural migrant still selling vegetables from a rented rehri after eighteen years in Chandigarh because no new licences were being issued.

Migrant who used to be an Agricultural Tenant

Belonging to a scheduled caste and displaced during Partition, this thirty-five year old man had settled in a rural area of Haryana. He and his brother cultivated rented land, paying a proportion of the produce as rent and worked as agricultural labourers at other times of the year. When the land reform laws were introduced local landlords stopped renting land to them in fear that they might claim ownership on the grounds of being the real tillers.

The whole family was forced to migrate in search of employment. They had come to Chandigarh five or six years before and both brothers had started working as *rehriwallas* selling vegetables. They rented a small piece of land in a nearby village where they had built a mud house.

The two brothers were the only workers in a joint family of twelve, consisting of their old parents, their wives and children. None of the six children was going to school because of the desperate financial plight of the family.

Asked why he had chosen to work as a *rehriwalla*, he replied that as he was totally illiterate and unable to find any other job, what else could he do? He preferred working in the market for most of the time because it was easier and gave him a sense of dignity. He said that while doing mobile work people could be very rude to *rehriwallas* leaving them quite defenceless. He owned his *rehri* but had been unable to obtain a licence from the Estate Office and could not afford to pay the black market price for one.

Migrant forced to move because of the Smallness of the Family Landholding

This forty-five year old man had to migrate from his village in U.P. because the family agricultural landholding could not support them. He was almost totally illiterate and had come to Chandigarh two years before in the hope of being able to earn enough to send some money home to his parents and support his own family who were with him. He had rented accommodation in a neighbouring village.

He was using a rented *rehri* because he could not afford to buy one as he was in debt for over Rs.1500 to the village moneylender and his brother-in-law. A few days before being interviewed, his *rehri* had been confiscated when he was caught selling vegetables to a passerby who stopped him on the road. He had had to pay a fine of Rs.100 and all his vegetables had rotted so he was unable to send money home that month. After this experience, although he preferred being mobile, he said he was never going to be so again.

Asked why he had chosen his occupation, he replied 'After all, someone has to do this business. I am illiterate and cannot do anything else. I hunted for a job, but could not find one'.

Widowed Vegetable Hawker

Among the *thariwallas* was the only woman respondent. At thirty-five, she had found herself left to her own resources after the sudden death of her husband, who had been an indigenous inhabitant of a neighbouring village. As she was illiterate, hawking vegetables walking round the city during the day and coming to the market in the evening had seemed the only way of making a living. She had to support herself and her five children. To help with the work, she had had to take her thirteen year old son away from school, but was trying to give some schooling to the rest.

She sold vegetables only during certain times of the year when the three cows left by her husband were not in milk. She preferred making a living by selling milk in her village and disliked intensely working as a hawker, 'going round the streets barking like a dog'. But circumstances and economic necessity forced her to continue doing so.

Indira Market

The emergence of Indira Market as a sub-group with its own name and identity only dated back to 1971–72. However most of the members had been working from the same location for considerably longer. Unlike the CRWU members, they were engaged in a variety of trades, such as provisions, cloth, general merchandise, footwear, *dhabas*, and services such as tailors, stove repairers and barbers (see table 11.5). The dominant modes of operation were immobile *rehris* and *pattriwallas*, both working from fixed locations; there were no mobile *rehris* among them.

The genesis of Indira Market lay in the cumulative effects of the Administration's policies on those whose occupations were not compatible with mobility.

To cope with the onslaughts of the enforcement staff, many members had earlier tried to provide themselves with legal protection by obtaining *rehris*, although they did not need them for their work. To benefit from collective action, most of them had joined *rehriwalla* organizations and a majority were members of the CRWU. When, following the emergence of the Nehru-Shastri Markets, additional restrictions were introduced (see page 186), enterprises in Indira Market suffered greatly. Membership of the CRWU could not provide them with a suitable platform for resisting the new measures as it was geared to the needs of *rehriwallas*.

It was under these circumstances, in the wake of the general elections, that Indira Market was born. The naming of the group after the Prime Minister established a pattern for the use of important politicians' names, which had first happened in the case of the Nehru-Shastri Markets. At one stroke, the fight for survival and defence of the livelihoods of a group of otherwise powerless petty traders was given a political tone. As executive authorities in the country are subject to political pressures from the party in power, and every vote becomes important in the pre-election period, unable to get any sympathy from the Administration, Indira Market traders devised a means for by-passing the local authorities and obtaining direct access to central government politicians. Since then other similar groups in the city have resorted to the same tactics.

The key figure in the manoeuvre was the General Secretary of Chandigarh Territorial Congress Committee. His agreement with the leaders of the group was that providing they named themselves after the Prime Minister and collectively paid for his trips to New Dehli when necessary, he would ensure through his contacts there that they would not be harassed by the enforcement staff. That had remained the basis for joining Indira Market. When funds were required, the financially better off enterprises had to pay more and the poorer ones less. The importance of numerical strength under the circumstances was fully realized by the leaders and newcomers were encouraged to join the group.

Thus the emergence of Indira Market resulted from the sifting out of those enterprises from the CRWU for whom the Administration's policies threatened total destruction.

The size of provision, cloth and *dhaba* enterprises can make them appear no less prosperous than equivalent ones run in regular shops. In a minority of cases this was probably true within the market, but the case histories of even some of the largest units illustrate the delicate economic balance on which their survival depends and why so much resistance is offered to the authorities' attempts to topple it. Also the small beginnings of many of those in reasonably prosperous circumstances and the slow and arduous process of accumulation, growth and expansion spanning the working lives of a whole generation, is indicative firstly of the *role* of non-plan enterprises in offering opportunities to those coming from desperate economic backgrounds, and secondly why at an advanced stage of their working lives they are unwilling to risk a major change.

Indira Market: Case Histories

Stove Repairer

This man had the best established stove-repairing business in the market. Displaced during Partition, he had tried to settle in Haryana and make a living by collecting waste materials to sell to wholesale *kabadi* dealers. Work was hard and income little, so seventeen years before he had decided to move to Chandigarh. Initially he had built a hut in Bajwada and continued with *kabadi* work as he had no money to start anything else. However, he wanted a more respectable occupation and started learning how to repair stoves in his spare time. He had to borrow tools from friends in the beginning, but slowly bought his own with savings from *kabadi* work. When Bajwada was 'liquidated' in 1959, his hut had been demolished as he was an 'illegal ineligible' squatter. He then moved to the market where he had been working ever since. He started as a *pattriwalla* because he needed a blow fire which he built on the ground. Slowly, as work increased, he started stocking a few spare parts which were in demand. First he used to take his equipment home each evening, but as its bulk increased, he started leaving it at the site locked in a box. When only *rehris* were recognized as the legitimate mode of operation, he rented first one and then a second and became a member of the CRWU. The *rehris* were unnecessary for his work.

By 1974 he had managed to buy a residential plot and build his own house. He was still paying the government loan obtained for house construction. His son was going to college, but helping during the evenings. His daughter was in the ninth class at school. As his family was small, he had been able to improve their economic situation considerably during the seventeen years they had been in the city. With the threat posed by the Estate Office's policy of requiring *rehris* to remain mobile and no work being allowed from the ground, he had joined Indira Market to safeguard his hard-won business and

Figure 11.12. The stove repairer pretending to be a *rehriwalla*, working from the pavement. His *rehris* are totally submerged under his spare parts for sale in the background.

economic capacity. At forty-five there was little else he could do and renting a regular booth with high overheads and loss of regular customers was an unacceptable proposition.

Dhaba Selling Tea and Cooked Meals

Also a displaced person, after trying to run a *dhaba* in a small town, this man had moved to Chandigarh twenty years before. He had started work in the city selling roasted peanuts and chick peas in Bajwada. After seven years when he had saved some money, he began running a *dhaba* in the market. He worked from the ground and had built himself a *tandoor*. Originally his customers wore loose traditional shirts and did not mind squatting on the ground to have their meals. However as the city and its government population grew, new clothing styles became fashionable. Even his normal customers started wearing European style shirts and tighter trousers. They were no longer happy to squat on the ground and he had to obtain cheap benches and tables. To avoid trouble from the enforcement staff he also acquired a *rehri* and became a member of the CRWU, but changed to Indira Market when this was formed.

At the time of the survey he had a good business, many of the market workers being his regular customers. His wife and daughter helped him with the cooking and he did not take holidays 'as his customers had to eat every day'.

Over the course of twenty years and starting from almost nothing, he had managed to educate all of his children, two of the sons having obtained technical qualifications. At fifty-five, he was unwilling to contemplate a major change in his work. Although theoretically it was perhaps possible for him to afford the overheads of running a restaurant from a regular shop, in the process of changing he would have lost most of his customers who preferred the informal atmosphere of a *dhaba* and, of course, the cheaper prices.

Trader in Cheap Footwear

This man was selling cheap, plastic footwear. He was using one immobile *rehri* and used boards supported by bricks on the ground to display his wares. He belonged to an untouchable caste and had come to Chandigarh twenty-three years before. He was by then fifty years old. He had left Jullundur, where his family ran a small business making and selling footwear, after a quarrel, and arrived in Chandigarh almost penniless. At first he had squatted in Bajwada and worked as a *kabadi* dealer, earning Rs.2–3 a day. Slowly his business grew because the profit margins were good. However, he did not like the work because the waste collectors sometimes sold him stolen goods. Within two years he managed to buy a village building for Rs.150 and started using it as a shop. When Bajwada was acquired by the government he became an official lessee. In the meantime he had begun to sell cheap footwear because he had some experience of the business and, although the earnings were lower, there were not the hazards of *kabadi* work.

In 1959, under the 'Bajwada Liquidation Scheme' he was alloted a site for a booth in Sector 19 for Rs.6000 payable in four equal instalments. He accepted the allotment but had to continue working in the same way to pay for the site.

Figure 11.13. The footwear dealer with his goods on display.

When his shop in Bajwada was demolished he moved to the market and obtained a *rehri* to carry out his business. The change did not disrupt his work too
much as the market was close to Bajwada and he kept most of his customers.
This way he paid off the loan for the booth site and also managed to buy a small
residential plot while these were still sold at fixed prices. He obtained a government loan to build his house and when it was completed let more than half of it to
help pay back the loan. In 1973, as he had not paid his yearly instalment of
Rs.1500, a penalty of Rs.4000 had been imposed on him. He had been unable
to pay because he had built the booth on his allotted site and this had cost him
Rs.7500. He had not moved there because he did not have sufficient capital to
invest to make the booth profitable. He had not let it for fear of being unable to
evict the tenant later. Thus he was planning to remain in the market for the
time being where business was assured.

He had educated all three of his sons to higher secondary level. Two had
government jobs and supported their own families in other cities, while the
third ran another footwear business in the same market to help pay back family
debts and support his own family. Father and son obtained their stock jointly to
minimize costs. The father could make Rs.200–250 per month and the son
Rs.300–350. Together with the rent of Rs.400 from the house, they expected to
be able to repay the rest of the loan in two or three year's time. Only then was
he going to consider moving into the booth whose site was allotted to him in
1959. Even so, he was going to make sure that the economics of the move were
sound.

Tailor from a Rural Background

This twenty-two year old muslim tailor had studied up to matric and came from

Figure 11.14. The two brothers tailoring in the Indira Market.

a village in U.P. Tailoring was his family's traditional occupation. As he and his brothers had grown up they had found that work in the village was barely sufficient for their father. The eldest decided to leave the village and came to Chandigarh. After working in Indira Market for two years he invited his two younger brothers to join him. The respondent was the middle brother and had been working in the market for three years. He and his brother had been helped by the eldest who had bought them second-hand sewing machines.

He was training the youngest and the two were working from an area of about 6 ft by 8 ft with a canvas shelter to protect them. Their customers were low-income government employees and other manual workers including *rehriwallas*, who bought cheap cloth from adjoining enterprises. To get work it was essential for them to be near cloth sellers as they did not have many regular clients. They did not feel that they were competing unfairly with tailors in regular shops as their customers were from different sections of the population. The three brothers and the wife and two children of the eldest were living in rented accommodation in a nearby village. Their joint income amounted to about Rs.450 per month of which they were sending about Rs.100 home to their parents every two or three months.

Azad Rehri Market

This sub-group was the latest addition to the market ensemble. The process of its growth is an example of the means devised by non-plan enterprises to by-pass the Administration's restrictions imposed to curb that growth. It also illustrates the role of bribery, protection rackets, political manipulation and opportunism in such circumstances.

A majority of the sub-group were comparatively recent migrants to the city, young, and from traditional trading backgrounds. The general characteristics of the enterprises were similar to those of Indira Market, the largest number being immobile *rehri* units selling cloth and clothing, and tailors (see table 11.5).

The origins of Azad Market lay in the fight won by the CRWU against the Administration's insistence that all *rehris* retained some mobility and that no goods be placed on the ground at any time. In 1970 *rehriwallas* staged a massive demonstration against the restrictions and the Administration conceded to their demands provided they remained stationary only within authorized parking sites. As a consequence, older enterprises which had already taken the best locations in these sites obtained advantage over the new ones. For a young enterprise to get off the ground, being located close to a busy thoroughfare is vital for economic survival. The fruit and vegetable sellers in the market had reached a natural balance between mobile and immobile units. The small proportion of immobile ones enjoyed the benefits of being able to attract customers to a fixed location, the vast majority of the mobile ones working to a number of different daily patterns combining mobility with immobility during the evenings. However the nature of their goods made this a workable pattern as they catered for a fairly constant demand for commodities needed daily.

In the case of traders handling goods such as cloth and clothing, only those with the smallest enterprises can work as mobile hawkers and this does not permit growth. Only the least ambitious, most of whom are elderly and merely trying to earn enough to survive, continue to be mobile. For the rest, hawking is the first stage in a process of attempted growth, and a means of obtaining regular customers and hence potential for that growth. Many such hawkers use pavements of busy streets for the purpose.

The small street between two private housing blocks adjoining the market provided ideal conditions for this (figure 11.2). It was a busy pedestrian and cycle route between the authorized site and Bajwada. Four or five years before some *pattri*– and *rehriwallas*, finding it difficult to survive in the authorized site, started working from both sides of this street. Other traders joined them, especially during the evenings. These enterprises did not find much sympathy from the CRWU because it had agreed to respect the Administration's rules. Indira Market tried to win them over to add to its numerical strength, but the new group had nothing to gain through such a cooperation. Joining either of the existing groups would have meant having to accept disadvantageous locations.

Strictly speaking, the tactics of the emerging group were 'illegal'. Frequent raids by the enforcement staff left its members exposed and insecure. However the group continued to grow. Its increase not only attracted more customers, but also more enterprises. Yet something needed to be done about Estate Office persecution. Inevitably some traders bought protection by bribing the enforcement staff, but not all were able to do this. Some collective solution had to be found, and an intermediary with access to the political party in power was needed. One of the cloth traders was a member of the Congress Party and professed to be a born leader. He told his colleagues that he would ensure that no one was harassed any more, but that this would cost money. He began collecting Rs.30 per month from the better off cloth traders who could both afford to pay and had more at stake because they could not run away easily during raids.

In the summer of 1974, a new Estate Officer was appointed. He found numerous complaints in the files from residents in the area against the noise and nuisance caused by the group. He visited the site and saw that because of the group's numerical strength he could not simply adopt the attitude of confrontation and order physical removal. He initiated a dialogue with the group and told them that although he had to take action because of the residents' complaints and therefore had to remove them, they could appeal to the authorities through proper channels and that their grievances would receive due consideration. The whole area was cleared.

The group became more organized and called itself Azad Rehri Market. After a month of negotiations, it was granted verbal permission to move temporarily to an adjoining area of fixed size (figure 11.2). The leaders collected funds from all members on the basis of the number of *rehris* each used, and systematically subdivided the site into individual plots which were supposedly allocated to different units by drawing lots.

When Azad Market was surveyed at the end of 1974, it had been functioning from the new location for two or three months. In the course of informal conversations it became evident that many people, no longer having to buy security, were feeling free to express their resentment at having been manipulated for so long. One group of members was extremely hostile towards the Congressman who had been collecting money from the enterprises. They felt he had been lining his pocket at their expense. Another section was more philosophic and felt that people would not have paid him unless they were getting something in return. After all, they had managed to survive under his patronage whatever the 'morality' of his actions. A significant aspect of the situation was that a mere verbal agreement with the Administration that they would not be harassed at the new site had negated the role of any protection racket. It was no longer necessary to pay an intermediary simply for the right to work from land belonging to the government.

Azad Rehri Market: Case Histories

President of Azad Rehri Market

One of the enterprises selling cheap crockery in this group belonged to a young man who was President of the market. He was exceptional among the respondents in that he was technically qualified, having a diploma in mechanical engineering. He had come to Chandigarh four years earlier because he had an *ad hoc* appointment in the Building and Roads Department of Haryana Government. Within two years he lost his job during a retrenchment of temporary employees as an economy measure. He had been unable to find another technical job and so had set up his crockery business. He had been able to get an initial stock worth Rs.3000 on credit from a wholesaler, and he and his brother were working together using three *rehris*. The younger brother went on the rounds during the day, joining the elder in the market in the evenings. Pushing a crockery *rehri* is arduous because of the weight and because of this the elder brother stayed in the market with most of the stock. Although they were able to make about Rs.900 per month and supported their parents and sister, he was very unhappy with his work. He wanted to get away from the family's traditional occupation and put his technical training to use. He was continuing to look for a technical job, but the prospects were bleak because of the high unemployment of technical graduates.

General Secretary of the Azad Rehri Market

The General Secretary was a thirty-three year old *Banya* who had migrated from a village in U.P. three years before. His father had a provision shop there and was also a moneylender. He had decided to leave because the joint family was too large to support on the income from the village shop. His own household in Chandigarh had eight members including his nineteen year old brother whom he was helping to set up a tobacconist *rehri*. Initially relatives had helped him to obtain credit from a wholesaler to start retailing ready made garments. Because of lack of experience this enterprise

Figure 11.15. The immobile cloth *rehri* stall of the General Secretary of Azad Rehri Market.

failed. He then switched to selling cloth because he felt he could handle it better and had been doing this for a year fairly successfully.

From the outset he had worked as an immobile *rehri* unit along the street where the group was previously located. At first he had managed to buy one *rehri* and rented a second. Recently he had bought the second one for whose licence alone he had had to pay Rs.250. He was content with his occupation and wanted to get a government loan to improve his business. This was largely because with only five years' schooling he saw no other future for himself. However, he was determined to educate all his children, three of whom were already going to school. His ambition was that one day one of his sons might become a Deputy Commissioner in the government. (This was interesting in that the Deputy Commissioner in Chandigarh is the Estate Officer in charge of instructing the enforcement staff in dealing with non-plan enterprises like his own!)

Although the difference between handling ready-made garments and cloth may appear insignificant, among traders, particularly those belonging to the *Banya* caste, such differences were obviously very important. Not only is experience in handling a specific commodity considered desirable, but there is a hierarchy of status associated with different commodities. For instance a traditional cloth trader will consider it beneath his dignity to handle fruit and vegetables. Because of frequent ups and downs in business there is also a general reluctance to change from one commodity to another with a significant element of superstition in such behaviour. Outright policy decisions to ban certain trades are largely doomed to failure because they do not take account of these factors. They expect people to put aside perhaps generations of experience on grounds which are incomprehensible to them, particularly when no acceptable alternative is offered.

Trader Selling Secondhand Army Clothing

This respondent had ended up as a *rehriwalla* as a result of one disaster after another. Displaced during Partition, his family had received some agricultural land as compensation for property lost in Pakistan. The family had never cultivated the land themselves and sub-let it to tenants, charging 50 per cent of the produce as rent. Following the introduction of land reforms, one of the tenants filed a suit, claiming ownership of the land on the basis of being the actual tiller. After ten years of litigation, the respondent decided to sell his land in fear of losing it altogether. He had moved to Chandigarh three or four years before because he had relatives there. His first attempt at finding a new occupation was to set up as a wholesale cloth dealer. Lack of experience resulted in failure. He switched to a smaller scale, renting a shop in Sector 35 and selling cloth. This too failed. Trying to reduce overheads, he climbed down the ladder by renting a *rehri*. In the beginning he remained mobile, but was fined a number of times when caught selling to customers on the roads. As a consequence he gave up moving around and joined the Azad Market.

Deciding that cloth had brought him bad luck, he switched to general household goods. Then, three weeks before, he had started selling second-hand army clothes. He was hoping that the rising cost of living, the oncoming winter and the particularly high prices of warm clothing would provide a good market among the poor. He did not yet know how he was fareing. At forty-seven, his misadventures over the past three or four years had landed him with a debt of Rs.7000–8000 to relatives. He had to support a household of six. One of his sons, who had completed ten years at school, had begun to help him after school hours. But it was likely that the son would have to end his studies and find some means of adding to the family income. It was interesting that this man did not belong to the *Banya* caste and his dismal story was partly a consequence of lack of trading experience.

Thariwalla selling Cheap Handwoven Cloth

This man was one of about eight *thariwallas* selling cheap handwoven cloth. They were at the bottom of the economic hierarchy among the cloth dealers in the market. He was a fifty year old muslim from a village in U.P. His father sold cloth woven by village artisans. The respondent had left home as a youth because of insufficient opportunities to support the joint family. He had worked in textile mills in many cities such as Ahmedabad, Bombay and Poona, but had given this up eleven years ago because working conditions were bad and his health was suffering. He had decided to come to Chandigarh, where he had relatives, to explore the work possibilities. He joined one of his cousins as a partner in selling handwoven cloth supplied by a wholesaler from his district in U.P. Both were still working in close cooperation. While one sat in Azad Market, the other went round on a bicycle to surrounding villages or high-density residential sectors as a hawker. Both took turns in doing the rounds. As their *thari* was on the side farthest from the main thoroughfare, sales were not very good. On days when hardly any sales were made, he risked taking his small bundle of *khadi* cloth back to the old location on the busy street during the afternoons.

He was sharing a single room in a private house nearby with three others like himself which they rented for Rs.80 per month. In eleven years he had not been able to bring his family to the city because the cost of living was too high. He earned about Rs.400

per month, spent Rs.100 keeping himself and sent the rest home to his wife and family. Thus he was working at the retail distribution end in a chain linking village artisans to the urban market. Few regular shops handle handloom cloth, other than the government network. He could sell much cheaper than such shops in spite of their subsidization and his customers belonged to the poorest sections of the population. He would have liked himself and his children to be farmers, but he could not afford to buy agricultural land. He expected his children would have to work as he did for lack of other alternatives.

Diffused Group Working from Unauthorized Locations

This group, although not belonging to any separate organization, shared the common feature of working from unauthorized locations within the market ensemble. At the time of the survey, authorized locations comprised the parking site demarcated in 1959 from which the majority of the fruit and vegetable sellers and a part of Indira Market worked, another area to the right of the road where the Indira Market spillover was located, and the more recently demarcated site for the Azad Rehri Market (figure 11.2). The common locations of this group were either the busy area near the street junction or along the same street from which Azad Rehri Market had been removed. Among them were a considerable number of the smallest enterprises from the Azad Market. These were mainly handloom cloth *pattriwallas* and even one or two *rehriwallas* who had found relocation to an area only a couple of minutes walk from the street sufficient to threaten their economic survival. Among them, however, were also some traders doing extremely good business, who certainly were not totally dependent on working from such locations, and who could be labelled as 'exploiters' of the situation. This group had the potential to evolve into another Azad Market.

Diffused Group: Case Histories

Harijan Cobbler

This man belonged to an ex-untouchable caste and had one of the longest associations with the market ensemble. He had left his village in Haryana in search of work some twenty years before and had come to Chandigarh because, as he still believed, 'it was the capital of the nation'. Illiterate and with very little money, he had started working as a cobbler, which was his traditional caste occupation. Tools at that time cost only Rs.10–15. He had built himself a hut in Bajwada and also worked there. When the first attempt to clear Bajwada was made, he fell into the category of 'ineligible' squatters. He moved to the market and worked from a street corner near one of the residential blocks. Even his hut in Bajwada was demolished and he moved to the labour colony behind the University. As no authorized plots were allotted to Bajwada evictees, his dwelling in the labour colony had remained unauthorized.

In the market, over the years, he had managed to get enough work to make a living. To protect himself from the weather he had built a tarpaulin shelter supported on

Figure 11.16. The cobbler and his repaired second-hand shoes on display working from his old location along the busy thoroughfare.

bamboo sticks. As a group of families dealing in repaired second-hand clothing worked nearby, he started buying second-hand shoes collected by them and after repairing them, sold them.

When the Azad Market was moved, so was he. Realizing that, as an individual, he was likely to lose the right to work anywhere, he became a member of the newly formed group. This had required much insistence on his part and he felt that other members had tried to exclude him because he belonged to a low caste. He tried to work from the new site, but found that its location away from the thoroughfare reduced his trade so much that he could no longer even make a bare living. Within a month he was back at his old place on the pavement where he had been working for fifteen years. He felt that it was important to remain in a place where people knew they could find him. The effect of a minor relocation on his work is indicative of the dependence of small enterprises being in the immediate vicinity of busy thoroughfares where their activities inevitably come into conflict with easy traffic movement.

Strictly speaking those providing his kind of service were at the time allowed to work from pavements (see page 194), but he said the enforcement staff kept harassing him. *Pattriwallas* like him had no organization of their own and therefore could not protest strongly when harassment occurred. Asked if he would prefer to have a small shop he said this was impossible because of the overheads. He wished he could rebuild his improvised shelter where he was, but as part of the policy towards *pattriwallas* no shelter of any kind was permitted. They are expected to sit under the trees if shelter is important to them, and if there is no tree at a good location – too bad!

He wished he could improve his situation by starting something with a better income, but simply did not have capital or access to credit to do so. To him, plying a *rehri* appeared an attractive proposition, but in twenty years he had not been able to make even such a small change. His monthly income of Rs.150–175 had to support a household of nine.

Two Enterprises selling Rags

Both these enterprises were selling shop-soiled garments, mostly woollens which are referred to as rags. These are supposedly imported from abroad to be shredded and used as raw material by hosiery mills in Amritsar. Because of a 'leakage' through customs, large quantities of rags were finding their way into the market instead of the mills. Wholesalers sold them by weight and retailers by individual garments. Demand for them among the middle and lower income population was phenomenal, profits were good and there was a roaring trade throughout the country. Thousands of poor people were able to buy fairly good woollen clothing for the first time in their lives. The only losers were the mills who suffered a considerable fall in demand for their much more expensive products.

Both the respondents in this trade probably had the highest incomes in the market and said they could make between Rs.1000 and Rs.1600 per month. Both were using unauthorized locations to catch their customers and a high degree of bargaining went on; crowds and confusion were good for business.

Initial investment was low in both cases, only Rs.400 or so. Terms were strictly cash. Success demanded a high degree of entrepreneurship. The semi-illegal nature of the commodity required good contacts for survival. Both respondents professed to be strong and active supporters of the Congress Party and had not bothered to join any union or group. One said it was necessary to be 'on the right side'. Neither wanted to have proper shops because neither the commodity they were handling, nor their customers would be compatible with the atmosphere of regular shops. Their backgrounds are not given here as they were not typical market traders. But it is people like these, with stories of high incomes, political patronage and opportunistic activities, who lead to the general suspicion about *all* non-plan workers.

The Market and the Emergency

All that has been described relates to the market up to 1975. The Emergency in the country from June 1975 to March 1977 affected the destiny of the market drastically, just as it affected other non-plan developments in the city. Under the Emergency, the complex structure of relationships between different sub-groups and different modes of operation was suppressed and all market enterprises made to conform with the standardized demands of the byelaws. The original authorized *rehri* parking site was cleared as it was decided to build a school there. The temporary site allocated to the Azad Market was withdrawn as the land was to be released for auction for commercial development as stipulated in the plan. All the immobile enterprises were cleared and screened to conform with the byelaws. In the process the market was reorganized and fitted into an area less than one-third its original one on a site which before had only been occupied by a spillover of Indira Market (figure 11.17).

The present approved *rehri* parking place has been provided with a cement floor, a water tap and a toilet. Compared with about 330 enterprises using the

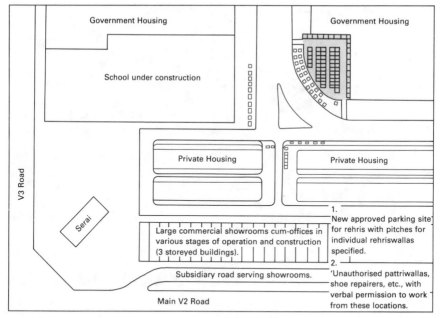

Figure 11.17. Sector 22 market: present location of the market and land use of surrounding areas.

market before, a total of 190 parking spaces were demarcated; each allottee having to pay a monthly parking fee of Rs.15. No permanent shelter of any kind was allowed and the compulsory *rehri* designs were enforced.

Although the impact of the drastic change on the case history enterprises has not been described, the turmoil it created in their lives can be assessed in relation to the diversity of their circumstances. Among those using *rehris*, the *dhaba* owners were amongst the worst affected. Not permitted to provide any seats for their customers their business was drastically reduced. All the other immobile *rehri* enterprises selling cloth, provisions and so on, which had expanded to more than one *rehri*, had to cut down their businesses so that they could work from a single *rehri*.

For the small mobile enterprises, the flexible daily work patterns leading to their gathering in the market in the evening is no longer possible. This group which belonged to the CRWU was in the main most adversely affected. Many actually moved out of the city during the Emergency as they could not work within the restrictions and were afraid of the unrestrained executive powers.

In the case of the *thari–* and *pattriwallas* providing services, and who remained as unrecognized by the new byelaws as before, the market reorganization left them in an even more precarious position. They were simply given verbal permission to work from the pavement just outside the boundary of the new site. Whereas earlier they had been interspersed with other enterprises, for

Figure 11.18. The market since its reorganization during the Emergency functioning from a third of its old area. The railing in the foreground is supposed to define its boundary. The canvas canopies in the majority of cases are attached to the *rehris* themselves as part of the new compulsory *rehri* design.

example tailors worked near cloth sellers, now they all had to sit separately. The group of families selling second-hand clothes, who had earlier been given verbal permission to work from fixed sites, were also moved out on to the pavement. The problem with such verbal or *de facto* recognition is that if the individuals concerned are harassed by the enforcement staff, they can do nothing to defend themselves. At the same time they can be shunted around according to the whims of the authorities.

The Emergency made the market workers' organizations totally dysfunctional. It was no longer possible for the Indira Market to use its political leverage as a means of survival. Vote catching for the ruling party was no longer a priority. The CRWU was broken up under the strains of the period. Some of its leadership was co-opted by the authorities, leading to the demise of the only city-wide *rehriwalla* organization. For the Azad Market, which was mainly relying on the Jan Sangh party's support, it was no longer prudent to advertise this support as many of the Party leaders had been thrown into prison. The diffused group working from unauthorized locations more or less disappeared as the costs of being caught became too high.

Thus the market ensemble, which had survived and evolved over a period of several years, producing ingenious responses to cope with each new official restriction, was suddenly reduced to near shambles. Faced with the possibility of having to confront the repressive apparatus of the State, little other than compliance was possible.

With the Emergency over four years behind, first cautiously and then more boldly, unauthorized parking adjacent to the approved site has once more become the norm. Enforcement of mobility among the enterprises allotted specific parking sites has again become largely academic. Fixed canvas shelters across the lanes between rows of *rehris* give them an air of stability and permanence – little different from the original *khokhas* and later immobile enterprises of earlier days. Certainly, the overt form of the market has changed but its content and nature remain the same. It is there because it is a response to the felt needs of a large section of the population in the present socio-economic conditions.

However, if the market, and others like it, have shown dramatic resilience in adapting to drastically changing conditions and survived against heavy odds, they have done so at heavy costs to most enterprises. The experience of the extent of their vulnerability, which remains unaltered, arising from their 'informal' or non-plan character, has made many determined to try and change the situation. They are now demanding permanence and legality by getting the master plan suitably altered to permit the construction of pucca shops on the existing approved sites. While planners and economists in national and international arenas are beginning to sing praises of the 'informal sector' and pinning high hopes on its solving many employment and economic problems, those trapped within it with first-hand experience of its pitfalls are groping for every possible means of getting out of it.

12

Points of Departure for Positive Change

As pointed out in chapter 1, one of the main objectives of this book is not simply to explain the conflicts and contradictions in Third World urban planning as exemplified in Chandigarh, but to identify the agents and processes by which the situation could be transformed. Even to begin to do so, however, it is essential to understand the wider processes and structural relationships which are generating the situation.

The preceding chapters have concentrated on highlighting the structural limitations against genuine improvement for the mass of the working poor, be it with respect to a solution to their housing problems, or in terms of opportunities for meaningful and productive employment. The increasing support by international 'aid' and 'development' agencies for a pragmatic approach towards the growth of illegal or semi-legal settlements, and an active encouragement and legitimization of the growing 'informal' sector of employment has to be seen within the emerging pattern of decision-making and control of the world's resources and means of production at the international level. This pattern indicates a two-tier structure in which the control of decision-making is retained by an ever decreasing minority by virtue of its control of large transnational capital. The base of the population, increasingly de-linked from direct participation in this dominant structure, is being assigned the subordinate role of making do with managing whatever little is left over. In other words, remaining engrossed in lower level decisions concerning small local problems, they are being encouraged to 'participate' in a better management of their poverty. The important point to note is that in neither of the two aspects, housing or employment, do the currently proposed policies directly address themselves to dealing with either the actual causes or problems of deprivation and poverty. The evidence and analysis of the Chandigarh experience have attempted to highlight why this is so.

As already substantiated, on the one hand, effecting legalization of semi-legal or illegal settlements is intrinsically inviable for State agencies within existing societal frameworks, except on an *ad hoc* basis. On the other hand, even if it were assumed that such policies *could* be enforced, they would offer little social and material improvement to the living and working conditions of the working poor. The promises of betterment held out by the protagonists of such policies are no more real or viable than those offered by Le Corbusier in support of his plan – of its offering 'all amenities of life to the poorest of the poor of the city's inhabitants to lead a dignified life.' Their true function can only be seen as that of creating illusions and deadening a potentially growing awareness about the nature of the contradictions involved in making economically and 'legally' inviable assertions.

The role and impact of planning intervention within the existing structure are also clear. None of the planning frameworks reviewed, irrespective of their levels of 'sophistication' in terms of incorporating inputs from several disciplines, directly addressed itself to dealing with the priority needs and problems of the working poor. Although statements of intentions to this effect were made in rhetorical terms, even a cursory examination of the parameters on which the planning has been based indicates the economic inviability of the promises. For example, not in a single case was any consideration given to creating working opportunities for the vast majority in activities and occupations geared towards catering for their priority needs.

On the contrary, the planning frameworks at different points in time in different contexts, have been in complete harmony with the models of industrial economic development attempted by different States within frameworks of mixed market economies. In so far as such planning led to the development of blatant social and economic contradictions, it was never its objective either to eliminate them or to prevent their development. It is a futile exercise to assess the 'success' or 'failure' of such planning from this point of view.

Opportunistic rhetoric by ruling political parties and public authorities, aided by the use of aesthetics by architects and physical planners in the introduction of planning and its legitimization, have served to distract popular attention from these basic inherent contradictions. The bourgeois concept of 'intelligence' whereby individuals are labelled as 'great' or 'masters' facilitates the centralization of decision-making in the hands of a few, leaving the rest of society at their mercy. Through the authorities' support for Le Corbusier, the imposition of an individualistic perception of grandeur and monumentality on the mass of the population – and the dismissal of their concerns with the real day-to-day problems of survival as unimportant – could be legitimized. Recent years have witnessed a reduction in the number of such 'great' figures as they are no longer a sufficiently effective instrument for distracting the disillusioned majority from the dismal reality of their life situations. Instead, the tendency now is to use teams of social scientists, who continue to perpetuate the myth of scientific rationality, accompanied by vast armies of social and volunteer field workers assisting the people in learning the art of 'participating' in small local decisions. In conformity with this pattern, it is likely that today Albert Mayer's more humanistic planning approach would receive greater support than Le Corbusier's, although neither of the two could resolve the conflicts of 'planned' Chandigarh nor cater for the needs of non-plan workers and residents.

What then have to be the points of departure for working towards at least creating the conditions for real change in the interests of the working majority?

In what ways can planning and planners be instrumental in supporting this, and on what socio-economic parameters must their actions be based if they are to play a genuinely progressive role?

To begin with the neutrality of planning must be demystified and it must be recognized that conventional planning is, effectively, an instrument for serving the interests of a particular class. This has been amply demonstrated by the Chandigarh experience and that of other planned new towns. Rather than explain, justify or diffuse the emerging blatant contradictions, the starting point must be to create the conditions which heighten an awarenes of their structural nature. To begin to identify the nature of their problems, the exploited and excluded sections of society must have a real conciousness of their predicament and of the absence of any long-term possibilities for bettering it within the present structure.

However a greater awareness among the mass of the working poor, in infinitely varying circumstances, is not necessarily adequate by itself. It must be instrumentalized by devising concrete activities which on the one hand heighten and increase a collective perception of their predicament and, on the other hand, provide the means for organizing collective responses. The support for the model of individualized, small-scale, self-employment solutions, by countering such developments, contributes to a consolidation of the weak and frequently worsening situations of the working poor.

A positive approach must aim at supporting any economic activities which establish and strengthen links between different sections of these people – the organized working class which on the whole is decreasing as a percentage of the total working population, the tertiary sections of the labour force and agricultural workers. The aim must be to enable these sections to acquire greater economic control of their situations by being able to support each other mutually, by exchanging products and services *between* themselves rather than striving for higher profits or incomes by catering for the national or international elite market.

Thus the socio-economic parameters on which alternative planning, aimed at catering for the needs of the majority, must be based must include viable economic programmes defined in terms of those needs. The appropriate pattern of production relationships has to establish and strengthen the links between different sub-groups of the working poor. These could enable them not only to determine *what* they produce but also to control its marketing and distribution. This cannot be an end in itself, but could be instrumental in strengthening their ability to alter the dominant structure of production and distribution towards real societal needs and to wrest its control from the ruling minority.

The obstacles in the way of the creation of this alternative are self-evident; a major one being the individualistic perceptions among the tertiarized sections of the workers themselves. However, unless such an economic programme and an alternative technological infrastructure can be created, however slowly and painfully, the chances for real social improvement seem remote. With an alternative to fall back on, not only can demands for minimum or better wages be fought for from a position of strength, but these can be taken into the arena of demanding a change in what is produced, for whom, and how it is distributed. Instruments have to be devised to enable the labour wasted in activities such as polishing shoes, or even producing consumer goods or services for the local, national or international elite markets, to be directed towards production catering for the workers' own far more pressing and basic needs, and an improvement in their living and working conditions.

Clearly, such an initiative is not going to come from State authorities nor is such a programme going to be implemented by existing State institutions.

Planners, other professionals and technicians have consciously to make their choice. There is no such thing as professional neutrality. Either they defend the interests of the ruling minority, of which they themselves frequently form a part, or they can work towards altering the structure of domination and dependence by actively working in the interests of the majority. Those who desire to work in this direction have to identify how their technical tools and abilities can be used in building up the alternative economic, technological and organizational infrastructure described above.

Planners are well equipped with professional instruments which can be used to heighten an awareness of the nature of the contradictions involved and to create conditions which increase the interaction between the organized working class and the less organized, so-called 'informal sector'. One of the best instruments to achieve this is a creative technology whose point of departure is the operative situation, at every stage in time.

Looking back at the experience of Chandigarh's non-plan residents and workers, on the whole a general awareness of their unequal position was seldom absent among them. Neither was a recognition of the need for a collective response missing when they were confronted by a common threat. However, their collective efforts could be negated relatively easily by the authorities by isolating the unifying leadership elements through the exploitation of their individualistic tendencies and weaknesses. As such individualism pervades all sections of the settlement residents and non-plan workers because of their individualized modes of production or working and therefore their individualistic perceptions of possible 'solutions' to their problems, their organizations remain essentially vulnerable and weak. The operational links between them and with other similar groups in the city are too weak to be activated and used in support of their needs. At the same time, it must be recognized that even the generally unfavourable resettlement scheme for the settlement residents was set up by the authorities primarily because of their growing resistance to being continuously manipulated. Only collective resistance, however vulnerable its organizational base, enabled this to take place.

The issue here is to identify how the basis of this collectivism can be strengthened and to explore to what extent being granted security of tenure can remain a key demand, however important it may be for all concerned. Some of the preceding chapters have attempted to deal at length with why the demand for security of tenure is likely to remain unfulfilled for all those who need it most. At the same time, restricting the basis around which collective organizations are formed to the security of tenure issue leaves the social and economic roots of the residents' circumstances unquestioned.

Similarly, the demands of non-plan workers centred around the issues of the right to a place from which to work and the legitimacy of their employment does not question the absence of socio-economic priorities in their occupations, the unequal relationship they have with wholesale dealers and agents, or how the labour-extensive structure of their employment could be altered to release the surplus labour among them for higher priority needs.

Given the scarcity of skills and resources among the mass of the working poor, clearly none of these aspects can be dealt with at the individual level. The only alternative lies in creating structures which increase the socialization of labour, particularly among those in the ever growing tertiary or 'informal' sector of employment, with the clear objective of enabling them to alter the structure of production, distribution and decision making.

Bibliography

Abrams, C. (1964) *Housing in the Modern World*. London: Faber and Faber.

Bauchie-Kessie (Chief Estate Officer, Tema Development Corporation) (1976) Housing Development in Tema. Paper presented at United Nations International Workshop on Training Human Settlement Managers, University of Science and Technology, Kumasi, Ghana.

Bienefeld, M. A. (1970) A Long-Term Housing Policy for Tanzania. Economic Research Bureau Paper 70.9, Dar es Salaam (mimeo).

Bienefeld, M. A. (1975) The informal sector and peripheral capitalism: the case of Tanzania. *I. D. S. Bulletin*, **6**, (3).

Boeke, J. H. (1953) *Economics and Economic Policy of Dual Societies*. New York: Institute of Pacific Relations.

Bose, Ashish (1969) Land Speculation in Urban Delhi. New Delhi (mimeo).

Bose, Ashish (1973) *Studies in India's Urbanization, 1970–71*. New Delhi: Tata McGraw Hill.

Bose, Ashish (1977) India: the urban context, in *India Since Independence: Social Report on India 1947–72*. New Delhi: Vikas, pp. 85–129.

Bose, A. N. (1974) The informal sector in the Calcutta metropolitan economy. W.E.P. Working paper 2/19/WPS, International Labour Organisation, Geneva.

Brown, M. (1974) *The Economics of Imperialism*. Harmondsworth: Penguin.

Castells, M. (1972) *La question urbaine*. Paris: Maspero.

Castells, M. (1975) *The New Structure of Dependence and the Political Processes of Social Change in Latin America*. Los Angeles: University of California.

Census of India (1971a) *Series 25 – Chandigarh, Part IV: Housing Report and Tables*.

Census of India (1971b) *Series 25 – Chandigarh, Part IV: District Census Handbook*.

Census of India (1981) *Series 26 – Chandigarh, Provisional Population Totals*. Chandigarh: Chandigarh Administration.

Chandigarh Administration (Department of Finance) (1974) *Draft Proposals, Fifth Five Year Plan (1974–79)*. Chandigarh: Chandigarh Administration.

Chenery, H. *et al.* (1974) *Redistribution with Growth*. Oxford: Oxford University Press.

Corrada, R. (1969) The housing program, in *Planning Urban Growth and Regional Development: The Experience of the Guayana Program of Venezuela*. Cambridge, Mass.: MIT Press

Costa, L. (1957) Relatório do plano Pilôto. *Revista Brasileira dos municipios*, **10**, pp. 41–44 (in Spanish).

Dandekar, V. M. and Rath, N. (1971) *Poverty in India*. Bombay: Economic and Political Weekly.

Dasgupta, S. (1964) Underdevelopment and dualism – a note. *Economic Development and Cultural Change*, **12** (2).

Dayal, J. and Bose, A. (1977) *For Reasons of State: Dehli under Emergency*. New Delhi.

Desai, A. R. (1960) *Recent Trends in Indian Nationalism*. Bombay: Popular Book Depot.

Desai, A. R. and Pillai, S. D. (1972) *A Profile of an Indian Slum*. Bombay: University of Bombay.

Deshpande, S. G. (1976) Resettling a squatter resettlement. *Economic and Political Weekly*, pp. 519–22.

Digby, W. (1901) *'Prosperous' British India*. London.

Doxiadis, C. A. (1960) Preliminary plan for Islamabad. *Ekistics*.

Doxiadis, C. A. (1963) *Architecture in Transition*. London: Architectural Press.

Drew, J. B. (1961) Sector 22. *Marg*, 15 (1), pp. 22–25.

D'Souza, V. S. (1968) *Social Structure of a Planned City, Chandigarh*. Delhi: Orient Longmans.

D'Souza, V. S. (1973) Problems of housing in Chandigarh. *Urban and Rural Planning Thought*, 16 (4), pp. 254–66.

D'Souza, V. S. (1976a) People prevail over plan. *Economic and Political Weekly*, 11, (38), pp. 1526–8.

D'Souza, V. S. (1976b) Green revolution and urbanisation in Punjab during 1961–71, in Alam, S. M. and Pokshishevsky, V. V. (eds.) *Urbanisation in Developing Countries*. Hyderabad: Osmania University, pp. 349–65.

Ellsworth, P. T. (1962) The dual economy: a new approach. *Economic Development and Cultural Change*, 10, (4).

Engels, F. (1872) *The Housing Question*. Moscow: Progress Publishers, reprinted 1975.

Engels, F. (1892) *The Condition of the Working Class in England*. London: Panther, reprinted 1969.

Epstein, D. G. (1973) *Brasilia, Plan and Reality*. Berkeley: University of California Press.

EPW (1976a) 11 (1/2), Bombay.

EPW (1976b) 11 (27), Bombay.

Evenson, N. (1966) *Chandigarh*. Berkeley: University of California Press.

Frank, A. G. (1967a) *Capitalism and Underdevelopment in Latin America: Historical Studies in Chile and Brasil*. New York: Monthly Review Press.

Frank, A. G. (1976b) Sociology of development and underdevelopment of sociology. *Catalyst*, pp. 20–73.

Frank, A. G. (1977) Emergence of permanent emergency in India. *Economic and Political Weekly*, 12 (11), pp. 463–75.

Fry, M. (1951) Letter to Mayer, 16 October 1951, quoted in Evenson, N. *Chandigarh*. Berkeley: University of California Press, 1966, p. 27.

Fry, M. (1955a) Chandigarh: capital of the Punjab. *Journal of the Royal Institute of British Architects*, Series 3, 62, pp. 87–94.

Fry, M. (1955b) Chandigarh – new capital city. *Architectural Record*, June, pp. 139–48.

Fry, M. (1977) Le Corbusier at Chandigarh, in Walden, R. (ed.) *The Open Hand, Essays on Le Corbusier*. Cambridge, Mass.: MIT Press.

Geertz, C. (1963) *Peddlers and Princes: Social Change and Economic Modernization in Two Indonesian Towns*. Chicago: University of Chicago Press.

Gerry, C. (1974) Petty producers and the urban economy: a case study of Dakar. W.E.P. Working Paper 2/19/101/1/WP8, International Labour Organisation, Geneva.

Gerry, C. (1977) Petty production and capitalist production in Dakar: The crisis of the self-employed. Paper presented at the Institute of British Geographers, University of London (mimeo).

Glover-Akpey, A. W. (1976) Problems of industrial development in Tema. Paper presented at United Nations International Workshop on the Training of Human Settlement Managers, University of Science and Technology, Kumasi, Ghana.

Government of Ghana (1952) *Appreciation of the Problems Involved in the Planning and Development of the New Town of Tema.* Accra: Government of Ghana.

Government of India (1952) *First Five Year Plan.* New Delhi: Planning Commission.

Government of India (1962) *Tables with Notes on Internal Migration,* n.53. New Delhi: National Sample Survey.

Government of India (1970) *Fourth Five Year Plan.* New Delhi: Planning Commission.

Government of India (1973) *Recommendations of the Adviser, Programme Administration, on the Fifth Year Plan 1974–79 and Annual Plan 1974–75.* New Delhi: Planning Commission.

Government of India (1974) *Draft Fifth Five Year Plan, 1974–79.* New Delhi: Planning Commission.

Goyal, S. K. (1962) Trade unions and trade associations in Chandigarh. Thesis, Department of Sociology, Punjab University, Chandigarh.

Grenell, P. (1972) Planning for invisible people: some consequences of bureaucratic values and practices, in Turner, J. F. C. and Fichter, R. (eds.) *Freedom to Build.* New York: Macmillan, pp. 95–121.

Hardoy, J. E. (1967) The planning of new capital cities, in *Planning of Metropolitan Areas and New Towns.* New York: United Nations.

Hart, K. (1973) Informal income opportunities and urban employment in Ghana. *Journal of Modern African Studies,* 11 (1), pp. 61–89.

Harvey, D. (1975) *Social Justice and the City.* London: Edward Arnold.

Higgins, B. (1961) The 'dualist theory' of underdeveloped areas. *Economic Development and Cultural Change,* 12(4).

Hoetink, H. (1965) El nuevo evolucionismo. *América Latina,* 8, (4), pp. 26–42 (in Spanish).

Holford, W. (1957) Brasilia, a new capital city for Brasil. *Architectural Review* 122, pp. 394–402.

Hornsby-Odoi, E. (1976) Managing Director's speech on the problems of planning and development in Tema. United Nations International Workshop on the Training of Human Settlement Managers, University of Science and Technology, Kumasi, Ghana.

I.L.O. (1972) *Employment, Incomes and Equality: A Strategy for Increasing Productive Employment in Kenya.* Geneva: International Labour Organisation.

Jones, G. S. (1971) *Outcast London: A Study in the Relationship between Classes in Victorian Society.* Harmondsworth: Penguin.

King, K. (1974) Kenya's informal machine makers: a study of small scale industry in Kenya's emergent artisan society. *World Development,* 4 (5).

Koenigsberger, O. (1952) New Towns in India. *Town Planning Review,* 23, (2).

Lakdawala, D. T. *et al.* (1963) *Work wages and wellbeing in an Indian metropolis: economic survey of Bombay city.* Bombay: University of Bombay.

Lamarche, F. (1976) Property development and the economic foundations of the urban question, in Pickvance, C. G. (ed.) *Urban Sociology.* London: Tavistock, pp. 81–118.

Le Corbusier (1930) Introduction to questionnaire: Luft, Schall, Licht.

Le Corbusier (1950a) Personal notes. Archives, Fondation Le Corbusier, Paris (hereafter AFLC) (translated by the author).

Le Corbusier (1950b) Letter to Madame Lachmanam, Ambassade de l'Inde, 25 November 1950. (AFLC) (translated by Helen Walden).

Le Corbusier (1950c) Document ref. AW21 Nov. 50. (AFLC) (translated by Helen Walden).

Le Corbusier (1950d) Letter to Jane Drew and Maxwell Fry, 1 December 1950. (AFLC) (translated by J. L Sarin).

Le Corbusier (1950e) Minutes of meeting between Le Corbusier, Jane Drew, Maxwell Fry and Pierre Jeanneret, 6 December 1950. (AFLC)

Le Corbusier (1951a) Conférence de Propagande pour Chandigarh, 4 May 1951. (AFLC) (translated by Helen Walden).

Le Corbusier (1951b) Letter to Jane Drew, Maxwell Fry and Pierre Jeanneret, 12 December 1951. (AFLC) (original in English).

Le Corbusier (1953a) Conférence d'Information au Palais de la Dècouverte, 18 March 1953. (AFLC) (translated by the author).

Le Corbusier (1953b) *Urbanisme.* Bombay: Marg.

Le Corbusier (1954) *The Open Hand* A brochure presented by Le Corbusier to Jawahar Lal Nehru (AFLC).

Le Corbusier (1955) *Oeuvre Complete, 1946–52.* Zurich: Editions Girsberger.

Le Corbusier (1959a) For the establishment of an immediate statute of the land, 18 December 1959, (AFLC).

Le Corbusier (1959b) *Le Trois Establissements Humains.* Paris: Minuit.

Le Corbusier (1961) The master plan. *Marg,* 15 (1).

Le Corbusier (1967) *The Radiant City.* London: Faber and Faber, first published as *La Ville Radieuse* in 1935, Boulogne: Editions de l'Architecture d'Aujourd'hui.

Le Corbusier (1971) *The City of Tomorrow.* London: Architectural Press.

Leys, C. (1975) *Underdevelopment in Kenya: the Political Economy of Neo-Colonialism 1964–71.* London: Heinemann.

Lojkine, J. (1976) Contribution to a Marxist theory of capitalist urbanisation, in Pickvance, C. G. (ed.) *Urban Sociology,* London: Tavistock.

Marg (1949) The Charter of Athens. *Marg,* 3 (4).

Macdonald, L. and Macdonald, J. S. (1977) People of the Plan: Ciudad Guayana 1965 and 1975. Report of the Centre for Environmental Studies on the absorption of newcomers in a Latin American new town (mimeo).

Mangin, W. (1967) Latin American squatter settlements: a problem and a solution. *Latin American Research Review,* 2, pp. 65–98.

Mayer, A. (1950) The new capital of Punjab. *American Institute of Architects Journal,* 14, pp. 166–75.

Mayer, A. (1951) Letter to Fry, 31 January 1951, quoted in Evenson, N., *Chandigarh,* Berkeley: University of California Press, 1966.

Mayhew, H. (1861) *London Labour and the London Poor,* four volumes. London.

McGee, T. G. (1973a) *Hawkers in Hong Kong.* Hong Kong: University of Hong Kong.

McGee, T. G. (1973b) Peasants in cities: a paradox, a paradox, a most ingenious paradox. *Human Organisation.*

Mitchell, M. (1972) The growth of Tema. A history essay presented at the Architectural Association, London (mimeo).

Mitchell, M. (1975) Shanty cash. A report on shanty settlements and a framework for cooperative subsidy in the metropolitan region of Ghana (mimeo).

Moser, C. (1976) The informal sector or petty commodity production: autonomy or dependence in urban development. Draft working paper, Development Planning Unit, University College, London (mimeo).

Nambiar, K. K. G. (1977) No cloth for the poor. *Illustrated Weekly of India,* 98 (32), pp. 16–19.

National Planning Committee (1947) *Report of the Sub-committee on Population.* New Delhi: Government of India.

NIB *(New India Bulletin)* (1976) 3, May/June, Indian People's Association of North America.

Nilsson, S. (1973) *The New Capitals of India, Pakistan and Bangladesh.* Lund: Scandanavian Institute of Asian Studies, Monograph Series, No. 12.

Nehru, J. L. (1962) *An Autobiography.* New Delhi: Allied Publishers.

Oza, A. N. (1977) How big is India's big business? *Illustrated Weekly of India,* 98 (36), pp. 8–19.

Palkhivala, N. A. (1977) How 'Janata' is the Janata budget? *Illustrated Weekly of India,* 98 (28), pp. 8–15.

Perlman, J. (1976) *The Myth of Marginality: Urban Poverty and Politics in Rio de Janeiro.* Berkeley: University of California Press.

Prabhawalkar, A. R. (1954) The city centre as proposed by M. Le Corbusier. 13 January 1954. Archives, Fondation Le Corbusier, Paris (mimeo).

Prakash, V. (1969) New Towns in India. Program in comparative studies in Southern Asia, Duke University, North Carolina.

Punjab Government (undated) *Construction of the New Capital at Chandigarh.* Project Report (mimeo).

Rao, V. K. R. V. and Desai, P. B. (1965) *Greater Delhi – A Study in Urbanisation (1940–57).* Bombay: Asia Publishing House.

Rostow, W. W. (1960) *The Stages of Economic Growth.* Cambridge: Cambridge University Press.

Rodwin, L and Associates (1969) *Planning Urban Growth and Regional Development: The Experience of the Guayana Program of Venezuela.* Cambridge, Mass.: MIT Press.

Santos, M. (1971) *Les villes du tiers monde.* Paris: Editions M. Th. Genin.

Sax, M. (1869) *Die Wohnungszustände der arbeitenden Klassen und ihre Reform.* Vienna. English title: The Housing Conditions of the Working Classes and Their Reform.

Small Industries Service Institute (1970) *Industrial Pattern of Chandigarh.* Ludhiana: Government of India.

Sovani, N. V. (1966) *Urbanisation and Urban India.* Bombay: Asia Publishing House.

Steinmann, M. (1972) Political standpoints in CIAM 1928–33. *Architectural Association Quarterly,* pp. 49–55.

Sunday Tribune (1981) 28 June, Chandigarh.

Thorbecke, E. (1973) The employment problem: a critical evaluation of four ILO comprehensive country reports, in *Strategy for Employment Promotion: An Evaluation of Four Inter-agency Employment Missions.* Geneva: International Labour Organisation.

Times of India (1977) 19 June, New Delhi.

Tribune, The (1977a) 7 August, Chandigarh.

Tribune, The (1977b) 23 August, Chandigarh.

Tribune, The (1979) 30 October, Chandigarh.

Tribune, The (1981) 23 July, Chandigarh

Turner, J. F. C. (1963) Dwelling resources in South America. *Architectural Design,* 33, pp. 360–93.

Turner, J. F. C. (1967) Barriers and channels for housing development in modernizing countries. *Journal of the American Institute of Planners,* 33 (3).

Turner, J. F. C. (1976) *Housing by People, Towards Autonomy in Building Environments.* London: Marion Boyars.

Ward, B. and Dubois, R. (1972) *Only One Earth.* Harmondsworth: Penguin.

Ward, C. (1976) *Housing: An Anarchist Approach.* London: Freedom Press.

Ward, P. M. (1976) The squatter settlement as slum or housing solution – evidence from Mexico City. *Land Economics,* 52 (3), pp. 330–45.

Ward, P. M. (ed.) (1982) *Self-Help Housing: A Critique.* London: Mansell.

Wilheim, J. (1960) Brasilia, 1960 Uma-interpretação, in *Brasilia Uma Puboiçacão Acropole,* 2nd edition (in Spanish).

Index